HD
6073
.F652   De Santis, Marie
U63
1984   Neptune's appren-
           tice

DATE DUE

Neptune's Apprentice

Though the action as described in this book is all true, a number of names have been changed to protect the privacy of certain individuals.

Copyright © 1984 by Marie De Santis
All rights reserved

Published by Presidio Press, 31 Pamaron Way, Novato, CA 94947

Library of Congress Cataloging in Publication Data

De Santis, Marie, 1945–
  Neptune's apprentice.

  1. De Santis, Marie, 1945–   2. Fishermen—United
States—Biography. I. Title.
HD6073.F652U63   1984   338.3'727092'4 [B] 83-27002
ISBN 0-89141-200-X

Line drawings by Patricia Walker
Jacket Design by Jill Losson
Front insert photo by Mary Muzzi Durney

Printed in the United States of America

To the California fishing fleet

Contents

Acknowledgments

The writing of this book would never have been possible without Roger, Linda, Adele, Freckles, Dan, Cathy, Pam, Elaine, Crystal, and so many others than when I think back over the people at my side during the months of work, I realize no amount of thanks could match the encouragement, kindnesses, and attention I received.

Roger Slagle's enthusiasm was indispensable. He is an ex-fisherman who for a number of years now has been stranded on the beach by a bad back. So unrelenting is his craving for the sea that I'd call him at three in the morning and say, "Hey, I just finished another chapter," and he'd say, "Great! Bring it over right away." No writer could ask for more, but in Roger, I also had his full-on sense of humor, his open friendship, and a complete understanding of what I was trying to say.

Adele Horwitz is editor in chief at Presidio Press. At the very inception she gave me a professional boost of morale that carried throughout the project. I couldn't be more pleased by the ironic course of events that brought the manuscript full circle back to Presidio for publication with Adele at the helm.

Linda Purrington is an ace friend, editor, and mother who, from beginning to end, put her beautiful skill with words completely at my disposal. Linda has done this for writers of over a hundred books, and one of these days a publisher is going to get wise and snap up one of her own books.

As for those many cursed hours when a writer is forced to dangle over the dizzying void of a blank sheet of paper, I was not really alone then either. A fisherman's richest harvest from the sea is the sea story. Whether from the sheer intensity of the life, or its lack of chronicling by others, or from some mysteriously bizarre contagion from the sea itself, one thing is certain: no fisherman on the coast can resist the slightest opportunity to tell, retell, embellish, polish, or otherwise stretch the art of storytelling to encompass the oceanic proportions of their lives. No writer has ever spun tales like those unraveled by the fishermen anchored in the lee of a storm or pinned to the dock by the wind.

If this book has a story or two well told, it is only because in the quiet of those times at my desk, I could call to mind the voices of so many fishermen and borrow from their rhythms and hearts.

1

Anchors Aweigh

DESPITE THE FIFTY-POUND sack of belongings slung over my shoulder, I could barely feel my feet touch the planks as I walked down the dock toward my first boat. The *Donna Lou* was beautiful as she surged gently against her fenders. The rigging held taut against the playful gusting of the afternoon wind, the hull seemed impenetrable as the waves bounced off her planks, and the deck machinery and fish gear on the stern gave the aura of serious business about to begin. At the end of the dock, I stood staring at my boat the way you might catch yourself staring into the eyes of a lover.

"Hey, are you Marie?" came a voice out of the blue.

"Yes," I answered, surprised to see that someone had come so close without my hearing a thing.

"And you're the one who's planning to fish this boat?" he asked rather gently through the rough appearance of his deeply weathered face.

"I sure am," I said proudly. "I'm moving aboard right now."

The fisherman shifted his weight a little uncomfortably as if he were trying to decide on which leg to stand. I almost jumped with his change of tone. "Can't you tell just by looking at her, that boat's gonna kill you?"

"Don't worry," I quickly reassured him. "I'm going to fix it up before I go anywhere."

The strain was growing in his voice. "That's not the kind of

thing you just go and 'fix up,' " he said. "Would you take an old
pine tree and start 'fixing it up' to be an oak? That *Donna Lou*'s
just a pile of junk that's lucky enough to have some good nylon line
holding it up to the dock. I can't tell you what to do, but I don't
like to think of you even walking on the deck."

Man, I thought to myself, this old-timer sure is coming on heavy
for such a nice sunny day.

The old man, sensing the vastness of a sea between us, changed
his tack. "Look," he pleaded, "don't take my word for it; ask anyone here. Most of these guys have been working the ocean since
they were kids. Talk to them first, for your own safety. They don't
even like this one tied to the same dock with their own boats."

He was right, too. I did talk with a lot of the other fishermen
and, without exception, they were all very prejudiced against the
Donna Lou. A couple of times, I even overheard them reprimand-
ing the owner for leasing me the boat. But the combination of a
powerful dream, total ignorance, and a first boat is not something
that can in any way be penetrated by common sense. I invariably
responded to their pleas for my safety with a barrage of questions.
"Why won't the engine start? Where's the hyraulic pump? What's
it for? How can I strengthen the deck? May I borrow your electric
saw?" Then once I had it in my hands, I'd say, "How do you use
it?"

The condition of the boat was one thing, but when the fishermen
realized that I didn't know which end of a screwdriver to hang on
to, they soon took the attitude "Well, she's not going anywhere
anyway, so humor her."

What they didn't realize was the extent to which I'd become
possessed. I was awake until 3 A.M. every night reading the engine
manual, up with the sun pounding nails, then down the road bug-
ging the mechanic, over to the electrician's, and then back to the
bilges. Looking back at that month of preparation, I barely recognize that person myself. There was none of the standard cursing at
the problems that wouldn't get solved in the time I allotted; tools
never got thrown against the bulkheads, and the break of day
never arrived soon enough. Absolutely nothing could frustrate me.

A few days before I felt I'd be ready to leave, a friend offered to
help out if I would take him as a deckhand. Poor Charles; I wel-
comed him aboard.

The big day arrived; we threw the lines off the dock and headed down the Sausalito channel toward the Golden Gate Bridge. From there we'd steer west for five hours and anchor in the protection of Drake's Bay for the night. I sat on the flying bridge, captain of my ship, proud and excited beyond imagination, when suddenly I smelled smoke, turned around, and saw it belching out of the cabin with flames leaping into the doorway. Immediately, I knew that Charles and I would be swimming to the shore, which was less than ten yards away. For a fraction of a second it was obvious that the *Donna Lou* was nothing to risk our lives for. The next second, I found myself down in the forecastle, beating at the flames with my jacket. When the fire was out, I came to the back deck to choke in some fresh air and, for another brief moment of lucidity, got a vision of my own craziness.

It turned out to be only temporary sanity. Back at the dock, inspection showed burned floorboards and a charred bunk, with the only serious damage limited to the wiring. I reached under my bunk, pulled out a bottle of champagne we were saving for our triumphant arrival at Point Reyes, and yelled, "Hey, look, Charles, it didn't break; for sure it means good luck." He hadn't said a word until now, but this did it. With as much disgust as I've ever heard compressed into three words, he said, "Oh, Jesus, Marie," grabbed the bottle from my hand, popped the cork, and we drained the bottle dry.

Whether or not it was the lucky bubbles of the champagne or the merciful ghost of an old sea captain, no doubt something was saving our act. It turned out the fire started because the electronics man who had installed the radio early that morning assumed that the boat had a negative electrical ground like most every other normal boat. It hadn't. *Donna Lou*, the eternal hermaphrodite, had a positive ground. When we started the engine, the reverse charge from the alternator went through the radio, and things got a little hot. The electronics man was responsible. He came down and rewired the boat—for free.

Three hours later we passed under the magnificent span of the Golden Gate Bridge. The Pacific Ocean was on its best behavior, soothing our burned-out nerves with her seductive swells and wide open spaces. The air was even warm enough to sit on the open flying bridge for the entire trip, away from the scream of the engine. After a few hours of riding the shimmering, glassy surface of this huge pond, all was well with the world.

As imperceptibly as the sun worked its way toward the water, Point Reyes was growing out of the horizon ahead of us. This massive, anvil-shaped, mountainous land juts away into the Pacific, creating in its lee one of the largest anchorages on the West Coast of the United States. Its jagged, sharp cliffs looked soft and protective in the evening sun. It wasn't an impression that could last long in anyone's memory of Point Reyes, and I, too, would soon be calling her by her proper name, the Blow Hole. But tonight, Point Reyes was as cozy as a sleeping cat.

We pulled in close and dropped the anchor right under the tall, creamy bluffs that characterize the south side of the point. It's got to be one of the strangest-looking views of the coastline, as if someone had sliced the earth away with a giant knife and let the ocean flow in. It's also the back side of the San Andreas Fault, where the earth shakes from time to time and rearranges California. As the full moon rose out of the east, the awesome solid shapes of our surroundings retreated into a world of eerie silvery outlines that were as fluid as the roll of the boat. I lay in the bunk and listened as the sounds grew louder in the void—deep gulping sounds; hollow watery, secret, creaking sounds—a dark unfathomable dialogue between the hull and the gentlest sea. I lay there in the surgings of fascination and terror, unable to escape the rising tide of awareness that I had severed more than I ever intended. My first night as captain, I was too afraid to sleep.

At 2 A.M. both alarms went off unnecessarily. We wanted to be sure the other boats didn't leave without us. There was way too much water out there to find the fish on our own; we both knew that much. Around three thirty the cabin lights went on in the boats anchored nearby, and a series of miracles took place on ours. The engine started, the running lights went on, the fear was gone, and the anchor wasn't tangled with the slimy balls of red kelp that usually come as a final bonus of having anchored at Point Reyes. We were off.

The radio blared with the singsong string of morning greetings among the fishermen, waking each other up, rehashing yesterday, and discussing the weather. We tried for a long time, but we hardly understood any of it. It was a tumbled up mix of Italian, English, radio lingo, commercial fishing and secret codes, part language, part opera, some news, and much reviews. There was enough confusion aboard this vessel already, and I turned it off, completely oblivious to the fact that I'd soon be glued to two of these radios simultaneously, combing every nuance and phrase for that one little pearl of information—a likely spot for the fish. For now, I was free of the monsters and their blare.

The sky went through a palette full of colors as the day broke, and the glassy water reproduced the splendor as faithfully as a mirror, all the way to the horizon, in every direction, as far as we could see. The land was out of sight, and the sight was out of this world. Charles was just about finished baiting up the fifty herring we needed to set the gear, and I was steering the boat, completely content to be led to pasture. When the other fishermen slowed their engines, so did we.

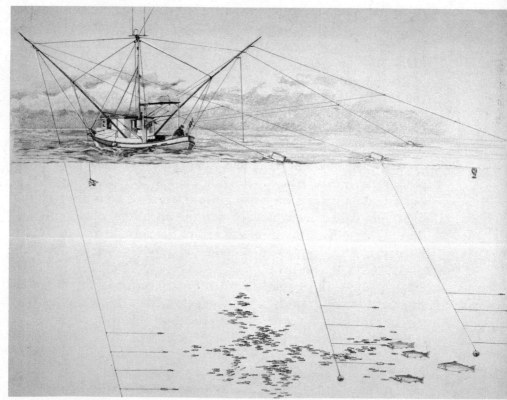

Trolling for salmon

We put the boat on autopilot, went back to the stern, uncoiled
the leaders, and carefully snapped each one to one of the three wire
cables on each side of the boat. In just a little over two hours, we
had completed the fifteen-minute job of setting the gear in the
water. But no sweat! We didn't know that by this time the morning
bite would just about be over, so there was nothing to get nervous
about. For the same reason, we wasted no energy worrying about
trolling speed, the depth of the gear, our angle of attack, the movement of the school, or the guesstimated time of arrival of the next
typhoon. Watching over our shoulders for other boats and figuring
out how to get the hydraulic gurdies to engage properly and bring
the gear back from the depths were our only concerns. One by one,
the leaders were winched back to the surface, unsnapped from the
wire, and recoiled on the deck. One of Charlie's baits came back
with deep scratches along the body and a missing tail. We wasted
a good fifteen minutes rolling it over and over in our hands as we
pondered whether or not it meant what we thought it meant. The
next leader I pulled was stretched out into the water with such
tension that I was sure this thin piece of monofilament would
break at any moment.

"Hey, Charles, a fish!" I screamed in complete astonishment.
Despite the fact that every breath for the last month had been
geared for this moment, it seemed an act of complete magic that
any one salmon in this huge ocean could connect with that tiny
bait. I grabbed the leader and wrapped it twice around my hand
in the classic amateur style that's guaranteed to make your hands
pay dearly for the fish. Sure enough, when I swung the gaff and
missed, the salmon went crazy, darted from the boat like a bolt of
light, and the leader sank deep into the uncalloused, waterlogged
skin of my hand. The muscular tail of the salmon grabbed on to
the ocean with a power that seemed way out of proportion to its
size. The hook held firmly on the lower jaw, and I had a second
chance, and a third, and a fourth. Finally up it came, dripping,
shining wet, and landed on the deck with a loud thump that
marked the end. My eyes were so fixed on this fish, admiring its
iridescent rainbow scales and the obvious skill of its captor that I
almost didn't notice Charles was in the same trance staring at his
fish. We had planned to eat the first fish on the boat in accordance
with a ritual that's said to bring luck. It was easily decided that
the little one came aboard first. The big one was going to market,
our cornerstone on the yellow brick road to certain success.

For the next few hours, whatever came up out of the water was a source of the most profound amazement, whether it was an empty hook, a fish, a tangled leader, or a bait that returned exactly as it had gone down. It's a good thing the weather was calm and clear; any more input and our emotions would have whirled into orbit.

By one o'clock, barely halfway through the average fisherman's long day, we had six fish on the deck. It was like holding the winning ticket to the Irish Sweepstakes, and we couldn't wait any longer to cash in. Besides, as far as we knew, the little fishing town of Bodega, twenty miles to the north, was but a black dot on the chart, with a big reefy rock at the entrance, where Alfred Hitchcock had filmed his horror-suspense movie, *The Birds*. It seemed a wise idea to get there before dark.

Once inside the jetty, the beautiful expanse of the bay with its long, winding channel opened to our view. Pelicans dove around us, and a crowd of screaming sea gulls dive-bombed in our wake as Charles tossed the old bait overboard. Along the neat New England–looking waterfront, there was one fishhouse that stood out from the others with its huge, lettered sign that read Cash for Salmon.

One hundred and twenty-seven dollars was the unbelievable sum. We each stuffed our share into our pockets, as if the boat beneath us wouldn't eat a dime.

The other fish boats that were in port for one reason or another were rafted to the dock in strings of five or six boats each. When I approached to tie alongside the outside boat of the first string, a fisherman hopped out of his cabin in a posture of an alert watchdog. "You can't tie here; you'll be much better off on the next string back." When the same thing happened on the next string back, Charles pointed way in the back to a string of old wrecks. The insult was painfully received. As far as I was concerned, *Donna Lou* in just one day had redeemed herself as a respectable member of the producing fleet.

"Hey, *Donna Lou*, why don't you come over here and tie up," came a gruff, old, Italian voice. My first sight of Hobo was as I was always to see him in the late afternoons. A short, stocky, gruff-looking old man under a battered old sea hat, standing in his stern, a couple of warm beers within easy reach and a hand line hanging over the rail, waiting for the elusive nibble of the three-inch shiners that swim around the pilings.

With the boat finally secured to his satisfaction, we all exchanged our stories. Hobo told us that he had first fished with his dad when he was seven years old and had been on the water ever since. Now he was a retired old-timer, working the morning bite on the ocean for expenses and relaxing at the dock for the long Bodega afternoons.

In the finest Italian style, he cooked up a big pot of pasta and a lingcod soup and yelled at a couple of his buddies to bring the French bread and wine. As delicious as the soup was, it didn't warm me near as much as Hobo's invitation to follow him out in the morning. "Just give me a call if you need any help." Old Hobo had to have known that he was taking on a job that could have retired ten guardian angels.

For the next three days we glued our eyes to his stern more earnestly than we watched our own compass. The weather held and the seas never rose above a four-foot chop. In the midst of frantic efforts just to keep the hooks baited, the boat on course, and the engine running, I grabbed every moment I could to look out across the beautiful expanse of the blue and rolling sea.

Every day Charles and I managed to unload half a dozen fish, and though Hobo was bringing in four and five times as many and giving us nothing more than a knowing laugh when we asked him why, we were thrilled. I guess Hobo figured he was doing enough to jump up from his work every five minutes to give us trans-oceanic instructions on everything from tightening belts on the hydraulic pump to removing the hook from the rough mouth of a shark. Because of Hobo's patient, constant, and carefully detailed explanations, we were never even conscious of the disasters we courted.

On the evening of the fourth day, walking up the dock to get my my bait, I spotted the owner of the *Donna Lou* coming my way. I was anxious to tell him of our overwhelming success. He introduced me to his friends and said that they'd come up to take the boat fishing for the weekend. From the tone of his voice, I knew immediately he had come to take the boat. From the beginning the deal was pretty shaky and so was the owner, but I had chosen to ignore it like every other negative. I waited till we were on the boat alone before trying to hash it all out in a last desperate attempt to get him to hold to the terms of our unwritten contract. He responded in no uncertain terms by untying the lines to take *Donna Lou* to the other side of the bay. Charles had already headed back to San Francisco, and I took my sack of clothes and angrily threw them into the back of Hobo's boat where I'd have to spend the rest of the night.

I sat there and watched in total despair as my only hope of going to sea disappeared in her wake, far too stupid to realize that *Donna Lou*'s departure was actually my only hope of going anywhere. Hobo's miracles could not have lasted forever.

It was a number of hours before the cold night breeze was able to penetrate my hot glow of resentment. Still I couldn't sleep. Though I was physically quite comfortable stretched out in my sleeping bag across the back deck, it was a little too easy to identify with the fate of all the fish who had gasped their last breath in this very spot. For a while I tried mapping out my future, but even the best imagination in the world would have difficulty manipulating my penniless, homeless, and boatless situation into something positive.

There certainly wasn't much of anything to indicate that in a matter of hours I'd get a break that would not only change the course of my life but would also change me in ways I could never have imagined. For now, I felt condemned to look back through the events that delivered me into this mess.

I remembered three years ago, arriving in Berkeley with one purpose in mind. To study. I'd been a student in Chicago for the last six years. I'd finished the course work for my Ph.D. in chemistry. Doctoral exams were coming up, and it was time for one last merciless marathon through the books. On the other hand, no sweat; I had three whole months to prepare. Now, nobody but nobody stays on the South Side of Chicago if they can leave. I'd go to Berkeley (because of the library, of course), get a part-time job, and study.

In less than two weeks I was astray.

I met Jim—handsome and adventuresome, a fireman by trade and a lover of boats at heart. "How would you like to make a trip down to Mexico by boat?" he asked. Mexico? I'd never been to Mexico. "Why, certainly!" About the only reservation in my mind was the certainty that the days and days of running would get boring, boring, boring.

And so it was, after the initial excitement of passing under the Golden Gate Bridge, three hours passed and we were barely outside Half Moon Bay, four more hours and we reached Pigeon

Point, two more hours we were off the top end of Monterey Bay, another hour and a half and we reached the bottom of Monterey Bay. We'd moved less than an inch on the big chart, and there was well over a foot left to go. I was beginning to wonder what the hell I was doing in this day and age of airplanes, making a thousand-mile journey at the breakneck speed of eight knots.

By the third day, we had settled into a routine of meals, maintenance, and watches, short ones for me as Jim took a long time before giving anyone control of his boat. I remember that afternoon very clearly, sitting on the back deck, letting the endless train of waves flow past my vision. It was the first time I was aware of being in that strange state of mind, a dreamy state of completion, almost like a trance induced by the perpetual rhythm of the sea. I was surprised that the books and games we'd packed to pass the time had become irrelevant. It was more than enough to let my thoughts drift out to the horizon, float around, and return in patterns that I had never before experienced.

On the surface, the source of the sea's magnetism seemed clear. The ocean has no solidity on which to fix your eyes, no lines, corners, or permanent shapes; even the border of sea and sky is constantly redefined by the interplay of the waves. The surging rhythms not only fill your stare, they enter your body in a force of motion more profound than your own cycle of breathing. Rising and falling, tensing and relaxing, whether you are talking, eating, sleeping, or working. There is no way you can stop the mood and energy of the sea from dominating your own. But there was so much more I couldn't explain. Something lurking in the unknown depths, or drifting on the horizon, or loosed in the open space was driving me to the sea as unconsciously as a moth is driven to a flame.

I wish I could find four or five sentences that would completely convey this feeling that has lured people back to the sea again and again, no matter what the obstacles, no matter how mercilessly they have been treated on the last encounter. But probably it is best to have it slowly seep through the book in the tales of the people and events of the fishing fleet. For it is here, really, in the highly sensual relationship between the fishermen and the sea that its lure manifests itself in a richness of life unparalleled by any other in our modern world.

Then, I was content to enjoy the stillness of time and the flow of the sea, certain that somehow, no matter what the cost, I would find a way to spend a great deal of my life on this water.

The rest of the trip was quite different from what I had expected. Though the Baja coastal communities were especially intriguing to me, I was always anxious to get back on the boat and out to sea again. I began to love the way the ocean unfolded in her own time, quite different from the logical sequence and scheduled development of events as I've come to experience them on land. Out here, it was more like the way a forgotten dream image suddenly pops into your mind at the most unexpected moment, sweeps you emotionally, and submerges again without the slightest hint of explanation.

One time, while standing a quiet watch in the deep sleepy hours of the night, I was suddenly terrified as electric torpedoes seemed to head directly at the boat. I had to force myself out of a dead freeze to race forward and wake Jim. It turned out they were porpoises, lit up with the phosphorescent microbes that frequently swarm these waters. Their bodies were completely, perfectly outlined in light identical to starlight and left a dazzling trail behind them at least forty feet long. For almost half an hour after I stopped trembling, we watched a display more spectacular than the most extravagant Fourth of July as the dolphins whipped, jumped, and flashed in the infinite dark around us. Then, with no warning, they left us with nothing to ponder but the void.

Another time, we had been traveling for many hours without the slightest sign of life on the sea or in the sky. The sun was about to set, and it looked like a peaceful end to a very quiet day. The first thing I noticed were the birds, flocks of them blotting the sky as they seemed to come out of nowhere. They began diving frantically on the bait which had begun boiling out of the surface of the sea as their teeming schools were chased by the larger fish below. "Look," I said, pointing to the north, at the same time Jim was exclaiming, "Look!" as he pointed to the south. Dolphins, literally thousands of them, were leaping high into the air as far as our eyes could see against the now blazing color of the setting sun. We stood there speechless amidst this powerful eruption of life from the sea. Then, less than five minutes after the sun disappeared below the horizon, we were once again the only living creatures in sight across the full expanse of the sea.

I felt like I was just beginning to savor my first taste of the sea, and there loomed the Golden Gate Bridge ahead of us, stretched across the two worlds with all the structural grandeur that such a task requires. On the other side was a maze of beaten paths and a decision. It took but a minute for the boat to pass through its watery shadow, but I guess a big part of my soul never made the trip.

"You're crazy!" yelled my professor. "You're crazy!" he screamed again as if there were some possibility I didn't hear him the first time. "You've got it made, and you're going to give it all up for what?"

He did have a point, six years of work and study down the drain for what? A wild and restless whim? I didn't have a penny, a job, or a plan back then, either. I just knew that after seeing the stunning beauty and drama of the Pacific, going back to Chicago would have been like committing myself to jail.

Besides, I thought as I leaned against the phone booth and looked around the town, it hadn't escaped my notice that Berkeley 1968 was specializing in outlets for wild and restless whims. But I even surprised myself when, a month later, I was deeply embedded in the staff of the *Berkeley Free Press*.

It was three years before I picked up the thread of my desire to be at sea, and then it was quite by chance. I had wandered down to Ocean Trader's Fish Dock to take a picture of some sea gulls fighting over a piece of bait. It seemed like the ideal image to illustrate an article on the latest Berkeley City Council meeting.

It was early April, and the dock was high-pitched with everyone's preparations for the upcoming salmon season. I couldn't help but overhear a group of fishermen as they hotly discussed the negotiations for the year's salmon price. For years, I'd pictured being on the ocean a luxury for those very few who could afford a boat; now, listening to these guys, it finally sank into my mind that fishing was a way to make it pay. And there was the dream again, fresh and salty as a wind that just rushed in from the sea.

I asked the first person I saw if he knew of anyone who needed a deckhand. "Why don't you ask Halum on the *Mary K*. I think he needs a crew." He told me Halum had been fishing for many years and that he was an older man in his sixties. Great, I thought, that solves one problem right away. The *Mary K*. was a sturdy-looking, forty-five-foot, northern-style fishing boat, albeit with a lot of hours on her last paint job.

I went over to the side of his boat and yelled, "Anyone aboard?"

"Yeah, who the hell is it?" came a voice from deep inside the hull.

"May I come aboard?" I asked.

"Now what the hell do you think this is, the Navy?" The voice was getting closer, and just then he stepped halfway out the cabin to see who was there. He was tall, weathered, bent, and lanky.

"I'm Marie."

He shook my hand and broke into a devilish smile. We talked long enough for him to be convinced that I wouldn't be getting seasick, and he told me that he was planning to leave at three thirty that morning for a five-day salmon trip. I went home, called the "City Desk," grabbed a few things, and returned immediately.

By now the sun had set, and five or six of his fishermen buddies were all gathered in his galley around a couple of bottles of wine. Right away I liked this group very much. They were telling old sea stories and laughing easily at each other's raw sense of humor. And drinking more wine and laughing and pretty soon it was one o'clock. It wasn't hard to figure that we wouldn't be going out the Gate at three thirty, but I left the group unnoticed and hit the sack anyway. The next thing I heard was the roar of the big diesel engine, not four feet from my head. It was 3:00 A.M. I dragged myself from the bunk up to the cabin just to make the good first showing. He greeted me cheerily with "What took you so long to get up?"

Exactly three thirty and we were passing under the Gate. I was thrilled to be here again, but I was ecstatic when he handed me the big wheel, gave me a course, and retreated to his galley table. Despite the fact that he never looked up from his magazine, I trusted that he sensed precisely where that boat was every second. Every once in a while he'd mumble something about "Watch that boat on your port," or "Keep more to the right of that buoy or we'll be wearing it."

When the dawn broke, Halum came to life a little and yelled through the cabin, "Hey, honey." I decided to derail this line of thinking immediately, cut him off, and said very emphatically, "I'm not your honey!"

For a moment all was quiet, and then I heard him slowly, methodically walking up behind me. In the slow motion of half-feigned shock he came to rest his full weight against the dash and just as slowly turned his eyes to mine in total disbelief, turned around, walked back through the cabin, and slid back in his seat without once breaking his pace. A couple of minutes passed, and I heard in a very carefully long drawn-out sigh, "Well, I'll be danged." So I looked out the port window, and then I looked out the starboard window for a little while, and then I looked at the compass, giving myself plenty of time to think of just the right words, because inevitably, out here on our way to the infinite horizon, I had to say something that worked. Suddenly, I was bolted up hard with the loud and fast yelling from behind, "Hey, what's your name, you want a cup of coffee?"

I really liked his sense of humor, but I sure hoped that's all it was.

We were working a school of fish about ten miles southeast of the Farallon Islands, right smack in the middle of the shipping lanes to San Francisco. It's very unusual for anyone to drift on the salmon grounds at night, and never would anyone drift here. A little after sunset, the rest of the fleet picked up their gear and headed full speed for the land. Halum finished coiling the last leader, walked up to the pilot station, pulled the engine out of gear, hit the kill button, went back to the stove, pulled out a pot, and started fixing up some garlic and beans laced with a little red wine. Every twenty minutes during the night he got up, checked the radar for ships, and returned to sleep for another twenty minutes. I could like it or not.

In all fairness, Halum's harassment never went beyond verbal absurdity. The days, in fact, were an Olympian mountain of work, a herculean test of my endurance, a demolishing shock to my image of myself as a person of boundless energy. The gear had to be baited and in the water before the sun cracked the horizon. At least one of us, and most of the time both of us, were running the gear up and down steadily, all day long, until the sun dropped below the opposite horizon. We were catching between thirty-five and forty-five fish a day. Each one had to be meticulously gutted, gilled, and cleaned, as salmon is one of the most perishable fish of the sea. If I wasn't cleaning fish, I was making baits; and if I wasn't making baits, Halum was instantly reminding me that it had been at least ten minutes since I'd run the gear on my side of the boat. And when I was running the gear, he was forever checking to be sure that I was watching for oncoming boats. If I went up to the cabin for a drink, I'd inevitably return with Halum mumbling something just loud enough for me to hear about the collapsible quality of land people. By late afternoon, I'd look off to the west where the sun seemed to be hovering for hours in the same spot, and I'd mumble something about the masochistic quality of sea people. Finally, around 9:00 P.M. that big old sun would set in a blaze of colors like you never get to see on land. I'd lean against the rail, take a deep breath, and feel that, after all, every moment of work was worth the splendorous sights I could see. And in less time than it took to think that thought, Halum would be yelling from the cabin, "You'd better get those fish bedded down in the ice before the sun jumps back at you from the east."

Down in the ice hold were seven-foot-high bins full of crushed ice that had hardened into solid blocks, and there was a nasty-looking tool called a devil's fork with which to break it. Each fish had to have its belly individually packed with ice, be bedded on its back next to the other fish, and the whole row covered with a layer of newly broken ice. By the time I got to the galley table, my tortured hands rebelled at the simple act of holding a fork. And my puzzled mind kept wondering what it was about the work that was more satisfying than anything I'd done before.

Despite the mind-numbing exhaustion at the end of the day, I was glad that Halum had doled out the tasks as he would to any other deckhand. I was certainly learning that commercial fishing had nothing to do with the image of a fish pole in one hand and a beer can in the other. And I was gaining a whole new respect for the old-time captains and the many layers of skills over which they have complete command. This man was old, tired, and never more than a quart low on wine, but he was so in touch with that boat, the sea, and the fish as to make you wonder if they were not all somehow only parts of the same being. He handled the gear with the easy efficiency of a dance, every movement timed to the pitch of the sea. He talked the fish into the boat and never failed to get them aboard; he anticipated every mistake I was about to make with the gear, heard every ping of the pistons, knew the precise location of everyone in the fleet, and had a grand old time back there catching fish even when the seas were spitting their cold frothy tops down his torn yellow oilskin.

One time, I was pulling a line, and, before the first leader had even reached the surface, Halum yelled and shoved me out of the

way, "I'll get that fish!" The fish was way down on the third leader
and what a monster. Halum grabbed the leader and stood there
with the frozen tension of a stalking cat. "OK, baby," he said to
the fish in the hushed tones of a hypnotist, "don't do anything to
upset me and this will take less than a minute." It was ten minutes
of life and death concentration before Halum lifted the fish over
the stern like a feather. He admired this beautiful animal for a
minute, estimated his weight at thirty-eight pounds, and ran to the
radio. I couldn't hear his end of the conversation, but his buddy's
answer came back loud and clear over the back deck speaker.
"Oh, no, Halum, I know my fish is bigger than yours, and I don't
want no bottle of wine. Either you put up that fish or the bet's off."

The fifth day, the wind came up and the seas got nasty. Even at
trolling speed the *Mary K.* was beginning to fall sharply off the
crests of each passing wave. In spite of the good fishing, I blessed
that storm. Twenty-four hours a day for five days was too long to
be under anyone's command.

Finally back in the Sausalito channel, I had one final job of
going back into the hold, breaking the fish out of the ice, and
throwing them up on deck in preparation for unloading. When I
came to the thirty-eight-pounder, I knew this baby would need a
hefty throw to get him over the hatch coaming. With a swing and
a grunt, up he went. The next thing I heard was a big splash where
there should have been a loud thump. That lousy fish went right
over the side; I had a bad feeling I was to follow. There was an
unending stream of angry yelling coming from the cabin. Halum
must have been looking back at just the right time and seen that
fish flying by the cabin door like a bird. I pulled the hatch cover
over my head, determined to sit in the ice with the fish until we
tied to the dock. Once there, I jumped off the boat and cornered a
guy named Tom on the other side of the dock. When I briefly outlined the story, he offered to let me stay on his boat for the night so
I could get my things from "what's his name" in the morning after
he cooled off.

That night, though I was way on the other side of the dock, it
was all too obvious that Halum was coursing through the wine as
passionately as the *Mary K.* plows into a head-on sea. He turned
on his radio PA system and began broadcasting full volume
through the loudspeaker on his back deck. I'm sure they heard him
in San Francisco. Complete with slurs and burps, he must have

told over ten different versions of what happened to his by now eighty-pound fish. In the time it takes a flock of sea gulls to gather around a piece of old bait, every boat at the dock was involved in the act. Even Tom turned on his PA and began yelling at Halum to shut up. Right then and there, that was the moment I vowed to get my own boat. Captain, I was sure, would be the quantum leap to the freedom and adventure I sought.

Just my luck, Tom happened to know of a boat that was for lease. Her name was the *Donna Lou*.

Dawn was gnawing away at the Bodega night as mercilessly as my rememberings brought me full circle back to the sight of my latest bellyflop into the sea.

Damn that sun; now I'd have to get up and do something constructive. Maybe if I cursed that bold ball of fire long enough, it would slither right back over the horizon from whence it came. When that didn't work, I decided to call Jim, then Kathy, then Ann, Bob, and Molly, call all my friends and spread my misery in the hopes that they would sympathize the problem away. An unhappy infant would have shown more class.

"Hi, Jim, I realize it's 5:00 A.M., but you know what that jerk who owned the *Donna Lou* did to me? He waited until I put all that work in the boat, started catching a few fish, and last night he came and took it away."

"Just think," said Jim cheerfully, "now you'll get to celebrate your twenty-seventh birthday."

I almost hung up, I was so mad. I should have known better than to call him anyway. When Jim had first seen the *Donna Lou*, he said he didn't think he wanted to come aboard because if he "had to go down with a boat, he didn't want it to be tied to the dock."

"Look," he said, "why don't you lease my boat for the rest of the season."

I was sure he said this to appease me, because deep down I knew as well as he that as far as my ability at sea was concerned, I was an accident looking for a place to happen. I was as surprised as Jim must have been when the first word out of my mouth was "When?"

2

Getting Hooked on Salmon

I WENT TO Berkeley and talked with Jim for a long time.

The *Tjallee* was a work of art to Jim. Every detail of that boat had been meticulously engineered, the rigging was flawless, the hull was perfectly maintained and finished with a high gloss paint job that wouldn't last a week on the fishing grounds. That boat meant so much to him, and the lease meant so much to me. I saw the doubts go through his mind, and a couple of times made up my own mind that there was no way I could take the responsibility. With no other basis to his reasoning than friendship and blind faith, Jim leased me the boat until the end of salmon season. I was more terrified for the welfare of the *Tjallee* than I ever was for my life.

The next morning as I was going out the Gate on an ominous grey sea, it finally hit me that I'd gone too far. By now I should have known that you don't just jump on a boat and call yourself a fisherman. Most of the guys work for years as deckhands before getting their own boats.

And that was another thing—guys, all guys. How many years had I been talking about women's rights to go anywhere and do anything? Now that I was here, I found myself staring nervously into the water, wondering if maybe there wasn't some kind of cosmic serpent centaur lurking in the waves, waiting to enforce the age-old law—women are Jonahs at sea.

You laugh at the weakness of my convictions, but sometime put your bow in an alien territory, and you'll be amazed as I always am how frightfully alive are the myths you think you've shed.

Which brings me to Elise standing right beside me, chattering away like she wasn't even aware we'd left the dock. I hardly knew her when she came down to the dock and said she wanted to fish. She had just arrived in this country from her home in a small town in England. Her accent was so thick, sometimes I could barely understand what she was saying. The trouble was none of my friends were available, and Elise would have to do.

Watching her now didn't strengthen my spirits a bit. She looked so dainty and delicate, I could imagine the squeals the first time we caught a fish—assuming, of course, she hadn't already fainted at the sight of the bait. And now she's telling me over her two-finger hold on a cup of tea that she had just gotten married four weeks ago and "Richard" had just bought a shop in Berkeley and she hoped to make "a bit of money, you know, to help Richard with the business."

I was headed straight for Bodega; I knew I needed Hobo's help more than ever.

The first few days I showed Elise as much as I could about the process on the back deck, but it wasn't much of a demonstration. We caught two fish in three days—two-thirds of a fish per day. The look on Elise's face made me feel like a beggar on Wall Street.

"Hobo," I asked in panic and despair, "what happened to those fish that were here two weeks ago when I had the *Donna Lou*?" Hobo looked at me with that astonished stare that used to cross his face whenever we reminded him just how green green could be.

"Marie, those fish got tails. They travel night and day—up the coast as far as Canada and then all the way down again, then way out to the deep and back to the rocks. Every day and every year is different. The more years you fish, the more they drive you crazy." And the more he talked, the more his voice rang with the frustration of those years. "You've got to travel the coast like a yo-yo for those fish and you see what you get?" he said, pointing to his grey hairs. "Each one of these was given to me by a fish that was supposed to be somewhere, and I ran all night only to find they were already one hundred miles farther than where they were supposed to be. Now my boat's paid for, my kids are grown up, and I got smart. I sit here in Bodega and wait for the fish to come to me."

I was sitting on the back deck, trying to think of something to erase Elise's look of utter despair when Hobo received a call on the radio which he always left on low volume until just before he went to sleep. The voice that came back resonated the speaker to its capacity. I couldn't understand the Italian, but from the tragic operatic tone, I could have guessed this man hadn't seen a fish for a week.

"What did he say?" I asked Hobo when they finished.

"I'm not going to tell you 'cause you'll blab. Just get up early and follow me out."

So that's how they cover their trail, I thought. We were up at 3:00 A.M., and Hobo's cabin light was already on. "Are you ready?" he called across the boats, between a whisper and a yell. "Now listen, don't talk on the radio all day unless it's an emergency, or if someone calls you first. And if someone calls you, be cagey. You know what cagey means? Don't blab. It's pretty foggy, so stay close. If you get lost, don't call because there's no way I can find you anyway. Just head south-southwest two and a half hours and then fish. OK, throw the lines and let's go."

Jesus, my first day in the fog, and no radio. If Hobo hadn't tossed the lines, they'd still be tied. Except for the dim yellow haze of his mast light and the invisible rise and fall of the boat, the whole world was black. A couple of hours trying to hold onto that light with my stare, knowing it was the only thing that separated me from being swallowed by the cosmic void, and I began to question my own existence.

Even the light of day did little to dissipate the eerieness. All we could see were the subtle shadings of three or four waves in every direction as they floated through the mist. The muted color of Hobo's boat seemed to levitate as he floated back and forth across the border of our vision. I don't know what was more terrifying, the thought of losing Hobo or the possibility of suddenly being rammed by a 100,000-ton freighter plowing through the fog at eighteen knots. Or perhaps it was the fear of giving in to the temptation to stop the engine and just sit there for the day, gazing into the wet, dreamy pastures of the sea. The ocean had never looked so soft. I imagined that at any moment it would seem perfectly reasonable if Bambi had walked into our vision and begun grazing on the golden green kelp that floated by. It was terrifying that part of me couldn't care less if we got lost.

Exactly two and a half hours of running time and Hobo slowed his boat to set the gear. Elise and I took our time, being careful that our boat stayed snuggled up to Hobo like a puppy dog. We had barely gotten the first line set on either side of the boat, when Elise looked over and saw Hobo throw three fish on his boat in a row. The sudden change aboard the *Tjallee* would not have been more dramatic if a bomb had exploded on deck. For a moment I stood totally stunned as I stared at Elise in disbelief. She had launched into action, jamming baits and running the lines with such passion and speed, I wondered if she had become possessed.

"Hey, take it easy!" I yelled. "You're going to get hurt." She never even heard me as she took a wild swing with the gaff, reached precariously over the side with both arms and half her body, grunted loudly, and fell back onto the deck with the twenty-pound fish flying through the air and landing in her lap.

"There's more, there's more!" she screamed through her laughter.

By now the lines were so loaded with fish, they shook the rigging all the way up to the mast. In no time we were over our boots in a frantic, whirling chaos as we tried in vain to keep on top of throwing fish, running lines, making baits, cleaning fish, staying out of each other's way, yelling, screaming, trying to undo the endless mistakes in the midst of hysterical laughter that barely masked the greed. I was thrilled; we were a fireball, class A team that deserved each other.

It was too bad neither of us had the slightest idea of what we were doing.

We were in 'em, no doubt about that. There was either a fish or a stripped hook on every leader. "Like picking grapes" was how I'd heard the other fishermen call this wonderful phenomenon, except our grapes keep jumping out of our hands. Then the gurdies that pull the lines began to slip under the weight of so many fish, and we were shredding our hands as we grabbed the wire and helped it along. And there were big balls of that golden bull kelp that kept tangling in the gear and fish. Every time we'd get clear of the kelp, Hobo would turn his boat and head straight back into it. It sure seemed a stupid thing to do, considering all the other problems created by so many fish. I felt like giving him a call, but despite the excitement, I remembered my promise.

The fog slowly dispersed under the heat of the morning sun. All the moody greys of the water and sky came alive with blues and greens. I could see there were only six of us out here in this very private heaven wherever we were. On the radio we could hear the endless mournful cries of faraway fishermen fruitlessly scouting one area after another. Until you get used to this wailing ritual, you might easily imagine they were all about to shoot themselves.

"Hey, kid, everything OK over there?" That was Hobo. I grabbed the mike before thinking and began spouting like a whale. "God, Hobo, we can't make the baits fast enough, and for some reason the gurdies can't pull the weight of all these fish. They're all big ones, too. How come you keep running through the kelp line?" There was a long pause. "Hobo, you pick me up?"

Silence!

Within the hour, a steady stream of boats was popping out of the horizon, their bows locked on our position like the noses of bloodhounds.

Nonetheless, the big beautiful salmon continued to jump on our lines even during the normal slack of the midday hours. Despite our torn hands, which were beginning to look more like raw hamburger dangling from our wrists, the excitement of the day would have kept us fishing way into the night. But by three in the afternoon, we were clean out of hooks and leaders. Between the kelp, the fish darting wildly at the end of their leaders, and our complete ignorance of how to handle it all, as often as not the gear came up in big, baffling, tight tangles that seemed impossible to unravel. We'd stare at these messes of hooks, wires, kelp, and thrashing fish, trying to decide where we dare reach in and make the cut. The second the cut was made, hooks flew like bullets, fish swam away trailing their leaders behind them, wire cables frayed and popped. All the way home we griped about the loss of gear, never thinking to thank the Lord for our eyesight.

On the way in we tried every cream or ointment we had to soothe the wounds in our hands. It wasn't until we hit the fish dock and wrapped our hands around that big wad of cash that we found our first relief from the pain.

We took our money and gave it to the gear store in exchange for enough supplies so we could go fishing the next day. It would be a number of years before I understood that this was the real job of the fishermen, courier of the fish companies' money, carrying it over to the gear store or up to the boat yard so they could get you ready to go out and get the fish company more fish. For now I was basking in the delusion that we had merely chosen to spend it this way, as freely as one might choose to buy a steak or a plane ticket to Tahiti.

We were barely halfway through our work on the back deck when Hobo came plowing down the last stretch of the channel. He delivered one thousand dollars' worth of fish. When he tied along-side, I wanted nothing more than to extol the fortune that had come our way, but I remembered the awful silence that had fol-lowed the broadcast and buried my head in my work. Hobo jumped on the stern of our boat without saying a word and began tracing the hydraulic lines back to the pressure relief valve. "You see this valve? That's how you adjust for the slippage in your gurdies. And the reason we were in the kelp is because that kelp was trapped in a rip where two currents meet, in the same way, schools of herring get trapped in the rip. What do salmon like to eat?" he asked as if completely overwhelmed by the demands of this simple friendship.

"Herring," I answered as my voice cracked between the sylla-bles in shame.

"And how the hell are you pulling those fish anyway? You keep wrapping that leader around your hands and in one more day you won't be able to hold on to a minnow." He followed with a demon-stration of how to hold the leader over the back of the hand and through the thumb to allow for controlled slippage so you don't jerk the hook out of the fish's mouth and so you come back at the end of the day with the same two hands you started with. It wasn't until Hobo looked around the back deck at the piles of tangled wire and the spools of expensive new wire, the busted leaders, bent hooks, splicing tools, and thawing bait that he broke into that knowing laugh. He must have remembered what he always said, "The ocean's the only place left in this modern world where the old are more valued than the young." The time it took for him to explain how to work the gear to avoid these tangles only served to make the point clear. What was worse, Hobo never said a word about the broadcast. The thank yous I wanted to give this incredi-ble man were so big they always stuck in my throat.

We got to sleep around one; the alarm must have gone off at about 3:00 A.M., but it wasn't until 3:15 when Hobo banged loudly on the cabin door that we awoke. I crawled out of the lower bunk and grabbed for the coffeepot, but my hands were as frozen shut as if they'd been doused with crazy glue the night before. It got to be the morning procedure; each cut had to be cracked open before my hands would function. Handling the lines and steering the boat were like the stations of the cross. Which was nothing compared to Elise's first job of the morning. She had to reach into an icy brine solution, pull out a stiff, salty herring, carefully set the hook, then reach back in the bucket fifty times each morning. I reached in that bucket once and almost jumped off the boat.

Of all the frustrations and complications that were unfolding before us in this amazing business, this is the one that brought us to tears. For the inexperienced and the uncalloused hands, even the routine of a slow day was excruciating. Aching cold, water-shriveled, cable-cut, lead-banged, hooked, rope-burned, jelly-fished, salmon-toothed, rock cod–spined hands. Not surprisingly, two of my strongest memories from that first year have to do with hands. One time Elise pulled a line just a little too fast, caught her hand on the wire, and got it pulled between the wire and a sheave. In trying to get out, she turned the wrong valve and pulled the fifty-pound lead against her hand and the sheave, smashing every cell in her flesh. That she didn't break any bones was no consolation. That she wanted to keep fishing amazed me.

Another time we got in a school of dog shark. Now every creature on this earth has a purpose, and the dog shark was put here for the misery of the fisherman. It has a lot of adaptations to the cause. The dog shark covers the earth, marauding in huge schools that foul and tangle every kind of fish gear known to man. Their sinister, electric green eyes and powerful, writhing, grey, ugly bodies could not be more fitting on the devil. But what I got introduced to this time was the two-inch dorsal spine rammed up the back of my fingernail, a full injection of that sophisticated poison it carries that sends a bonfire leaping through your hand, then your arm, right up to the shoulder.

Between the pain, the cold, and the fatigue, I had to laugh at my image of fishing as a healthy outdoor occupation. What we learned, for better and for worse, was that we could push past it, forget it. How? It's like all the other problems people seem to think we were so brave to have tackled at sea. We had no choice.

It was quite a realization that another boat can't come alongside to assist at sea; two boats tied together at sea would crush each other in a minute. It's just you and the boat and your problem.

You can't even go out for a walk to avoid it all. We could kick, scream, throw things overboard, and we often did, but it always came down to the same thing: fix it or you don't go home. It's a great and inevitable lesson of the sea, being pushed past every limitation you thought you had and discovering the extent of your resourcefulness.

Tied to the dock for the evening is another story. The stifled fatigue and frustration of the day seemed to pounce on us as soon as the lines were secure to the dock. We'd been fishing now for six days straight, it was ten thirty, and as usual we were the only ones still up making preparations for the next day. If it hadn't been for Elise standing beside me, salting and icing the bait, I would have gone directly to bed, and I had a feeling that if I hadn't been standing there tying one leader after another, Elise would have left that thirty dollars' worth of bait to rot.

"What are you girls doing?" Hobo yelled across the boats. "Don't you ever look at the sky?" I felt like making some deeply sarcastic remark about all the time we had for stargazing, but Hobo continued. "You're not going anywhere tomorrow; it's gonna blow."

"How do you know?" I said. "The weather report was good."

"Experience," he said as if that were the final word and returned to his bunk below. Experience. That's how he catches more fish than us, that's how he gets his gear in the water so fast, that's how he knows where to find the fish, and now he informs us that's how he predicts the weather. Who could argue? Who wanted to? We were about to experience one of the greatest rewards of being in this fishing business. The simple act of going to bed had, in my short experience, been transformed into the most indescribable pleasure, the highest indulgence, the most profound luxury on earth.

The first morning of a blow, everyone usually grabs a couple of extra hours of sleep, but heroic efforts are made to hold on to the pace of the sea and not yield to the tempting recreations of land which are beckoning from only yards away. There's still work to be done, the kind of work that makes you marvel all the more at the self-restraint of those who manage to do it. Clean up! Clean up the ice hold full of slime, clean up the gear, clean up the blood the sun has baked into the paint all over the hull, clean up the cabin which has been daily rocked into disarray, clean up yourself which after six days at sea only your imagination can describe.

Elise and I got involved in scrubbing the boat with an enthusiasm for thoroughness that made it all too obvious it was our first time through this ritual. It was so out of place that in the course of the morning, three different fishermen passing the boat made the same comment. "Hey, don't you girls know that a clean boat doesn't catch fish?" It was our first day in port with the rest of the fleet, and that was actually a pretty mild introduction to the riddles and remarks that would follow.

Hobo came over to the boat with Freckles, the friend of his who called us on the fish a couple of nights before. This good-looking old man with weathered face and pure white hair underneath a black skipper's hat couldn't come closer to the movie image of an old sea captain. He had fished for fifty-two years from Peru for anchovies, all the way up to Alaska for salmon. As he told us himself, "I've worn out more pairs of boots than shoes." But I could tell by the delighted curiosity in his face that old Freckles was looking at something he had never before seen on the ocean, two ladies running a fishing boat. He checked us over, checked over the boat, and then told us about another lady he had heard of who used to fish albacore.

"What happened to her?" I asked, faintly suspecting this story had a purpose.

"She drowned," he said casually. "I think she got too tired one day, fell asleep at the wheel, ran onto the rocks, and lost everything."

That was my introduction to Freckles who, quite contrary to my initial impression, turned out to be one of my best and most respected friends on the ocean.

As for the woman captain, I heard a lot of different versions of that story, including the comment from the wife of an old-time fisherman, who said "Bullshit" to the whole thing.

Next came a young guy who, I quickly gathered, was on an errand. "I hope you don't mind my asking," he stammered, "but I, I mean we, were wondering, are you girls gay?"

Well, two girls on a boat, what else are you going to think? Elise looked out over the harbor full of boats and said, "If that's the case, there's sure a lot of gay men in this town." A few more comments about how killer whales are attracted to the smell of women and I couldn't decide whether to hurl a lead at the next guy who passed or go cringe in the forecastle until the wind quit. No kidding, I could pit my whole being against the sea, but ridicule is something that I never could handle. And more than anything I hate being laughed at by men. And here I was, surrounded. It didn't take much of an imagination to see that our operation was a potential bottomless barrel of laughs for the fleet, free for the picking. The more I thought about it, the more I geared myself for all-out, enraged, defiant, full on, smart-mouthed attack against the next guy who came too close.

I looked over at Elise as she busily cleaned up the last of the hooks and neatly hung them in the box.

"Hey, Elise," I said, my voice full of rage, "don't these jerks bother you?"

"What?"

"These goddamned, macho, manipulative excuses of men," I said with plenty of emphasis.

"Macho?" said Elise, genuinely perplexed. "They seem more to me like little old ladies hanging over the backyard fence. Don't let them get to you, Marie. We're learning. They'll get the idea that we're going to stick around and that'll be the end of it."

I was dumbfounded. It was Elise's first time away from home, and she still looked every bit the ideal image of daddy's little girl. She amazed me daily with her energy and determination, and now I see she has such inner certainty about what we're doing that this stuff just rolled off her back.

And here I am, wise to the world, captain of my ship, and never before had I needed to lean so heavily on two people. Elise and Hobo; they were heaven-sent. It would take a number of years for me to get all this straightened out with the rest of the fleet. But right for now Elise saved me from blowing it completely with the most enjoyable community of people I've ever had the opportunity to meet.

"Come on," she said, "hurry up and finish. It looks like the fun's about to begin." And so it was!

By late afternoon the press of chores was giving way to the easy and enthusiastic socializing of people who for the last week had only been able to communicate by radio. Many of them were being reunited for the first time in months, or even years, by the chance positioning of the fish. The Monterey fleet was here in Bodega because their own backyard hadn't seen a salmon for the whole season. And there was a sprinkling of boats from different ports along the coast who had placed their bets on fish at Bodega and made the move. When the wind blows, it's not any port in a storm, it's the closest one. The deep friendships of the fishermen seem to thrive on this shuffling from the winds of chance. Whether it was a good trip or a bad trip, the first night in port after a blow is always a celebration.

We had no end of warm invitations to join the many lavish barbecues that were being organized on the backs of the boats. It was totally puzzling in light of the comments we received that day. It was like "Sure, you're going to drown, but don't be worrying about the little things right now; the work is done and it's time to eat, drink, and be merry."

As the sun set into the wine, people began a slow migration up to the Tides Restaurant and Bar. Without any cars to ferry people to the lack of entertainment in the neighboring towns, much as people bitch and scream, the Tides is the center of the party. Inside there's a bar and tables for fishermen and a restaurant for the tourists, with a movable partition in between. It was pretty easy to walk in among the loud laughter and lively conversations. More than anything I just wanted to sit down and listen, unnoticed, and that was pretty much what happened except for the row of drinks that was lining up in front of me way beyond my capacity. The events of the last fishing trip were rehashed unmercifully until each fish had been caught at least six times. The bravado of a thirty-fish tack mixed in perfect harmony with cries of the guy who was a day late and a dollar short, as did the yells across the room of sudden recognition of friends who hadn't seen each other since they were blown together in places as far away as Seattle and L.A. And soon it was time for Hobo to join Uncle D.B. in their well-lubricated renditions of songs they had played to many such audiences along the wind-blown bars up and down the coast. As if on cue, Mitch, the owner of the Tides, came in and closed the partition to protect the tourists from the real tenor of the fleet they had driven so far to see.

The next day, the day after, and the day after that were carried through time on a steady stream of stories. The immediate details of the last trip gave way to the more lasting stories from way back when. Bill's story about the whale that once came up under his boat to rub his belly reminded Jack about the time a whale tangled in his gear and ripped his poles down in the middle of a hot salmon bite, which reminded Rich about his 200-fish day when he anchored at the Islands. Too tired to clean the fish, he awoke the next morning with a sea lion sitting on his back deck munching on his catch, which reminded everyone how much they hated anchoring at the Farallon Islands. Jerry walked in with a string of cuss words about his hydraulic pump, and three of the men seated at the table got up and went down to his boat to give him a hand. Two of the local fishermen sat in their place and began talking excitedly about the big fish scores that had taken place off Eureka just before the blow. When they left, I asked one of the Eureka fishermen if he would try to get home when the wind quit. He laughed, "They try that trick every year; it's all just part of the music."

I began to feel comfortable enough in the easy ramblings of the conversation to begin asking some of the hundreds of questions I had about surviving in this strange new world. What I really needed to know was how to catch more fish. Even though they did it every day, nobody seemed to be able to say just how. It was as if I had asked them to describe the path to Nirvana. Mostly they laughed or gave me the old "When you're hot you're hot and when you're not you're not." So I got very specific with my questions, only to find I had opened a Pandora's box of magic and ritual that was mine to unravel for as long as I fished the sea.

"Just tell me what you put at the end of the leader." Occasionally someone would get into it, the different lures, flashers, and ways of baiting depending on whether the sun was out or behind the clouds, or whether the water was milky green, olive green, brown or blue, depending on the mood of the fish, the time of day, the speed of the boat, and on and on. It didn't bother me that it was complex; it was just that the first guy swore by one thing and the next guy by its opposite. But swear by it they did, with stories of boatloads full of fish to back up every hot lure they had. Old Ron even took me down to the stern of his boat when no one was looking and showed me a set of gear that looked like crap. "It is crap," he said. "I keep the real stuff hidden in the cabin. If I show it to you, you have to promise not to tell a soul. If anyone used it, it won't work anymore."

It was so frustrating; I'd spent twenty-six years of my life adjusting to a rational world, and suddenly I was immersed in a society where even the most successful, especially the most successful, were involved in a voodoo more elaborate than anything that's come out of the ages.

The only one who gave me any handle at all on this mysterious business was Manuel on the *Elma G.* "You've just got to work at it until you find a system that works for you and your boat. And then you have to believe in it or it stops working." Having found someone who could at least speak to my frustration, I asked Manuel how he went about locating the fish in this vast expanse of water. He turned to look out toward the sea, sucked in a deep breath, filled his chest. "You smell 'em; if you can't smell 'em, you'll never be able to find 'em." It was a long time before I understood that a fisherman's thinking is of necessity as fluid as the sea.

And as gossipy as the wind. Once I loosened up a bit, the fishermen's curiosity about me was unleashed, and no shyness about it. "Where are you from? How'd you get into fishing? Are you married? Why not? Do you fool around? Why not? Where'd you get the boat? Who's Jim? . . ."

The lighthearted, unself-consciousness of their approach would have put me at ease—except for one thing. The second day I had just finished telling Banjo about my trip to Mexico. I got up to run an errand, left him deep in conversation with his friends, walked two blocks to the gear store, and another fisherman waiting in line said, "I hear you took a trip down to Mexico a few years back."

The lightning speed of this grapevine wasn't nearly as intimidating as its voracious appetite. Everything I did and everything I said was sucked up and disseminated with such fervor that for a while it made me very cautious. Until I realized, of course, that it didn't matter. The grapevine's capacity for creative embellishment made all attempts to temper it in vain.

There was one question, however, the old grapevine couldn't seem to satisfy. I know, because if I answered it once, I answered it a thousand times! "Why do you want to be captain? Why don't you work as a deckhand if you want to fish so bad?" I'd answer it as honestly as possible, and the next day the same gang would be back with the same question. So I reduced all my thoughts to what seemed like the most obvious, simple, easy to understand explanation. "I want to be captain for the same reason you want to be captain, and I don't want to be a deckhand for the same reason you don't want to be a deckhand."

"Yeah, but you're a woman."

"So what?" I'd answer.

"So what?" came back like he was thinking, My God, woman, don't you know what it means to be a woman? And I was thinking,

My God, man, didn't we settle all this two years ago in Berkeley? It became as nebulous a diatribe as my attempts to find out how they caught the fish, a perfect pair of puzzles.

In fact, the one time I seemed to communicate anything on this subject was by crossing the wires. I was up to my elbows first time trying to dismantle a pump, when here comes a fisherman to exercise his gums. "Why do you bother to go through all this when you could just sign yourself on someone else's boat?" What a pleasant interruption, I thought, so I flipped him the old "When you're hot you're hot, when you're not you're not," and he laughed like he understood.

Despite the unfathomable chasms there was one impression that was so appealing about this group that it bridged all the rest. They loved and respected their life more than any group of people I had known. Eighteen hours a day they worked the fish and the sea until the wind got so bad that their boats couldn't take the beating. Pushed to the shore by force, they rarely penetrated the land farther than the reaches of the salt air smell. Those same eighteen hours were still devoted to the fish and the sea in the tales they told, in the boats they pampered and prepared for the next trip, and the drinks they raised in homage to luck. And it wasn't just for fun!

Strangely enough, it was here, sitting among the fishermen at the Tides, that I felt my first real fear of the sea.

When they told of twenty-foot walls of water piling over the boat while still ten hours' running time from the nearest port, or anchors dragging in the middle of the night and waking to find the boat in the rocks of bar waves that would lift and heave a boat like a toy, I listened very quietly. I would have brushed it off as exaggeration or added drama for the effect of the story, but I was sitting right there and I could see in their eyes the glazed looks of remembered horror and sheer terror. I used to say how much I loved the ocean when it was rough and riled up by the wind. And I'd see that look again. "You'd better cool off, Marie; that ocean will turn on you any time." They were dead serious. "You'd better gain some respect for that old lady or you're going to be in trouble. That same ocean that gives you fish is the one that takes your friends." I did take it all in, but it was impossible to completely comprehend until I had experienced it myself. The time would come.

There was something else the fishermen were trying to get through my stubbornness. As much as they were baffled that any woman would actually choose to work in the harsh ocean, they seemed more puzzled that anyone would want to enter a business that was on its way out. "It's over, the fish are being depleted, the fleet is changing, the spawning grounds are ruined, the foreign ships are taking everything, there's too much machinery and too many gadgets, the ocean's dying, and we're going with it." I could hardly see it at all. The Pacific Ocean was bigger than anything on earth, the excitement of big catches was all around me, and the old-time spirits of the fishermen seemed alive and well to me. The fishermen were used to not being believed.

I would see it all too soon. For now I was wrapped up in discovering the richness of sea life. After all, whoever heard of a party that starts when the wind blows, includes anyone who happens to be in port, and goes on until nature calls a halt. I adapted to this part of being a fisherman with ease.

On the fifth morning when I walked confidently up to the Tides for breakfast, Ted, who had talked with me aimlessly for hours the night before, just about knocked me over as he rushed past me with a case of bait on his shoulder. The Tides was empty. I rushed down to Hobo's boat.

"Hey, Hobo, what's going on?" I asked.

"Junior blew ice," he said.

"What's that supposed to mean?"

Hobo looked out to the sea and shook his head. Finally he turned back to me. "Do I have to teach you everything? When a guy takes four tons of ice at one in the morning, it's not because he's planning to mix a drink. Everybody figures he heard some news and instead of acting like fishermen, they start acting like those lemmings in Norway. Marie," he said with finality, "you're not ready to travel." We decided to wait and go out with Hobo the next morning. It was the first time I bowed to the voice of authority.

There was no wind the next morning, but the days of blowing had left their deep tread marks in the water. An eight-foot sharp lump was how the earliest boats had described it in the very specific lingo that can name the full range of sea conditions as accurately as colors name the spectrum of light. And so it was as we headed out from behind the protection offered by the rocky headlands of Bodega Bay, *Tjallee* rolled so heavily from side to side that I wondered each time if she were coming back. It wasn't five minutes and everything in the cabin, which had been so securely stashed at the dock, was on the floor. I didn't dare check the fish gear on the back deck because it would mean undoing my hand-grip on the dash which was beginning to feel more like a perma-nent weld. The first faint light of day cast the eeriest shadows across the sea. When the boat rose on top of a wave, it exposed a view of the next trough that looked like we were about to fall off into a bottomless pit. Down she'd go and fall hard on her side in the bottom of the hole, and before I could draw a natural breath, the next wave would wrench the bow up to the sky. Even ten knots of wind would sharpen the tops of these seas to the point where riding them would be like having the boat released from the end of a stretched rubber band. For now the radio voices of experience had declared conditions fishable.

Every chore became triple the work in this nasty slop. And the unpleasantness was tripled again as the fish reports began to come in sounding more like an obituary. The Farallon Islands were dead, the forty-fathom line was dead, the waters off Fort Ross were dead; a mere four hours into the day and I was dead.

Someone called Earl on the *Annabell* and asked him what he was doing. Since he was working right in our area, we listened carefully for his answer. "OK, John, we're in the middle of making a breakfast tack here." From our short acquaintance with the language of fishing, we knew that this was either one of the thou-sands of strange terms used to describe a fishing technique or it was part of a secret code. I took my chances and got up my nerve to give him a call. "How do you make a breakfast tack, Earl?" I asked, hoping I wasn't prying into a code.

Before he had time to answer, someone else came back and explained that when there isn't much fish, you can put the boat in as sharp a turn as possible, give it full throttle and usually if there's any fish around at all, a couple will jump on the gear. That's where the name comes from, to "break fast." We hadn't had a fish for hours, and any trick that could help us connect with those elusive creatures of the depths was worth a try. Three times we followed the instructions to the letter, and three times the gear got tangled into a balled-up mess that today would make me reach for the cable cutters, send everything to the bottom of the sea, and start over from scratch. I hated to bother Earl, but we had to find out what we were doing wrong. "How come we keep tangling, Earl?" Again this time, someone else answered. "Marie, a breakfast tack is about ten or eleven o'clock in the morning when there is not much fish, a guy goes up to his cabin, throws a couple of pancakes on the griddle, pours a cup of coffee, and relaxes for a while, and that's how it gets the unusual name of breakfast tack."

Our minds were confused with a thousand different rituals for catching fish; the last thing we needed was a practical joke. It wasn't that the fishermen weren't willing to help us. In fact, in all the time I've been fishing, there hasn't been one person who has hesitated to give us advice or come down to the boat to give us a hand no matter what the hour of day or night. It's just that the only two things we could go by that everyone agreed on for catching the fish caused us as much anxiety as the fish themselves. That morning, after the lines were untangled and the joke was up, we heard it again. "Just keep your lines in the water; nobody's ever caught a fish with their gear on the deck."

"All right, so my lines are in the water and I'm still not receiving, now what?"

"Leave them there."

It occurred to us this morning in the long hours of waiting impatiently for our first salmon of the day that there is something intolerably inverted about this old saying. It's precisely at the moment you put the gear in the water that you lose control of everything. You can fine tune the engine, secure all the rigging, tie the leaders to perfection, make the prettiest baits in the world, throw it in the faces of a swarm of fish, and be better off if you spent the day at the dock.

Of course, if that didn't work, we could always fall back on the second maxim. "Experience catches fish." No one could tell us just what experience taught because, naturally, experience was the only teacher. What made all this the more frustrating was our growing realization that experience in this business was not measured in months or even years. One day, when we heard an old-timer on the radio just about reduced to the babblings of infancy by a month-long streak of bad luck, we wondered if anyone is ever freed from the tyranny of the fish. This poor guy had gone from bait to lures and back again; he'd insulated the gurdies; he even hauled his boat out of the water and changed the propeller and stern bearing, thinking perhaps they were making a noise the fish didn't like. Now, in utter desperation, he'd grabbed the microphone and wailed his story over the sea as if he were scattering the ashes on his last hope of ever catching enough to eat again.

It wasn't just the salmon that mocked the very essence of a rational human's pride. Everything about this place, the weather that daily blew holes through the forecaster's ego, the sea conditions that changed without warning, the flocks of sea birds that would as likely lead you to a dry hole as a school of fish, all seemed to be governed by the same unpredictable watery spirit. Even the boats, made of nothing but wood and fastened with iron, when their bellies are launched into the sea, seem to absorb a watery soul, and beware the fisherman who thinks he owns her.

After five hours of not catching a fish, we had analyzed the situation to the point where we wondered out loud how anyone could stake their lives and their livelihood on such elusive grounds. Luckily the sea intervened before we jumped overboard in despair by doing what it always does. It changed. The sharp, pounding waves that had flogged us all morning lay down to long, lazy swells that soothed our ride and our thoughts. The boats all around us looked now more like child's toys as they were slowly lifted to the sky and gently lowered again on the sleepy rhythms that stretched all the way from here to forever. At rare times like this, with no fish, good weather, and no emergencies, we'd pull away from the fleet, cook a gourmet meal, and talk.

And what we always talked about, though flanked in the past and the future by disaster, was just how immensely pleased we were with ourselves. How lucky we felt to be working in the midst of such beauty, how satisfying it was to be producing such beautiful food, how much we appreciated each other's crazy energy, stamina, willingness to risk it all, and our total unwillingness to die. We were fully aware that in the eyes of the fleet we were a perilous parade of predicaments. We congratulated ourselves on managing to extricate ourselves from every one of them and laugh.

Suddenly, we felt a cold chill. We looked up and realized that in those couple of minutes the fog had settled around us in a soup so thick we could barely see the bow of our own boat. Didn't the ocean care that our affection for it was already dangling on a loose thread?

I knew calling Hobo would be in vain; the last time I looked, he was at least a couple of hundred yards away, and any attempt to find him now would be a blind-man's buff. And there was no way after the breakfast tack affair and letting it be known that we had no fish that I was going to make the final announcement that we were lost. We were on our own in the fog, the situation I'd feared more than any other. It was bound to happen; this section of coast is buried in more fog than any other section of our West Coast. Sometimes it was brought by the wind, and you could see its thick, white wall approaching, and sometimes with moisture-laden air just a one-degree temperature drop below the dew point would suddenly transform a crystal clear day into a sea of mist. It didn't much matter how it got there, we had but one thought—to find the red buoy that marked the entrance to Bodega Bay. We knew we'd run fifteen miles southwest in the morning, but since then the drift of currents and breeze and the rambling course of our fishing had set us somewhere within five miles of ourselves—not a very healthy lead when you're searching for something fifteen miles away and not four feet across.

We had talked through the process numerous times with Hobo at the dock. The one navigation instrument we had on the boat was a Fathometer which told us the depth of the water. "Take a guess where you are, draw a course, and while you're running it, keep a constant eye on the bottom contour and check it against the chart. Whatever you do, don't come inside the fifteen-fathom line before you know exactly where you are; there are rocks that come out of that depth that don't give you or the boat a second chance. When you find the buoy in twenty fathoms, run the course carefully down the narrow channel between the rock island and the jagged cliffs of Bodega Head."

The idea was all very obvious and simple. But try concentrating on the recordings of a Fathometer and the markings of a chart when you're focused into the mist hoping to catch view of another boat before collision. And there was so little to distinguish on the contours of the bottom. It was like the Great Plains out here in front of Bodega. By the time we reached the twenty-fathom line, we had no idea whether we were above or below the Bodega buoy. Darkness would be coming in an hour, and I was freezing and sweating at the same time. The tension in that search for a way out of the grey caverns sure lifted the problem of catching a fish right out of our minds.

We steered to the north for a while and were certain that we were leaving the buoy far behind us to the south. So we turned to the south, and immediately we were plagued with the conviction that the buoy was to the north. How we finally found it is as impossible to say as how those two salmon appeared when we pulled the gear to run in. When we had just about given up hope, that red buoy popped out of the fog like a hallucination conjured by desire. I circled and recircled it many times, afraid to leave it for the next blind course between the rocks and the cliffs. The last leg of the channel was petrifying in the all-consuming envelope of dark and fog. We could hear the familiar activity on the dock and the idling engines long before we saw the hazy lights of home. I never, ever, wanted to go through that again.

The alarm went off at 3:00 A.M. the next morning. We got dressed, heated the coffee, I checked the engine water and oil, and Elise pulled the bait from the ice. While the engine warmed, we listened to the radio for a hint from someone who may have found a spot of fish the day before. We checked the Fathometer, turned on the running lights, cast the lines, and went fishing.

I just had the feeling that, if we could stick with it long enough, that ocean would continue to unfold its beauty and magic in the same strange way that brought us those two salmon and the buoy from the fog.

3

Waves of Fear

"WELL, HOBO," WE proclaimed loudly and giddily after unloading our last delivery of the season, "we made it! We're regulation, certified fisherwomen. The boat's in one piece, the diesel's still running on all fours, five fingers still attached to each hand, and to top it off, we're still alive."

Hobo wasn't smiling, nor did he pull his cap down and roll his eyes up like he usually does in the face of an onslaught of bullshit. Instead, he got distant and pensive and shook his head to the deck like he was trying to figure a way out of the conversation without having to explain his thoughts.

"What's the matter, Hobo?" I blurted out with my usual tact. But Hobo just kept shaking his head. "You didn't learn it right," he said with such somberness I knew not to ask him more, and Hobo walked into his cabin to commune with his beer.

Hobo's ominous riddles made me feel bad that he didn't see our season as a great success. The only thing that worried me was finding myself back on the land without a guaranteed, sure-fire plan for being able to fish the next spring. I needed my own boat, but by the end of the season, after lease, equipment, and deckhand payments, I barely had enough to live on for two months. My situation, as the Italian fishermen would call it, was "hard bread and a knife that won't cut."

Jim had an idea. The progressive British Columbia government had instituted a buyback program in order to trim the Canadian fishing fleet. The government purchased vessels from fishermen who for one reason or another had wanted out of the business, the fishing license for the boat was destroyed, and a strict limited-entry program was instituted for any new licenses.

The fish boats purchased by the government were then put up for auction and could only be registered in Canada for pleasure use. Now most people's idea of pleasure cruising doesn't include a pigeonhole cabin and a sprawling back deck full of machinery, and these boats were selling for a mere fraction of their value.

It didn't take the American fishermen long to smell a good bite. They simply purchased a boat at the Canadian auction and brought it to the United States fishery. Jim's idea was to buy one of these boats, have me deliver it to San Francisco, and I would fish it for him on a lease with an option to buy.

This mass importation of boats had been going on for about two years of some sweet, sweet deals, and then the lions roared. American fish boat builders had paced around their empty shipyards long enough. They were finally successful in their efforts to lobby for an emergency federal bill—no foreign hull, no matter what tonnage, could any longer be registered in the American commercial fleet. Nixon signed the bill exactly twelve hours before the gavel was scheduled to drop on the next Canadian auction.

At precisely that time the American fishermen who had already arrived in Canada were dispersed and diffused in the nightlife of Vancouver, and for many of them the news was preempted by the booze. My friend, I'm afraid, was no exception. The next day, he was the proud new owner and I, the committed owner, of the F/V *Golden Hawk*, a sturdy, gracefully built, thirty-six-foot gill net hull by design, and a giant rubber duck by decree.

We shook our heads a few times and then hoped for the best. Perhaps, we dreamed, once we got her as far south as San Francisco, no one would notice that she looked more Canadian than the maple leaf itself, and we'd slip her through documentation side by side with America's finest.

If nothing else, this trip would be an opportunity for me to see the whole West Coast of the United States from a perspective few people even consider in their mind's eye. I looked forward to the adventure, not realizing quite how far the meaning of that word could stretch.

The creative forces of geography didn't fool around here. For the full length of our West Coast, there are almost no islands, inlets, or coves to soften the raw power unleashed as three thousand miles of continent to the east meets squarely with three thousand miles of ocean to the west. Neither the land nor the sea come quietly to this edge. The land doesn't slope gently or tentatively to the sea as it does on our eastern shores. Instead, for the most part, it is cliffy and precipitous, primitive and untamed. The sea comes with its back arched long before arrival by the prevailing northwesterly winds generated by the high pressure center located in the mid-Pacific. The Great Pacific High the meteorologists call it, as if it were some euphoric Eastern drug trip when, in actuality, it is one of the largest wind machines on earth. The persistent ground swells in the sea are its unique gift to America's West Coast. It takes little effort for the local winds to whip these swells into fury, and the local winds themselves, not to be outdone by the other forces at hand, are rarely satisfied with little efforts.

My friends kept asking me if I wasn't afraid that this trip might end up leading me through the wrong Golden Gate. "Hell, no," I'd say. "I know how to pump the bilge, pick the weather, and pull my weight, like anyone else on this ocean." During the days before the trip, I was full of it. But during the nights, I had begun waking from sleep in a sweat, suddenly staring motionless at the visions of danger that seemed to hover in the darkness of the forecastle. It felt like the grasp of a giant hand. I knew it wasn't just my imagination: these scenes were straight out of the mouths of the fishermen on whom I was completely dependent for every clue to the coast.

"What are you going to do if it gets foggy? All you have is a damn depth flasher, and you don't even know what the ports look like if it's clear. And what are you going to do if you get in trouble? The ports are an average of ten to twelve hours apart with no protection in between." My curt, daytime "I'll think of something" turned into long hours at night just trying to think of anything.

There were moments when I could pacify myself with something I became aware of when I was six years old and Buddy Proctor told me there was a bear living behind his house so maybe I shouldn't come over any more and play on his swing. Boys think it's a gas to scare girls, and age only seems to sharpen their game. During the first few years I fished and especially before this trip, I spent a lot of time and energy trying to sift out the baloney from the meat; otherwise I would have been afraid to even look at the sea. But when it came to the fishermen's warnings about the bars, there was nothing that I could do to loosen the nauseating clutch of midnight fears.

"And what about the bars?" they asked. "What are you going to do when the bars are closed?" It wasn't my ability to find a good stiff drink they were worried about. It was the treacherous stretch of water between the sea and harbor that's called a bar that nature put there like a rite of passage, an ordeal by water, for any who dared to make the transition from land to sea and back again.

With the exception of Bodega Bay, Crescent City, and Neah Bay, every port from San Francisco on up the coast has a bar. Most of these ports are located at the mouths of the rivers that have carved their way through the coastal mountains in their demand to reach the sea. If you drive here by land, you'll see the fishing boats sitting quietly as sleeping ducks on the pondlike waters of their berths, giving only an occasional gentle nod to the restless waters beyond.

Enter by sea and you'll immediately understand that this inner serenity of the port is possible only because the sea and the river have spent every last ounce of their energy in the ferocious battle they do on the bar.

As the waves roll in from the sea, they are literally tripped by the shallow floor of the bar. The wave length shortens and all the energy of the wave goes into building its height. Tons and tons of water are pulled up the back of the wave and sucked up the front until the wave looks like the monstrous head of a cobra about to strike. When conditions are right, when the waves are big enough, or the tides and river swift enough, the wave gets so top-heavy that it breaks, hurling tons of water ahead of it with volcanic force. It is estimated that the force behind the water of a mere six-foot breaker is two tons per square inch. It's tricky enough to keep a boat from broaching once the waves have begun their transformation, but to be spit out alive from the churning jaws of a breaker is no less a miracle than Jonah's escape from the whale.

Because of the persistent ground swells that roll in from the sea, the West Coast bars are some of the worst in the world. They have snuffed the lives of as many of our fishermen as the open sea itself. But there is no way to avoid them; they are as much a part of the fishermen's commute to and from work as the highway toll booth is to yours.

Picture a fisherman tired from a long trip. The ocean's getting bigger than his desire for fish, and he wants to go home. Naturally, when the ocean's rough, that's when the bar is at its wildest. So he sits outside the bar, jogging the heavy sea with a stopwatch in his hand, timing the breaks and looking for a hole. Probably through the wave-dashed windows of the cabin he can see his home on the hill, at least he can see the familiar docks and streets of his town, and it all looks so safe and warm just ten minutes over the bar from here. A smart man waits and jogs the storm for a day, or two days, or however long the weather takes; a tired man thinks of home and believes he sees a pattern in the chaos, and he aims the bow toward shore. Suddenly a giant is rolling up behind him with that thunderous dragon hiss of a sound spitting off the top of the wave, and in one eternal second it lifts the stern to heaven and points the bow straight down at hell.

The West Coast fishermen have thousands of hair-raising tales that tell of the unique character and behavior of each of the bars and the way they have extracted the fullest range of human emotion and drama from the men who dare to run them. Stories that weave as powerful a legend of our western frontier as any we have sought to preserve with the written word. But just before my first trip down the coast, the last thing I wanted to hear was another blow-by-blow account of who bit the biscuit, how, on which bar. They were ruining my sleep, and yes, I was scared, and no, I didn't know exactly what I would do if the bar was closed any more than they did.

Fortunately my friend Molly came up from San Francisco to join me on the trip. She was a naturalist who loved nothing more than to take a bunch of kids into the woods and show them the beauties of nature. Her fresh enthusiasm for the journey was exactly what I needed to cut loose from the dock. After one last cup of coffee at the dock cafe.

Once under way, it took Molly exactly five seconds to fall in love with the ocean. And the ocean, as if in response, was wooing her to saturation. For the first three days the water was like a lake. The sun beamed through the clear skies, and the glassy, slick shimmering of the calm sea danced with the sparkling light for a thoroughly dazzling show that began in early morning soft pinks and ran straight through to the vibrant golds of evening. I tried to tell her that this is how the tiger looks in the sheepskin and that she ought to at least prepare mentally for some nasty changes. But it was my word against the infinite calm that seemed to have stilled the motion of time itself. Besides, I wasn't having a whole lot of trouble adjusting to this myself. Navigation was a cinch in this weather, the boat was running smooth as the sea, and in the absence of the grueling work of fishing, there was nothing to do but steer the boat, soak the sun, raid the galley, feast our eyes, forget the bars, and talk about anything this beautiful ocean inspired.

It was so calm that we could pull close into shore and look straight up at the massive, pinnacled rocks that line the northwest corner of our country like hundreds of Statues of Liberty. We coursed among these pinnacles in a lyrical path that would make any of you cringe who have been here in more normal conditions of the sea. Then we'd swerve way out to the depths just to be in the center of hundreds of huge sea birds that were lunching on the bait below, and we'd look back and see that our awesome continent was but a thin line between the water and the sky like any other island in the world sea.

For hours on end we'd try visualizing the workings of the sea below, events that diminished the most volcanic actions of the land to insignificance. Especially we tried picturing the unique and voluminous upwellings of water that flow and rise out of the deep water canyons and make the whole West Coast of the United States one of the three or four most fertile fisheries in the world. Peru, until recently the biggest fish producer in the world, has the mirror image conditions in the Southern Hemisphere, and the dynamics of the eastern European coast are similar. It's the northwest winds and the Coriolis force that combine to push the surface waters out to sea, and the resulting suction of the waters from the deep is like no other pump in the world. The forty-five to fifty-five degree cold of this upwelled water allows it to be saturated with tremendous amounts of oxygen, and the mineral nutrients it brings from the depths irrigate and fertilize our west continental shelf to a year-round bloom of plankton, plants, and fish. The rich exuberance of life in the steamy rain forests of the tropics is but a one-dimensional slice of life compared to this vast oceanic sphere of fertility.

We commented over and over how right it seemed that everywhere in the world the sea is referred to as she. The fishermen always say that this is due to her unpredictability, but, of course, that's only a painless way of saying that they're the ones who can't do the predicting. It tells nothing of the feminine spirit that's often equated with the ocean itself. After three days in her flawless company, Molly and I had compiled a complete list of the sea's feminine qualifications that would sizzle the rubber soles of the fishermen's boots. I'll only mention from the more modest end that we certainly felt a special kinship with the infinite range of her beautiful fluid movements and the rich fertility of her unseen depths and the powerful dreams she could inspire and, oh, yes, the misconceptions heaped upon her and the taking, the drilling, and the overfishing, and dumping, as if her giving will go on forever.

But, we concluded, if there is anything that does go on forever, it will be the feminine force of the sea. Even if man gets to hurling his nuclear bombs and sends his very civilization and mountains and trees hurling to obscurity, the sun would still be shining on the ocean. And somewhere in this giant pool of light and nutrient sea, one strand of DNA would inevitably bump into another and coil up a whole new branch of evolution that would certainly stand a pretty good chance of doing better than the last.

Actually, I was beginning to get a little nervous when we started writing ourselves out of the picture. Tomorrow, though it be a spit into the sea of time, was a whole ocean of worries to me. "Look, Molly," I felt compelled to say again, "this isn't going to last forever. Forty-five percent of the time this ocean's cold and windy. Forty-five percent of the time it's cold and foggy, and the other 10 percent of the time it's the holy trinity, wind and fog and heavy on the cold. This weather here is a gift."

I could hardly believe it when we glided smoothly into the port of La Push on the Washington coast just one hour before gale winds began screaming out of the northwest. It blew savagely for a week, after which we grabbed the one calm day and made it to Westport just in time for the start of another week-long blast. I sure was picking the weather like a pro and leaving plenty of time for play.

All along the coast the ports are mostly small towns nestled firmly in the seaside valleys of the Pacific Coast Range. A brief walk from the boat, and the surrounding tidepools, rain forests, and beaches were ours to explore for hours. The towns themselves were as familiar and comfortable as home. The fishing industry is their backbone, and their heartbeat is the same cycle of salmon fishing in the spring and summer, offshore albacore fishing in the fall, and rock cod or crab in the winter. The docks and gathering places are geared to the nomadic life of the fishermen, and the only real outsiders here are the ones who've never been to sea. It hardly mattered which port we were coming from or headed to, the bonds among the fishermen are established and the friendships assumed before you even meet. Add to this, of course, the fact that two women running a fish boat down the coast was a sight heretofore unseen, and our social lives were never better.

A couple of weeks of this and we needed a good rest at sea. The weather report had just been reduced from gale warnings to ten to twenty northwest. We could easily put up with a little slop for the sake of making time.

Roger, a fisherman from Seattle with whom Molly had made a little time, wanted to join us on the next leg of the trip to Newport, Oregon. Sure, we all agreed, it would be fun.

Late that afternoon Roger arrived with a seabag slung over his grizzly bear frame and the anticipation of a love hot Pacific cruise written all over his face. Of the three of us, Roger should have known better.

Twelve midnight, high water slack, we were headed onto the bar. This timing would allow us to bypass the Columbia River bar whose nickname "the graveyard" didn't project the proper ring of hospitality. It would also put us in front of Newport, Oregon, in plenty of daylight to navigate the bar we didn't yet know. The Westport bar we had crossed on the way in and, of course, we knew it like the back of our hand. As soon as we left the protection of the harbor, the boat was lifted on a long swell like an offering to the sea. I always love that first liquid roll of the sea after too many days on the rigid face of the land. And especially on such a black starless night, when your eyes can't fix the scene, it's more like a transformation that happens completely inside of you. A freeing, liquifying transformation of the soul that lasted all of one minute before phasing abruptly into knotting of the gut.

The swell quickly became a tall, sharp slop that for long periods of time obscured the buoy lights on which we were depending for navigation. The blackness of the night blinded everything but my imagination, and I was certain that each upcoming wave was going to be the big one, the monstrous watery jaw that any moment would leap out of the darkness, and with one salivating slap of its tongue, we'd be gone. I was too scared to even turn around for fear of delivering the boat sideways to the waves. What unfathomable part of my brain had possessed me to set out on a rough bar in the middle of the night in the name of strategic timing? Is this how it ends out here, with nothing to accompany your passage but a glaring view of your own stupidity? For the next forty-five minutes, I went through a hundred deaths from every bar story I'd heard, and the whole time the boat never took more than a slap on the bow.

Aside from a promise never to go on a bar again at night, which I broke within the week, I made a determined promise to keep my imagination under strict control, which I broke within the hour. Luckily!

Reaching the open ocean had all the relief of a sanctuary, despite the twenty knots of wind and a six-foot sea. Going uphill against this sea would have been a nasty ride, but sliding with it was actually pleasant as the boat rose and fell with the smooth, sensual, repeating rhythm of a graceful, primal dance. The exact motion of a boat in a rough sea is uniquely her own; it's something that can only be crudely guessed at by examining her lines or talking with the skipper of her sistership. It's a secret she keeps from even the most sensitive and experienced naval architect. Not until awakened by the beat of the sea will she reveal that dance that is the core of her reason for being. This was the first weather I had been in with *Golden Hawk*, and I was surprised how firmly her light keel gripped the sliding front of the waves. The steering was tight, and her horseshoe-shaped stern seemed to have just enough curve to let the waves curl around her before they could grab a bite and shove her clumsily down the wave.

The three of us were sitting quietly together on the open bridge, the tension of the bar having been carried off into the night by the brisk winds blowing through our hair. It was after 2 A.M., and I would have thought with the ease of the ride that Molly and Roger would have broken off to catch some sleep. Maybe they stayed to keep me company, or to enjoy the borderless thoughts that grow out of this union with infinite space, or perhaps they had begun to sense something untouchably strange and wrong in this blackest of nights. I know I had. And no amount of determination on my part could repress that eerie something that was rising like a noxious vapor from the sea.

The winds were steadily increasing, and the seas began to foam at the tops unable to contain the energy of their heights. We could watch behind us as the deck lights would catch the waves at the last minute rolling up behind the boat like a parade of white-capped ghosts coming out of the dark. When you're heading into a rough sea, you worry about the boat shooting off the top of the wave, falling through the air, and then pounding in the trough below. In a following sea, you worry when the stern is first lifted high on the wave that the boat will pick up speed and begin surfing uncontrollably down the wave.

But really, even with the freshening of the weather, there was no problem; *Golden Hawk* was riding as sturdily as a boat twice her size.

For the next hour the three of us continued to huddle together on the bridge without saying much. Though it was pitch-black, we gazed out over the ocean in a steady, scanning search. Every once in a while someone would make a short comment about a particular wave, or a lone star that braved the cloudy sky, or make a quick note on our course or position. None of this was at all unusual; it's the typical mood that seems to envelop ocean crews on long night vigils, an alert quiet that you might easily mistake for deep inner thought. But actually, no one's thinking much at all except to make note of the waves, the stars, and the course.

It wasn't anything I could put my finger on in the sea, the boat, or the mood. But suddenly that awesome growing uneasiness grabbed me, and I grabbed the wheel and turned the boat hard over head on into the sea. It's the last time I ever tried to ignore those whispering soundings from the sea that I know now are a more important guide than the lines on a chart. This night, I'm certain, they saved our lives.

What we saw next is so frozen in my memory that could I paint a picture today, it would contain more horrifying detail than a wide-angle photograph. There was a wave, a wall, a moving mountain of black undulating water so high that as I wrenched my head back to look at its top, the light on the peak of the mast was reflecting back from the curl of the wave above it. Immediately the bow was lifted so violently that I thought for a moment we were going right over the stern. When the boat fell back into the sea, there was so much water everywhere I still wasn't sure which way we had gone. Besides, this wasn't happening like a movie; it was more like slides, still images being branded in my mind, and the sights and sounds of the in-between times were lost as my whole being was concentrated in the grip of my hands on the wheel. The next wave was over us before *Golden Hawk's* last dive was completed. The boat shuddered that nauseatingly slow vibration through the hull like a death shiver that all boats seem to make when their decks are buried by the sea. The foamy waves were racing around the back deck in every direction like a herd of trapped animals. And on every side of the boat were steep black walls of water poised ruthlessly for a horrible split second to expose a gaping view of their monstrous jaws above us as we sat helplessly in the throat of the beast with a view below into the insatiable seething of her belly that was the whole world sea.

It didn't make any sense.

It wasn't so much the mysterious development of these bestial seas that baffled my mind in the split seconds between the waves. It was the real possibility of my own mortality that seemed such a glaring miscarriage of nature's highest plan. From out of my gut, there came a scream, an angry, defiant "no" that I lashed on the sea with the voice of an animal I had never known. The sea answered thunderously with the curling cobra hiss of a third wave. It must have caught us a little on the starboard quarter as *Golden Hawk* was suddenly falling sideways off the back of the wave. I let go with my mind, I gave up; this is a private duel between the boat and the sea; it's no match, it isn't fair, but there was nothing I could do but let the dice roll. Wood-cracking sounds blasted through the hull as *Golden Hawk* landed on her side as cruelly as a fist slammed into a wall of cement, igniting new terror as I violently looked around for Molly and Roger. My eyes caught a razor-sharp glance of Roger's arm locked around the mast and Molly's hands dug into the rail of the bridge. Thank God, because if either one of them were gone, I would have died from the emotions alone.

The next few waves were violent, but at least they passed underneath the boat the way they were supposed to. Thank God again for Roger; the helm would need an experienced hand. "Take the wheel," I hollered into his ghost-white face. "I'm going below."

The first thing I saw was the radio, torn from its mounts, smashed on the cabin floor. Loneliness has a lot of faces, long and dreary ones I'd known before, but this was stark, a cold and surgical cut from the world. An image of a small coastal town ran through my head, and then suddenly it was gone. A flood of panic took its place. The boat fell on its side again and threw me across the cabin where I was stopped by the corner of a table jabbed squarely in my back. And now it was pain that ripped through my senses. Out loud I cursed at myself to get it together, now or never. I tore up the floor boards and watched as water squirted through each and every seam between the planks. It wasn't what you would ordinarily call a pretty sight, but being as I'd expected to see broken planks and ribs sticking through the hull like the bones of Evel Knievel after a bad jump, I was actually relieved. The automatic pump was running steady but couldn't begin to keep up with the volumes of ocean pouring in. I pumped for a long time on a high volume old naval gusher pump, which I could have kissed. At least for a moment, the boat was dry.

"Where the hell am I?" my mind asked, I'm sure, in regard to the overwhelming circumstances. But my body went to the compass, which was flailing on its gimbles, to take a couple of bearings on the lights of land which were one moment above me like a shooting star and the next doused from sight by a passing wave. Who writes these sea manuals anyway? Picture yourself on a roller coaster that just jumped the track, now take a bearing. Our exact position didn't matter anyway; we were locked into this head-on course no matter where we wanted to go. Turn sideways to this stuff and we'd have a thirty-six-foot, fir-planked, oak-ribbed coffin, first class.

Back on the bridge, I told Molly and Roger about the radio and mumbled under my breath about the boat taking a little water. No comment was necessary. An intense momentary stare into each other's eyes carried the complete conversation. "It's bad, we're alive, let's stick together and stay that way." It was unanimous. We never encountered another series of waves like those three, but the rest of the night was spent in torturous fear for a weakened hull on a blind and pounding sea. The winds were now blowing over forty miles per hour. Under the overcast sky, we couldn't see the waves soon enough to adjust the boat's position. It all had to be done by feel at the last second. "Slow down," say the sea manuals, "so you don't pound the boat to pieces." Sure, slow down and the wind grabs the boat and shoves her sideways to the sea. What ocean were these guys on anyway when they wrote these useless proverbs? Overboard with the damn books, and I have never since, in eight years, without exception, seen one of these "sea manuals" on a single fishing boat on the whole Pacific coast.

Conversation? What do you say in the midst of threading your life in the space between the forces of the winds and the sea? "Where the hell are we?" Roger had asked when I came up from the cabin.

"Deep enough," I answered briefly, knowing that he, too, had realized that you only see waves like that on a breaking bar. Other than that and a few involuntary comments about the oncoming waves like "Oh, shit," we were just huddled together like frightened lambs, and that was more comfort than ever can be imagined. Cradled in the bosom of the storm I've never heard anyone say anything like "Oh, the wonder of it all," or "God, is nature powerful." That seems to be for sitting in meadows or picnics at the beach where time and place have been carefully chosen to ensure that nature behaves like a pet. About my only complete thought for the night was a repeated promise to God that if I ever got off this ocean alive, I'd never come back here again.

There is one predictable event on the ocean that has never failed anyone no matter how much the sea of darkness has caused them to doubt. The sun always rises and sheds new light on the most deteriorated of situations. With the coming of dawn, we could at least see the waves. We decided to put her on the quarter course whenever we could and head back to Westport for no other reason than that we had been there before and that made it home.

We got back to the bar exactly twelve and one-half hours after we had left, just in time for high water slack, our first bit of luck for the day. From the looks of the backs of the waves curling in ahead of us, that luck was just going to have to stretch itself out another forty-five minutes; the thought of laying to out here and waiting for it to calm didn't even cross our minds. I had had it.

The exhaustion of being beat to death by the sea was nothing compared to the draining fatigue of constant fear. Staring at danger for those long, long hours was oh so different from a sudden near miss on the freeway. But I guarantee, you would be as amazed, as I always am, at how much energy you have left over inside. As soon as we were on the bar and someone yelled, "Here comes one!" and I looked back over my shoulder and then straight up at the green water boiling and spitting out the top of the wave as if the whole thing were about to explode, the last thing I felt was tired.

When we finally arrived, it was actually a little disorienting to tie up in the pondlike waters at the dock, to walk on the deck with two feet and no hands, to look around at buildings that stood so unwavering and sure of themselves in their grip upon the earth. And when I caught the sight of people walking around and conversing as if it were a quiet Sunday morn, I was sure they were mocking us into believing we had made the whole thing up.

I stepped on the dock and looked back at *Golden Hawk* and the truth of the night was again all too real. Her profile had always had a gentle, graceful presence the way the planks swept back cleanly from her bow. Now the paint was cracked along every seam on both sides of the boat where the planks had gasped like a rib cage in the violent labors of the night. Tears came to my eyes, and I told her I was sorry. I thanked her by name, turned my back, and walked away for good.

The three of us headed for a coffee shop and found a small little booth about the size of the flying bridge. We huddled there the whole afternoon, as firmly locked in the isolation of our experience as we had been the night before. Only this time we talked; full speed, nonstop, trying to make it come out like a minor setback, well managed by a levelheaded crew. Which didn't explain why we wore out two shifts of waitresses, sitting here giggling like mental patients, or why we waited until the very last possible second before we dared to leave each other's company just to go to the bathroom.

It wasn't until breakfast the next morning that we consulted a fisherman about the trip and asked him what he thought, especially about the origin of those three waves. "Sounds like you were on the Columbia bar," he said.

"But we were in deep water, a couple of miles off the beach, at least," I replied.

"That's right, now you know something about the Columbia. When that river ebbs with a big westerly sea, that bar will break as far as four or five miles out to sea." He looked me right in the eye and said, "You're very lucky, you know."

"Lucky?" I said, in renewed amazement at this attitude that runs through the fleet like a defiant countercurrent in the sea.

If the mast comes tumbling down and the rigging lays in a

twisted heap of a mess on the deck, you're lucky if no one is hurt. When Vic on the *Miss Angela* lost his boat on the maiden trip and was pulled from the water, barely conscious forty-five minutes later, his friend remarked, "That guy is the luckiest son of a bitch I know."

It's not ever like that with the machinery or the fishing. Rick gets a 100-fish day and his buddy who went fifty miles farther south gets 150 and Rick will cry for a week about his bum luck move. But with the sea, the winds, and the waves, you're lucky until the day you die.

I guess I hadn't been through it enough to have any deep appreciation for this perspective at all. If anything I was feeling quite jinxed about my relationship to the sea. And remembering my promise to God, with whom this was a first conversation in many years, it began to seem that my best bet might be to make the rest of the trip by plane.

I kicked around Westport the rest of the morning, thinking about my responsibility to deliver the boat and about how much I loved being at sea, and I thought about the thrill of fishing, and there wasn't any of it that could put a ripple to the terror of those three waves. Maybe it's the same looking down the barrel of a gun or up from a hospital bed, but the savageness of that sea was so ghostly strange and infinite that it felt like I'd already passed into the other world. Staying alive at sea wasn't so much a matter of working the odds as it was a clawing my way back out of the godforsaken landscape of death's domain.

Later that afternoon, the winds quit and the sea lay down and that, of course, is what persuaded me to continue. You probably think I was suffering from some kind of severe short-term memory loss, and maybe that's a pretty good name for it after all. But the changes of the sea are so thoroughly complete, they leave not a trace of their former self. Until you have seen that everlasting look on the face of a peaceful sea, it's hard to understand just how convincing it can be.

I told Molly that if she didn't want to continue, it really wasn't necessary for her to go into any long explanations as to why. Of the three of us, Molly seemed to be the least disturbed by the course of the night. Roger, on the other hand, seemed not the least bit disturbed that he had crew call the next day back in Seattle on a sixty-foot dragger named the *Confidence*. Nonetheless, after I thanked him for his help and apologized for a rather unromantic Pacific cruise, he said, "Look, you made a bad judgment on the weather, like everyone else. You handled it fine, and I'd go to sea with you anytime."

I looked at Molly and said, "Boy, did you ever find yourself a nut." But inside, I felt he couldn't have given us a better send-off. And my promise to God? Well, the fishermen had worked this one out a long time before I had arrived on the scene. "You think we all haven't made that same promise at one time or another?" said the same man who told us what a lucky night we'd had. "Think of it like this," he said, "if you were that scared and you still want to go back on the sea, what better praise could you give to its creator?" Now that's not half bad, I thought, for a rationalization. Still there was something tremendously inspiring to me in the sheer will of this fisherman who could take a defeat by the sea and a broken promise to God and turn them into their opposites. In fact, it was something I admired in all of the fishermen, the extremes of boldness and humility welded by the sea into a singular, lustrous spirit that even defeat couldn't tarnish—and I wanted to find some of that for myself.

It's a pity I had so far to go. That afternoon, Molly and I took a long walk on the grassy fields that lay along the bar. I wanted to talk about how the trip had changed. But each time I tried to find the words it was like brushing up against the winds of a tornado. How could I tell her I was terrified when I couldn't tell myself? How could I tell her I just found out that I had absolutely no idea what either I or the ocean would do next, when I was the captain with whom she was entrusting her life?

I just kept hoping Molly would go first; after all, she is one of the most honest and open people I know, and with all that edge on practice she ought to be able to find a way. I watched the grasses go down under my feet as Molly rambled on about the precarious nesting places of the cormorant that flew overhead, and then I watched her as she playfully mimicked the glide of a gull with her golden hair flying behind her as she whirled and dipped and all in all kept it from being a deadly afternoon. But still it wasn't until we had almost arrived back at the boat that she said she wanted to go on with the trip. And that was all! The rest was too monstrous, too unmanageable, too twisted beyond recognizable connection with anything we'd known before.

It's not that the ocean suddenly quit giving of its beauty and magic. For sure, the porpoises continued to appear and play at our bow. There wasn't a section of the magnificent Oregon coast that didn't make us feel as though we'd like to come back and live there, and our first night at sea after the storm we spent drifting offshore through a sunset of slick, calm waters afire in purples and pinks that were more intense than the colors of the sky. It was a night when we could reach over the stern and cup our hands around the water and let it trickle through our fingers, the very same stuff of the waves that had threatened our boat to oblivion.

But, my memory insists on reminding me, half of the time I was barely disengaging my ass from the clutch of continuous crises, and the rest of the time I was watching and waiting in fearful anticipation.

The fog supplied hours of tense searching for the invisible entrances to the unknown ports. And each time there was a final twist of the lemon as we headed in on a course and had to suffer with the fragment of uncertainty that perhaps we were headed straight for the rocks. There were problems with the rigging that naturally chose to manifest themselves only when the weather got rough. And one day on the trip from Coos Bay, every last fiber of my being came stripped from its glue. A frisky wind, sparkling blue water day when the spray of the dolphin's breath made rainbows in front of our bow—and the mast came loose. And while I concentrated on wedging and rigging, Molly misread the chart and steered us right into the middle of a five-square-mile reef. I looked up and saw a jagged black rock not ten feet from the boat, leapt to pull the throttle back, saw all the rest of the rocks around us, and I knew even God would have to make a guess which way was out. We lucked our way out of that and arrived off Brookings after dark, with a big sea and the town lights making it difficult to pick out the entrance buoy which lay in twenty fathoms. The usual trick of running the twenty-fathom line was not highly recommended because of the rocks that also sat in that depth. We doggedly turned back out on a stormy sea and planned for a two-hour run straight out so we could drift without worry about being blown into shore. Then the stack loosened in the heavy sea and burnt a deep persistent fire into the deck above the gasoline engine, shooting flames that seemed to grow with every dose of dry chemical. And as I tried to reposition the stack away from the deck, the boat threatened to heave me overboard every time I dared to use two hands for the work.

We shut down fifteen miles outside of Brookings and fifteen miles above Saint George Reef, and some god-awful current must have had my name on its tongue because four hours later the next morning we awoke on the other side of the reef—miraculously unscathed but much the worse for knowing about it. Without giving us an hour to digest that incident, the fog arrived; the nearest port of Crescent City had a welcome mat of giant rocks and a slot the size of a pencil, and early the day before I had already reached the point where the rubber band breaks.

In the midst of these scenes, with my body and mind contorted by the inhuman demands of the sea, I lashed out furiously at Molly when she fumbled at the simplest tasks of tying a knot, reading a chart, or handling a fire extinguisher. I screamed at the merciless ocean for doing this to me, and I cursed the sadistic God who wouldn't make it stop. All in all, I put out mountains of rage, trying to resist the obvious. Captain means you may have come a long way, baby, but it's irrelevant. One mind-numbing decision followed another, and each one carried the weight of two lives. There was nowhere I could lay that awful burden for even a minute in the day.

By the time we reached Eureka, I was feeling more like a dishrag than a boat captain. And Molly, I'm sure, was wondering whether this was a boat ride or a serialized nightmare. We had to talk about it now, whether we could find the words for it or not. The last line of the boat wasn't tied to the dock when I cut loose. "Damn it, Molly, this isn't the woods where you can make some kind of a choice about how you're going to relate to it. It's alien, and if you're going to go out there, you better learn some of the things that keep you alive, like knots, the tackle, charts, and the tools, and you better practice because half-assed is dead."

For the first time I was aware that the intense strain weighed as heavily on Molly. Throughout the ordeals she had worked fiendishly, without a word of reproach, trying to carry out my panicked commands. Now she flared with a temper I'd never seen.

"You can't expect me to know it all after two weeks. And you can't scream at me when I make mistakes just because you're mad and I can't do something in an emergency I never heard of before."

Round and round we went, from the back deck to the dock cafes and a makeshift seat on the railroad tracks. Slowly and painfully, I began to realize she was right. Molly had no idea what she was getting into, and she wasn't responsible for that. I was, and I never felt so alone. There was absolutely nowhere to turn; there was nothing and no one to buffer for me in face of the ruthless sea. Except my boat.

I went back to *Golden Hawk* and checked through every system bow to stern over and over again, trying to foresee and forestall anything that could go wrong. I had done this a hundred times before, a routine on every trip, but this time as I checked out the pumps, the steering, the radios, I grew frantic, angry, and betrayed. I finally came to lying on my back in the hold, exhausted, staring at the deck beams above. Strong and sturdy, I thought, but what about the nails within? And I cried in helpless fear of all that lay hidden and all that I couldn't know.

I had no idea what I was getting into either. One season fishing out of one familiar port, on a flawless boat, tucked under Hobo's wing and drenched in an outsized share of beginner's luck, had sheltered me from all but the most routine encounters with the sea.

It was frustrating to know that so many of these chilling spectacles came out of my own lack of experience. But it was even more disturbing to realize that too much of this was just plain part of the game. Once you see what the ocean can do and, even more impressive, how fast it can do it, that fear is like a heartworm, boring from within. How in God's name could the fishermen live with this, as if it were their pride?

Gale warnings were posted, and though I uttered all the standard grumblings that are called for on the occasion of the wind's delay, I was inwardly praying that it would blow the sea dry.

Unfortunately, the only place within walking distance where fishermen socialize at night is the Vista Del Mar. It ranks among land bars in the same position where the Columbia ranks among bars of the sea. You never know which way the wind's going to blow inside those big wooden doors. Is the two-hundred-pound guy walking toward the juke box to insert a quarter, or is he planning to lift it off the wall and heave it across the room? A couple of high-energy evenings in that place and Molly and I were deeply grateful to a sympathetic fishing family who recognized the look on our faces and invited us home. In addition to long-lost warmth and quiet, they had pleasures the likes of which I'd never known:

nonsoggy cookies, hot running water, a bathtub, refrigerator, and ice cream. What else could we ask for? "Come here," they said, "you think you've got problems? Sit down and watch this." On went the TV, and in the time slot for "As the World Turns," there in our midst sat John Mitchell, John Dean, and all the other chiefs on trial for breaking and entering.

For the next couple of days we entertained ourselves by imagining what would happen if twenty-foot waves began rolling beneath the courthouse. Would Jaworski huddle up to Mitchell for mutual warmth, would Dean kiss the trough end of the wave to save his skin, would Nixon plead presidential immunity, or would he demand that his secretary edit out the top eighteen feet of the wave?

We talked and laughed, and it felt more soothing than the warmth of the bath. "Well, how about that." I must be alive; after all the rough stuff and Sunday punches from the universe, I'm back here alive like everyone else. Maybe that's part of it. You keep squeezing out through the cavities in the teeth of death's jaw, and it's no wonder that every fisherman alive carries that certain twinkle in his eyes like he's sleeping with Lady Luck. (The dead ones, of course, aren't talking.)

"Marie?" said Molly with just enough hesitant question in her voice that I thought she was going to quit, and my panic was instantaneous. "If it's all right with you, I'd like to finish the trip, if you think I could be of help."

"Oh, Molly, don't scare me like that." And I finally was able to tell her, "I couldn't set foot back on that boat without you."

Despite the hospitality, we couldn't help heading back to the dock and asking for vivid instructions and descriptions on the next leg of the trip that would inevitably scare us to death.

Ask and you receive. Cape Mendocino is a naked mountainous fist of land that punches farther west into the sea than any other point of land in the continental United States. And the ocean punches back. The currents boil, and the sea winds clash with the land "breezes" that rush down the mountains at a frisky little pace that not infrequently exceeds one hundred miles per hour. The sea conditions are most often what the marine forecasters call confused because the wave patterns are coming from more than one direction at once. The fishermen call these conditions jackass because of the unmistakable character of the ride you get.

You would think that every boat coming there would certainly be aggressively pursuing its course to someplace else. But the numerous deep water canyons that upwell into this area frequently make the waters off Cape Mendocino a gigantic feedlot for thousands and thousands of salmon. You make a fishing trip to Cape Mendocino, and you stand as good a chance of coming back with eight thousand dollars' worth of salmon as you do of limping back with eight thousand dollars' worth of damage. For now, I was content to be aggressively pursuing my course to Fort Bragg, a fourteen-hour trip from Eureka (in good weather). On the first try we were two hours from the Eureka bar, didn't like the feel of things, turned around and went back; and that represented the biggest progress we'd made on the whole trip.

On the second shot we were awarded with all the incomparable beauty of a sleeping savage. As we approached the Cape, the swell began lifting us higher with each crest. You've probably guessed by now that it's the shape of a wave even more than its height that determines how much coffee you can put in your cup. These waves that were stacking up around the point were over ten feet high, but their tops were as smooth and rounded as the California hills. We rose and fell as if we were seated on the deep-breathing, sleeping chest of Mother Nature herself. It's without a doubt my favorite motion of the sea; all the power is there and none of the meanness, and I could easily ride that rhythm for the rest of my life. But just a couple of miles down the line and the swell subsided to the barely perceptible motion of a sleeper whose soul has suddenly left the body for a far-off dream. Still, as we looked across the miles and miles of silky surface, we could see the sharp lines of color change that marked the edges of the massive inner rivers more clearly than if they were painted on a map.

Saturated with the beauty of the day, we were primed for celebration before we even reached the entrance to Fort Bragg. Once inside the bar, we made a left turn and could see that the small winding river was so gorged with boats from other ports that you could just about walk across the river on the long strings that were rafted out from the fish docks. In fact, there were so many of the Bodega boats here that it was as good as arriving home. And for a while we partied accordingly.

Until slowly and not very gently my friends painted me the picture of why they were all here. While the propeller of the

Golden Hawk was slicing a path down the coast just to have it fill up with water behind us, my friends were making their fortunes. The salmon had schooled up in front of the Fort Bragg area like few could remember in their fishing histories. The same guys who last year were crying that they might have to begin cooking with the oil from the bilge were now sitting around juicy steak dinners in the tourist section of the classy Wharf Restaurant, discussing tax shelters. It was hard to believe they were all the same people; the very lines in their faces had changed.

When I looked out to the end of a string of fourteen boats and saw the bow of a blue and white clipper, I had to believe it all. Hobo? Old retired fisherman Hobo? Stay-in-Bodega-and-wait-for-the-fish Hobo? I climbed down the dock ladder, stepped on the first boat, tripped on the hatch cover, lifted my leg over the gunwale, set it on the next boat into a bucket of slimy bait, reached for the rigging (which was loose), and stepped the other direction into the gaff hatch without the cover; fourteen boats and twenty-eight bruises later over the monkey trail that's more than enough challenge even when you're sober—and there sitting quietly in his cabin was Hobo with a warm beer, listening to the late night fishing reports of the boats at anchor. "Hobo," I said, giving him a big hug, "what are you doing here? I thought you never left Bodega."

"I said I was old, not dead," came the instant reply. Then his voice turned serious. "You know, we were all worried about you."

"Hobo," I said, "a lot of times I didn't think I was going to make it." I started to tell him some of the incidents, when Hobo began interrupting with details I'd already forgotten.

"Word travels," he said. "I know every move you made." He seemed more than a little upset at some of the things I had done and especially at why I had done them. "You know, there's no way you're going to be able to fish that boat; you could paint it red, white and blue and run fifty stars up the mast, and it still wouldn't look American." Hobo turned to stare at his beer as if conversing with a long-time telepathic friend. "Listen, kid," he said, turning back to me, "you better get yourself a decent boat that can handle the traveling and hold a load of fish, because I'll tell you once and I won't tell you again, you got everything else you need to go out and make a couple of bucks."

I waited a minute and then figured I might as well tell him, "Hobo, I'm not going to fish any more. I can't handle the fear, it's too much. I wake up sweating in the middle of the night, worrying about a damned alternator belt; I check a valve ten times that I set right the first time; in the middle of a good meal I start thinking what the hell I'd do if a plank popped loose; when it's calm I worry about the wind, and when it's clear I worry about the fog; I'm afraid to look in front of me for fear of what's behind me."

"What did I just tell you, kid," Hobo interrupted, "that's what it takes," and he had the nerve to give me a smile.

I wasn't convinced. I lay awake long into the night, going through it one more time. "Nope, there's no way," I decided again and again. I'm not going to live like that. And it isn't enough of a reward to wake up on the mornings after and find myself alive. In fact, I was more determined than ever to keep it that way by staying off the sea. Whatever other secrets the fishermen had for dealing with it all interested me less than ever.

I'd just get this boat back to San Francisco and do what the fishermen always talk about doing after a string of sour luck. You put an oar over your shoulder and walk inland until people start asking you what it's for, and that's where you stick it in the ground and plant the rose garden. The rest of the trip from Fort Bragg to Bodega and Bodega to San Francisco, the ocean was flat grey and overcast. A welcome, blessed monotony.

Not until we could see the Golden Gate Bridge did the sun begin to shine. The spectacular sight of the gleaming white city rising out of the blue waters, framed by the bridge above, stuns the most jaded world travelers. To battered seafarers like ourselves, it looked like an oasis for the human spirit. Passing under the Gate, we simultaneously turned to each other with a look on our faces like we'd just stolen the key to longevity. I wondered what possible oversight could have kept the fireboat from being here to usher us in with its official salute. No matter, we had tucked away enough champagne to celebrate the enormity of our relief, with plenty left over to pour in every hold of that boat.

Jim was waiting for us at the dock; after the phone calls he had received along the way, just the sight of the boat in one piece was enough celebration for him. He planned to sell the *Golden Hawk* for pleasure use, and since he would be turning a little profit, he offered to lease us the *Tjallee* for the remainder of the season in exchange for delivering the boat. Oh, yippee, I thought to myself. By this time of the year the warm water currents have moved into the West Coast, and the majority of the salmon have left the area in search of cold waters. Salmon fishing in September is about as productive as berry picking in December.

Positive thinking was never my ace in the hole. After all that had happened, I would have much preferred straight cash. But then things hadn't exactly worked out the way Jim had hoped either, so I accepted graciously, and in three days Molly and I were headed down to Half Moon Bay where there had been a report of a small bite.

We arrived at the spot, looked into the clear blue water, and sure enough, there were the orange jellyfish with the red-hot tentacles and the sky-colored blue sharks with the hungry white teeth. I felt like taking the bait and throwing it over the side to save ourselves the trouble of threading them on the hooks. But we had come this far, so we might as well go through the motions. We baited the hooks, set the gear, and for the next three weeks we couldn't make a wrong move.

If we trolled a little to the north, there were fish to the north; if we went in a little early one day, the fish went off the bite; if we ran out of bait and put a bunch of old beat-up plugs on the gear, the fish went crazy for the plugs; I think we could have put tin foil on the lines and the fish would have snapped. It wasn't that everyone else was catching; the run of fish was larger than usual for this time of the year, but we were just hot, consistently doubling the average catch for the day. If it all sounds wildly exaggerated, then you're beginning to get a clear picture of just exactly how the pendulum of life swings at sea.

We were on a hot streak, and it didn't make any more sense than the waves that tried to eat us on the Columbia bar. Nor, in the midst of throwing fish on the deck, and being followed like a guru by the other fish boats, and counting big wads of cash, did we bother to wonder why any more than you would think to ask a pair of dice why they keep turning up seven and eleven.

And, of course, at the end of the season there was not a moment's doubt about what to do with the money. There was a pretty, twenty-eight-foot, Monterey-style fishing boat for sale in Santa Cruz. She was the bare minimum size for making it in this business, but then so was my down payment. So what if I was scared!

4

Filet of Soul

IT WAS OFF season; the limits of my world shrunk to the length and width of S-dock in the harbor at Santa Cruz. There was Windy, my new boyfriend, and his boat, my boat, and a dozen other fishermen and their boats. Never had my world been so complete.

The frenzied pulse of the summer gave way to late morning rising and easily interrupted work on the boats. Aimless groups of storytellers drifted through the days. And time stretched out as calm as a tropic sea.

A couple of times I surfaced to wonder and worry at how I could be so content in such a dreamy world, but it never lasted long. The pleasures of the drifting pulled me back again. About the only thing that actively engaged me was the fascination with the tales that, in the absence of pressure from yesterdays and tomorrows, began to unfold in an epic that reached through generations in time and spanned the seas from Peru to Sicily.

I was part of the fleet now, and my story would be weaved and meshed with theirs in ways as yet unknown. For now, I was spellbound for hours, propped against a hull or seated on a rail, mesmerized by how it came to be.

So, go ahead, lie back in the warm sand for a minute and let your eyes rest on the light blue waves rolling up to your feet like the silky tumbling of kittens that aren't yet old enough to know their own ferocity. And since that didn't hurt, open your ears as you have never opened them before; there is no sound to offend them. Only the easy waves of sound splashing water, spilling onto the sand, gentle as the warm wet air that issues from the sea, hugs you as it passes, and slips its way up through the simple homes of the villages to ripen the fruit of the yards.

What could the Sicilian families have thought back in the 1850s, when after way too long a journey they found themselves on the grey, wind-lashed shores of San Francisco Bay? And when they stepped closer to the shores of their new life and a dark, huge wave hurled itself against the rocks like an enraged beast, drenching the newcomers with water so cold it cuts you as it touches, didn't the Sicilian fishing families then think they had made some horrible mistake? No! They sent home for brothers and sisters, uncles, cousins, mothers, and fathers.

Money and prestige seem hardly enough to explain it, for nowhere in the world is the fisherman held in such low esteem as in America, while in Sicily the fishermen and their villages were noble. But come they did and began building the boat they knew by heart, the felucca, a wooden double-ender with as many graceful curves as the Mediterranean shore. The intricate lampara nets and beach seines that balloon in the flow of the tide were easily made anew by the experienced hands that weaved the meshes as freely as the men talked over them. With skill and nets and hands, they reached into the cold, dark bay, and what they caught was a dazzling glimpse of the history that would be.

The bay was ripe and untouched. Not even the Indians of the area had ventured much past the mollusk-laden beds of its shore. There were schools of barracuda, and bonita, salmon, and anchovies, herring, pompano, kingfish, and smelt. And that smell was sweeter than a whole skyful of the most fragrant tropic air. As long as the water rolled on with the promise of fish, the particular name of its shore, whether it be America or Sicily, was not more significant than the name of the place where you wash your car. But America had its way. By the early 1900s, the families no longer wanted their children to fish. Education was the new way to respect, and the children would go to school. I got a special kick out of listening to the old-timers recount the tales of how they avoided it.

Hobo's friend, Freckles, was born not long after his family had arrived in America from the village of Palermo. I had hardly gotten to know the man in the past seasons. He moved around the length of the coast like it was his own small backyard. But even so, I already idolized Freckles as the fisherman among fishermen. He certainly looked the part. A big, handsome, sturdy Sicilian with an ageless glint in his eyes, a sea-weathered face cropped by full, wavy, white hair, Freckles made Gregory Peck as Ahab look like a postal clerk. Just the way he stood on the deck of a boat seemed like it would be enough to draw up leviathan.

But now it was off season, and even Freckles was tied to the dock. One day I cornered him in his galley and, with no effort at all, prodded him back to those years when he was one of the kids the parents were trying to school. "Oh, some of the kids stuck it out," said Freckles, "like the Alioto boys and then they forgot where they came from. But most of us found one way or another to get onto the boats. And then there was this one kid who was just plain lazy, all he liked to do was play ball." Freckles paused.

Freckles's speech doesn't pause without a purpose, so I asked dutifully, "Who was that, Freckles?"

"Joe Dimaggio, Maria, didn't you ever hear of Joe Dimaggio, the ball player? Joe's father was a fisherman." And as if to thoroughly weld the kindredness of their spirits, he added, "Joe didn't know how to spell *yes* and I didn't know how to spell *no*. Our fathers went to the principal's office more often than we went to school. And our mothers cried a lot over us, don't think they didn't.

"I used to hide in the hold of the boat when my father was sleeping. Then when the boat began to rock, I'd know we were outside the Gate and out I'd come. My parents tried everything—part-time school, beatings, everything—but I'd just run away. Finally at seventh grade they gave up. I won," he added with the grin of a ten year old.

His dad's family boat fished lampara nets for sardines and assorted market fish. It was the kids' job to clean the boat, do all the scrubbing, and go for parts and supplies. "I remember standing for hours, holding the net in one position while the men mended. They never took any time out to teach us; you just learned or you didn't. And for this we got twenty-five cents a week. You couldn't get a share until they decided you could do a man's work. On your own family's boat, that day would never come."

Sitting across the table from this man whose massive hands, albeit with one finger missing, looked like they could crush the coffee cup if he but held it a little too firmly, I found it hard to picture the child pitching with the deck, reaching with tender hands into the gnarling work of fishing. I couldn't help but ask, "Why, Freckles, why would a ten-year-old boy want to put up with all that when he could be in a warm school, playing with the other kids?"

Freckles looked at me as if I had just lost a marble. "Maria," he said emphatically, "it was the freedom, the challenge of the ocean. I used to look out at the ocean from the bow of the boat and it made me feel like Columbus."

As for the man's share, Freckles's solution was the same as the other kids: they simply switched boats. At fifteen, Freckles took off to Monterey. "I loved it, it was much better. Your own family was strict, but on another boat the crew was more protective. I got a man's share right away and it was good times. It wasn't just the loot only; the laughing and joking's just as important—more important. During the week we worked hard; on the weekends we'd work on the nets in the morning and party in the afternoon. We'd go from house to house with our guitars and mandolins; every door was open. Then we'd go down to the Carmel River for a swim and pitchfork a couple of salmon for food. That's what made fishing so good; if it were a rat race like today, I don't think I would have been a fisherman."

That same year, at the greying end of fifteen, Freckles crewed on a tuna seine boat out of San Diego. Upon his return, he leased his first boat and fished on the ocean for salmon under the watchful eyes of the uncles and cousins who traveled with him. His boat was a twenty-six-foot Monterey, a design that was once the Mediterranean felucca that had evolved to meet the needs of a fishery rapidly expanding onto the sea. The belly was deepened and rounded to hold the roll of the open Pacific swell. A heightened clipper bow was given great flare so as to present a knife edge to the sea on the run and a wide buoyant surface on a dive. And where the mast of the sail once anchored firmly in the deck, there was an opening to the engine room where a one-cylinder Hicks filled the beamiest part of her hold.

There was one thing the Italians would never change as the boats were made to adapt. They were lined and curved with as much care to the eye as an artist takes with a sculpture. The Monterey, of them all, has to be one of the prettiest boats ever to grace the sea. But these boats were no things of idle beauty. They took the likes of Freckles and Hobo on their first, unfettered teenage struts across the sea, and today these same boats are still here to suffer the ordeals of beginners the likes of me.

It was the Depression. Even in the good days there is a saying in the fleet that hovers over the difficulties: If you're a fisherman you always eat. And during the Depression this was a distinction among men. The fishermen, like the farmers, were doing okay. Besides, there is another part of the fisherman's litany that is about as strong a bulwark as any that can be held against the uncertainties of the sea. Better days are coming, they always say, and the burden of the present is lightened by the future's glow.

Freckles got up, poured another cup of coffee, and turned to curse the wind, "Blow, you son of a bitch, blow!" and returned to his seat. "In 1938 I went to Alaska."

"Alaska?" I said, surprised at the turn.

"What's the matter, Maria, don't they have fish in Alaska? I ran the *Sea Star*, an eighty-two-foot transfer boat for the Bristol Bay salmon gill net fishery. There were fish, all right, but these weren't the better days I was looking for. Alaska is Siberia and the fishermen's attitude was dog eat dog. But I wouldn't even wish those conditions on a dog. The gill netters were still working with sail only, and when they came to make a landing on the unloading barge in the wind and the huge tides, one slip and they'd be swept down the bay with no chance of returning till the next tide. Just to get the fresh water for the engine of the *Sea Star*, we had to build a dock from scratch and run all the pipes from the stream. And I asked myself, can the dollar actually be worth that much?"

Better days were coming! Better beyond anyone's dream, and they were waiting right in Freckles's own backyard. In 1929 the first company had opened in the Bay Area to process sardines, and no one could have guessed. Ten years later there were 150 San Francisco boats alone in the fishery, and they weren't Monterey clipper bows. They were dinosaurs of boats that could pack two hundred tons of fish and carried nets that could scoop up to nine hundred tons of fish in a set if you had the nerve to grab them. The schools of sardines that now populated the area were so massive that you had to be careful not to bite off more than you could chew. And the market was unlimited.

You can't be among the fishermen very long without hearing

references and stories from the sardine days. The whole West Coast
fleet was drawn to it as helplessly as iron filings get sucked into the
face of a huge magnet. Boats and their crews were coming from as
far away as Seattle. When they went home for the weekend, they'd
rent three or four cars on the train with a band and all the trim-
mings. They'd party all the way up and party all the way back.
Nobody could believe that cannery row would ever stop belching
out smoke.

The fishermen who had come for the freedom and challenge of
the ocean had discovered the fast buck. On any one night for over
five years on the waters off California, the gold fever, with all its
excitement, frustration, and eros, was packed in the quarters of
the sardine boats in each of the twelve men aboard.

"Right, Maria," said Freckles, "twelve men, and twelve men
gotta know what they're doing. There were no green men in those
crews, and still a lot of boats went down and a lot of men were
lost. Sometimes, instead of swimming and milling around, all the
fish at once began diving to the bottom of the net, and you can't
handle it. They break everything—lines, cables, a three-quarter-
inch nylon line will break just from the sardines. You would never
think that those little tails could get a boom and snap it, but you
know the old saying, Divided we fall, united we stand. You even
hope that the net will rip because then it will make a hole and the
fish can get out. Otherwise you have to cut loose thousands of
dollars' worth of net and pray that you finish before the fish roll
the boat over. That's just one of the ways you paid your dues. But
don't get me wrong, nothing could keep the bees from the honey."

I knew that once we were on this subject, Freckles couldn't resist
telling a tale of a big catch. I didn't have to ask. "One night in
1944," he began, "we were the first boat on a beautiful school of
fish. In the night you can see them when they light up the phosphorescent organisms in the water, they make big pools of underwater light in the waves. We surrounded over nine hundred ton of
fish in one set. The net split from one end to the other. We weren't
even talking to one another in the crew, we were all so mad at
having split the net and lost the fish. All night long we were mending, mending, mending, and lacing, and there were a lot of fish
around us.

"The boat, the *City of San Francisco*, came over to us and asked
whether it was sardines or anchovies. We told them it was sar-

dines. So he lays out and we know he got a lot of fish. They offered us forty ton of their fish, and the skipper of our boat said, "No, we don't want them." I can't explain why he didn't want those fish without explaining to you all about the Sicilian people, and we don't have time for that.

"By now these fish were being broadcast on the radio, and more boats were coming to the school. We saw another boat lay out beside us. He looked like a city while on our boat everybody was mending, mending—twelve men mending and lacing. We kept throwing the net into the hatch and then mend, mend some more and throw more into the hatch. We were going as fast as we could. The other boat that had laid out plugged his boat and loaded about five others . . .

"This was during the war, because I remember we had a deadline at the Gate. You couldn't go in and out of the Gate anytime you pleased. We had a time we all had to meet as a convoy at the lightship where your identity was checked very carefully. We were working so fast so we could find a school of fish before the deadline. When we got finished, we looked around and we couldn't find anything. The skipper was disgusted. He was so disgusted that he went to sleep. His brother was taking the boat home. I was in the galley with Duke and the Governor, and everyone was going crazy because the way we saw it, we still had time to look around. But you don't make suggestions to the captain.

"We had already gotten to A buoy at the entrance way to the Gate. All at once the engine slowed down and the bell was ringing. If you want your job, you're on the back deck before the sound of the bell is gone; it's worse than the firemen. The fish were all over the place just breaking the surface. The commotion was unbelievable. Duke was running around in the wrong direction, and he was our skiff man. The Governor started looking for his hat, and everyone was ready to kill him because he was the one who had to let the skiff go. You only get one shot and that's it.

"So we lay out. The beauty of it was, it was shallow water, and when you have that much fish in shallow water, they can't dive on you, they hit the bottom. Right away we saw the volume of fish and divided the net in two parts. We were a fast crew. Pull, pull, pull like a son of a bitch, pull. It was beautiful weather. We put two hundred tons of fish on the *Anna B.* with a deck load. But by now it's daylight. The sea gulls were swarming us and the other boats could see what happened. We don't want to have to give the fish to the other boats because then we'd miss the convoy time and we'd lose a whole day. We saw the other boats coming toward us, so we let the rest of the fish go."

Something happened in 1946 to change all that, something that had more impact on the fishing industry than the stock market crash on Wall Street. Exactly what it was is still an unsolved mystery. But so permanent a burn did it leave on the memories of those that lived it that when describing the event thirty-four years later, the words they all use are identical. "The sardines disappeared — overnight . . ." Families lost everything. So many of the boats were burning to the waterline that the insurance companies couldn't pay off. But very, very few of the fishermen turned to the land in search of a job. Instead they went back to their Montereys and their small lampara boats and said, "Better days are coming."

The Fish and Game has long claimed that the sardines were fished out, but the fishermen have their doubts. Duke, who crewed with Freckles on the *Anna B.*, says there was something strange about that last school of fish they saw. "They were all swimming in one big school that was over fifteen miles long. There were no fish to the north of that and none to the south. Before this there would always be a lot of broken schools covering a much bigger area."

Freckles says the sardines are going to come back. He believes they're on a big, natural cycle, the size of which only the ocean breeds. "My father told me that his father saw the day when there were also no sardines, only anchovies. First, my father said, the blue mackerel came and then the sardine. In the late 1930s they were catching anchovies off Destruction Island [off the Washington coast]. It seemed that the anchovies were slowly moving south and replacing the sardines as they went. After the sardine disappeared from San Francisco and Monterey, some of us chased the sardine down to San Pedro and then into Mexico. Ensenada was built as a sardine port, but now they're getting only anchovies. Now, in Monterey for three or four years they've been seeing the blue mackerel again. I'm sure the sardines are coming back."*

---

*Interestingly, five years later, small amounts of sardines have been caught off Monterey for the first time in thirty years.

Freckles was luckier than most on the eve of the crisis. California Packers started foreclosing on the seiners and selling them to the Mexican government. "But," says Freckles, "it was like giving a man a semitruck when he's been pushing a wheelbarrow. At first the American government sent down a man from the Fish and Game who was going to teach the Mexicans how to fish—on the shore. Sure, maybe he could draw a picture of how the net should lay in the water, but how in the world are you going to teach anyone on shore how to fish the ocean?" Finally, the government realized it, and a number of hand-picked crews were sent to Mexico; half the boat would be American and the other half Mexican. Freckles spent four years in the warm southern waters, not because it took the Mexicans that long to learn, but because the Italians and the Mexicans hit it off so well, they found all kinds of ways to extend the program. After this Freckles spent four years in Peru on the same kind of exchange, and he wished he didn't have to come home.

On his return to the United States it was no big shock to Freckles that the California fisheries had not stood still in his absence. But I can't help but think that even he must have been just a little unsettled to find that the nets had almost completely given way to troll gear as the basis of the fishery.

Salmon used to be just another fish, and the albacore was out of range. But now with the disappearance of the sardine, they were the fish everyone was looking at to become the new economic base. The introduction of better radios, Fathometers, more efficient diesels, and pure necessity made it possible for the fishermen to get on the unpredictable, nomadic tail of these fish and chase them around the coast.

There were other changes that had taken place as well. The big money of the early forties didn't go anymore unnoticed by outsiders than did the gold that was discovered one hundred years before in the California hills. Aside from attracting writers the likes of John Steinbeck and drinkers the likes of them all, there were a lot of people who came for a piece of the pie. But by now this little corner of the Pacific was as much a matter of territory as the rangelands of the West. The Bodega fleet worked the area down to the Cordell Banks, the city gang worked from there to Pigeon Point, and the Monterey gang had from Pigeon to Point Sur; and when they crossed from one area to another, they were polite and worked accordingly. Many of these feelings carry over today; the Eureka boats know it's not cool to show up at the Golden Gate with a deck load of crab gear without prior arrangements, and a city boat would certainly make all the right phone calls before showing up in Monterey to fish the squid.

But the prospects of hoards of land people buying into the fleet and plowing this bonanza harvest from the sea was out of the question.

For the most part few defensive maneuvers were required: you don't make a fisherman overnight. The regulars merely had to wait for the typical afternoon breeze to whip up its standard seven-foot pounding seas and the newcomers were soon goners. If that didn't do the trick, there was always within their grasp a little friendly dissuasion—Sicilian style.

Ah, but there were those few among the seekers who, though the sound of their last names didn't roll off the tongue like a Verdi opera, the vibrations of their souls resonated to the same basso profundo themes. Trickery found trickery's match in men like Cass Gidley. In the year 1942 Cass had never been on the ocean before, but on the radio news he heard about the money they were making. The shark fishery simultaneous with the sardine fishery had come to bonanza days because of the vitamin A that could be derived from the livers. Each shark was worth a hundred bucks, and each fisherman was coming in with thirty to forty sharks a day. Says Cass, "I went over to the docks and watched for about three or four days, and I said, 'Boy, I'm going to get into this right away.' It took us six months to get our nets and hang them. We leased the *Nina*, a double-ender, went out and fished a couple of sets, and caught fish. The Italian fleet watched us and they didn't want us fishing. They said, 'Hey, look, kid, go down there off Pescadero and get in close; that's where the shark are really thick.' We went down there, made the set, and that's the last we ever saw of our nets. They'd put us right on the rocks. We got sacked a lot of times before I finally broke in.

"Then, when crab season came along, the buoys were getting cut off our pots because we were producing too much. One day, I came right up to this guy in the fog, and I saw him ahead of me, cutting. So, I trimmed his wings. I went over to his string of pots, cut his buoys off, and put my buoys on. Then, I went into the dock, took his buoys, and threw them in front of him and said, 'If you monkey around my gear again, I'll go through more of them.'

Crab pot set for Dungeness

"We had a big dinner on the dock that night. We were all friends, all brothers. We had a hell of a dinner and a good time. I went on the hill the next morning with binoculars and there they were, running my gear, the same guy I was having dinner with the night before. My friend Bob and I were so mad we went out and pulled fifty pots from various strings, we didn't care whose they were. We took them in and parked them at the wharf where everyone could see. They were livid. But we said, 'You keep messing with our gear and we'll take more and keep taking more.'

"Finally, that stopped, then instead of stealing the gear, they just ran the gear and took the crabs. So Bob and I put big lights on the boat and an extra crew member and we'd work all night. About 10:00 P.M. we'd hoist the anchor and out we'd go. We'd run their gear all night and then run our gear in the morning. We were sure coming in with a hell of a load of crabs, and they were coming in with none. It would get quiet for a while and then it would start up again. Still, those were some of the best years of my life, and we were all the best of friends. It's just the fisherman's way." Cass, like the rest of the entrants who survived these times, deserved to be among them.

None of this really perturbed Freckles; the ocean, even in its oldest traditions, never promised stability, and the newcomers who made it found one of their easiest friendships with this old man of the sea. Besides, Freckles had an idea. He wanted to design and build a boat that would incorporate all that he knew from his experience of the fish and the sea. The *Octopus*, launched in 1968, was quite a boat, and it looked just like him, beamy, sturdy, and determined. It would take a very long while to cover all the special features that graced the design and construction of the *Octopus* from the bow to the stern.

Suffice it to say that the *Octopus* was one of the first combination boats and one of the first steel boats in a fleet that is still predominantly wood and single purpose. "You better keep your eyes open, Maria," he said as I admired the vision in his boat. "It's not just the boats that are changing in ways like they never changed before, and none of it's for the good. Mark my words."

It was full on into the bow wake of these modernizing trends that I launched my dreams on *Angelina G.*, my brand-new, fifty-year-old Monterey. It was one thing to be riding around on the tail end of the present; it was quite another to catch a glimpse of the future pushing over the horizon.

Wintertime came: cold, rain, slop, southerlies, and especially no money. Salmon season didn't open until April 15; the season for bill collecting never closes. There was an old guy in Santa Cruz who hardly ever fished anymore. He had a gang of trammel nets up in his garage that hadn't seen the ocean in years. Somehow we got together—his nets, my boats, his knowledge and work, my work. No doubt it was a strange combination, but considering everything, it worked out quite well.

Trammel net is the real name for the gear we were using, but trouble nets or tangle nets is usually what Al called them. It was 2,400 feet of net, three layers of webbing that stood like a fence along the bottom of the sea; the small fish swim through and the big fish get caught. Al threw the first anchor on the end of the net, and though he'd explained what was going to happen, I still jumped back a few feet when the lead line, corks, and piles of mesh began racing across the deck and over the stern like a wild, uncoiling snake. It was exciting fishing from the beginning. We would leave the nets overnight to work while we slept, come back the next morning to harvest any number of a wide range of bottom fish, reset the net, and be back at the dock before midafternoon. That first night, lying in the complete safety of the berth, thinking about those nets out there making me a living, I couldn't figure out why everyone wasn't doing this instead of running around the coast like a yo-yo on the salmon's string. The next morning I was up an hour early with the restless anticipation of a kid at Christmas.

We had barely gotten the first fifteen feet of net back onto the boat, and already we had four big fish with wings about three feet across and a blubbery face just like a pig's. "What in the world is that?" I asked in complete ignorance.

"That's the devil," Al said without hesitation.

"How much do we get for him?"

"You can't eat stingrays, Marie; by the time we finish with this mess, all you're going to have is a backache like you never had before."

Sure enough, the whole net was loaded with them. When we pulled the last anchor onto the deck, there was a mountainous pile of webbing with over four thousand pounds of stingrays so tangled and twisted in the mesh, I was sure the nets were ruined. But it was even worse than that; each one of those ugly things, with its flailing tail and poisonous stinger, had to be carefully and firmly unraveled from the web.

Al's mood wasn't sweetened by the fact that he once stepped on one of these rays, the stinger went through his boot into his heel, and he was laid on his back for over eight months. I suggested using a knife to cut out the more difficult cases, and Al looked like he was going to throw me overboard. "You don't ever cut your net with a knife; you figure it out no matter how long it takes." The sun was going down, and we were just barely halfway through the job. I think he was more than a little surprised and very pleased that I was able to keep up with the work. He lightened up a bit in the swell of darkness. "You think this is bad," he said with that unforgettable smile that fishermen can wrap around the most miserable of times, "just wait till you see the jellyfish treatment or the starfish or the sportfisherman who pulls one end of the net, drops it improperly and the next morning everything's in one big ball. One time I had to get five guys to help me untangle a mess like that, and it took us three days, all day. But you know what really gets me is that box over there." I didn't have to look up; I'd been well aware of "that box" where we had thrown all the six of our marketable fish.

"What the hell am I doing here?" he said to himself, suddenly very serious. "I remember when I was a kid there used to be sea bass, mackerel, bonita, barracuda, crab, there was so much fish here in this Monterey Bay, a tremendous variety. There used to be fifteen boats fishing crabs alone, bringing in a load steady every day; now there's not one. And rock cod is a dead subject. It's not just the Russian ships doing all the damage. It's our own. Sure the Russians are taking a lot of the fish. But as soon as our drag boats came into the area, towing back and forth, back and forth, the fish were going fast. It's the chain along the bottom of the drag net, the thing that goes over the floor of the ocean and kills everything in its path. It's like me cutting the lawn day after day and never giving it a chance to grow. That lawn is going to die. It's the same with the vegetation at the bottom of the ocean. The fish put their eggs in the vegetation there, and you run over that with the nets every day and you're going to destroy everything for sure."

For sure, I'd heard this rap before, about the rock cod grounds at the Cordell Banks and the bottom fish grounds off Point Sur; I just never wanted to see it like that. Besides, as I stood there bent over that exhausting mess, it just didn't seem that there was any problem with a shortage of life in the sea.

The next morning we lay the nets in a little deeper water to avoid the path of the stingrays. He told me they rarely go deeper than fourteen fathoms in this area. And they rarely make mass migrations like the one we got involved in, except just before a southerly wind. "What happened this time," he said, "I don' no, I don' no, I don' no, but we ain't going back there for a while."

For the next week we were making forty to fifty bucks a day, which if you own a boat is a joke, but if you're hungry, it does the trick. One morning I was running the boat to the grounds, and, as usual, Al was content to stand against the rail and stare out at the horizon. Out of a long easy silence, he suddenly stuck his head in the cabin door. "Don't you see anything?" he yelled so as to emphasize the role of experience. Way, way, way out on the horizon was a trail of birds and a boat. "You should always see the birds and boats, they're your clues, but this is something different; head over there!" We were twenty minutes out of our way, when he handed me the binoculars. There was a trail of dead fish behind the boat, and two men on the back deck were shoveling, shoveling, shoveling.

"What are they doing that for?" I asked.

He was angrier now than when I had wanted to cut the fish out of the net with a knife. "It's nothing for a dragger to dump ten to fifteen tons of small fish because it's not worthwhile for the buyers to process the small fish. The small sand dabs, the small rock cod, the small lingcod, little black cod, little rex soles. They get caught in a dragnet, and it's way over 50 percent of the catch every time. And it's all dead and crushed by the time it gets to the boat. The markets won't touch it; there's not enough profit compared to the big fish."

He was getting hotter as he talked. "It's not just the little fish that get thrown back, it's the big fish too. If a market only wants 500 pounds of sand dabs and a guy makes a tow for 250 pounds of sand dabs and 2,000 pounds of sole, he'll throw the sole back and make another tow. You figure that one out." I'd never really believed it before; I thought it was an exaggeration, but there it was behind the boat, a trail of dead fish as far as the eye could see.

The mood was a little somber as we pulled our own net. I didn't quite know how to take all the emotion he had shown, and Al, I think, was feeling a little uncertain about having shown it. Soon we were distracted from our thoughts by a growing tension in the net. The more we pulled, the tighter it got. We both knew it wasn't good news that was coming up from the bottom of the sea, but when I saw that wide open jaw of a giant white shark coming up the side of the boat, I was sure glad Al was beside me. We stepped over to the gunwale for a better look, and the tail of that shark was over twenty-two feet away from its head, and the net was all torn, twisted and rolled in a mess as big as New York City. "Ain't that a beautiful sight," said Al in a voice that could never be described. "Hand me the knife," he ordered. For over an hour he cut and cursed, while it was my job to keep the boat from drifting over the net because, as always seems to be the case, it's never just one thing at a time. The wind had shifted and was blowing the boat directly into the net. It was tricky maneuvering, and I managed to do a great job right up to the point when Al got the net free of the shark. A gust of wind caught me off guard, the stern swung over the net and no doubt about it, we were hung up in our own gear. Al was hot, and I felt stupid. We drifted hopelessly and silently for one very long minute. I knew he didn't want to call the Coast Guard, and sure as hell he didn't want to call his friends.

Maybe I could save the day. "Hey, listen, Al, I used to dive around this coast a lot. It won't bother me a bit to take a little dip."

"No way," he said, and we fooled around a long time with the old "knife lashed to the end of a pole trick" which hardly ever works.

Finally, I said, "I'm going in." He tied a rope around me and told me how to keep from getting my head smashed open every time the boat comes down off a wave. But I could tell he still didn't quite believe I was going to do it.

As soon as I hit the water, all I could see was the gaping mouth of that white shark. I never figured out a tangle on a prop so fast; thirty seconds and I was back on the deck—a hero for the day. "Well I'll be goddamned," said Al. "Hey, I'm going to buy you a drink."

We were walking into Brady's, the local fishing bar that sits by the sea, when Al suddenly grabbed my arm, turned me around, and headed me out the door. "Listen, remember what I told you this morning about the drag boats? Well that's only part of the story. The rest of it is in this bar. Just keep your mouth shut and listen."

We walked back in, and Al went up to a guy in a uniform I

didn't immediately recognize and slapped him on the back. "Hey, old buddy, tough day at the office?"

"Hi, Al, how you doing?" he said with just a touch of tension.

"You'll never guess what we saw today. There's a dragger out there working inside the three-mile limit."

"What boat was that?" asked the warden.

"That's your job, pal." Al's voice was getting pretty loud, and even the jaded patronage of Brady's was beginning to shift in their seats. "Why don't you ever stick your head out the window? You could see them from here."

There wasn't anything the warden could have said, but he really stuck his foot in the trap. "We went out on a dragger just the other day, and they're not getting that much fish."

Al laughed sarcastically, "You gotta be kidding. Don't you know when you guys get on the boat, the captain's gonna take you to the Mojave Desert? How come when you don't go out, they come in so damn loaded with fish every day?" Despite the looks from the rest of the bar, or maybe because of them, Al wasn't going to stop. "You guys talk conservation, shit, you know what conservation is, it's putting the guy out of business that destroys." I don't think the warden wanted to discuss conservation, but Al didn't care. "Who the hell pays you guys to come down here and sit on your ass? Which fish market's putting the money under the table? It's gotta be someone, or are you that stupid that you don't know what's going on out there? You bust a guy for a lousy filet of salmon in a frying pan, and you don't see the other stuff?" The warden tried to move away, and Al tried to stop him. The bartender recognized the familiar symptoms and said, "Hey, Al, go to the other end of the bar."

I already knew there was tremendous hostility between the fishermen and the Fish and Game, but it seemed like the subject just didn't come up that often. Most of the time when they were together, things weren't this bad; they usually could sit down together over a friendly drink of coffee or booze. But I also knew from the stories that on more than one occasion relationships have been quite a bit worse than what I saw today. More than one warden has accidentally slipped off the stern of a boat he was trying to board, and more than one fisherman has been shot in the back. Is this where it's headed, I wondered, is it soon going to be just like the land with dissension and fights, are the fish going to die out, is the ocean but a final frontier for corruption and destruction?

Probably not, I thought. Al and I finished out the rest of the two months with a lot of mutual respect. I survived the winter; he was out there one more time, and we never again saw a dragger on the grounds. Probably not, the ocean is a great big place with too many miles of blue blue horizons. And apart from a few incidents, people cooperate out here at sea, they treat each other right, and they're happier with their lives than any group of people I've known. Besides, when the sardine left, didn't the anchovy take its place?

But I never forgot that day.

5

The Scent of the Hunt

THINGS WERE DIFFERENT now that I had the *Angelina G.*
When you lease a boat, your in-the-pocket earnings come off the
top of the catch; when you're buying a boat, your earnings come
off the bottom. Matter and antimatter only begin to suggest the
gap.

The bills for boat payments, insurance, haul outs, repairs, maintenance, fuel, bait, ice, and miscellaneous insaneness sat permanently by the compass like its alter ego. The pile they formed
actually seemed to grow larger the more I fished. It didn't take me
long to make an art form out of juggling a dozen of these hot
potatoes in the mail at a time, but coping with the pressure these
bills created at sea was often beyond me. I couldn't begin to
recount the number of times while fishing that I'd look out over
the sea in the throes of one or another of its rages, and every
instinct in my body said, "Time to go in, enough is enough." But
my mind would always betray me by adding up the weight of the
fish in the hold and subtracting the bills in the bow. For almost the
entire four years I fished this boat, it never ever came out to be
enough.

"Freckles," I said one day, exasperated by ten days straight of
bum moves, rough weather, midnight repairs, and not a whole lot
of fish, "how the hell do you ever get ahead in this game?"

"Maria, that's an easy one." He took a deep breath as if he'd
been waiting a long time for someone to set him up to deliver this
line and he didn't want to blow it. "Just keep putting in the time,

pretty soon you get old like me, then they bury you, and presto, you're ahead of the game." Before I could register my complete dissatisfaction, his deckhand hollered at him from fifteen feet up on the dock, "Hey, Freckles, catch." Freckles turned around and caught the two fifty-pound cases of bait, one after the other, like they were packs of cigarettes. Four o'clock that afternoon they had just finished unloading their last trip; now it was six o'clock, they had scrubbed the hold, reiced, taken fuel, and they were just about to leave for the bite that was reported almost two hundred miles south. He wanted to be there by dawn for the morning bite, so there wasn't much time to tell me that he wasn't putting me on. Freckles was sixty-two years old and I was twenty-eight. But the way I felt, one more trip putting in the time like the last one, and there wouldn't be anything left to bury.

What really was taking its mental toll was the fact that I was without a doubt putting in the time and never once did I get paid for it, nor did I get paid for lying cheek to cheek with a hot, greasy engine block till four in the morning, trying to resuscitate aging machinery; I didn't even get paid if I spent the whole next day plying a big sea headed for the big bite. The only thing that brought a buck was fish, gutted, gilled, and delivered.

From April 15 until September 31 the Pacific king salmon was my bread and butter as it was for the majority of the West Coast fleet. Add the impenetrable mind of this animal to the unruly forces of the wind and the sea, and business couldn't be shakier. The salmon is a mammoth migrating trout that has perfected all the cagey secrets of its freshwater cousin and claimed the full length of the Northwest Pacific in which to hide them. Even now after eight years of fishing, if I had to write up a statement of everything I know for sure about this fish, and if I had to sign it, I could barely fill an index card. Number one, I could safely say that the salmon leaves no tracks, and after cleaning thousands of their bellies, I'd feel justified in saying that the salmon eats anything alive that's smaller than its mouth: shrimp, herring, anchovies, baby crabs, snails, rockfish, etc. One of the few other facts I have about this fish was given to me by a zookeeper at Marine World. No aquarium in the world has been able to keep an adult salmon alive in a tank. Their urge to travel is so great that the salmon will ram its head into the wall until it is dead rather than be confined.

Amazingly, that's about all anyone knows about the life of a salmon at sea. Everything else about this fish is by guess and by golly. The migrations of the salmon around the coast aren't like those of land animals that can pretty much be depended on to arrive at Sunny Valley in August because the honey berries are ripe and then in September move on to Singing Flats because the bodincular bugs have hatched. The location of the salmon's feed is itself a secret brewing of the massive currents that swirl, surface, and disappear as mysteriously as the salmon, current changes so massive that were they to occur over the land, they could cover the space of a state in a day. Besides, locating their feed doesn't necessarily have much to do with a paycheck. I've seen areas many square miles of cold, green, shrimpy plankton soup go completely unnoticed by the fish while a couple of miles away they snapped like wild dogs in blue desert.

When you get right down to it, there isn't a thing about the unseen habits of this elusive fish that you'd ever want to bank on. Do they travel in schools? Sometimes. Do they travel alone? Sometimes. Males and females together? Sometimes. Do they school up for feeding or traveling? Sometimes. Do they feed mostly at dawn or dusk or do they swim against the current? Sometimes. The only certain thing about the habits of the salmon is that for the one occasion of spawning and death the salmon returns to the exact gravel-bedded streamlet in the mountains where it was born. And all that does for the fisherman is add to his awe.

Understandably, the local bank loan officers have a standardized laugh when approached by commercial fishermen. In the early 1970s, when I first bought the *Angelina G.*, there was only one place the fishermen could go for financial assistance; that was to the fish buyers. Now there were only seven or eight major fish buyers on the California coast; the concept of a company town provides only the weakest description of the scene. Things were tough in those years. I was holding on to the boat, yes, but I was also eating so much fresh seafood for breakfast, lunch, and dinner that it began to taste like grits.

Fortunately, you can sail along on hope for a long time, and fishing gives you that, in huge, unexpected overdoses that mainline through your veins and go direct to the brain's center of greed. The staying power and single-mindedness that results isn't much less primitive than that of a gold prospector or a heroin addict, but it still can move mountains.

Probably the best way to handle the confusion of these variables is to lay out a day to day picture of a trip taken from my early log on the *Angelina*. That way, too, you meet a few of the fishermen along the way as I did, take in a little scenery, watch the game, and see that any amount of confusion you may feel is nothing compared to mine.

I think I'll start with this entry here: "1 A.M.: leaving Half Moon Bay for Pt. Reyes, winds 25, slop." I deftly chose this point for the very simple reason that it's the only time in eight years' fishing that I ever kept a log of more than two days running.

The reason I was running at night was the usual one. At 12 P.M. I was sound asleep, snugly anchored in the bay with a dozen other boats. Suddenly, the silence was shattered by the sound of anchor chains clanking over winches throughout the bay. I jumped into my boots, checked the engine, pulled the anchor, and followed their lights to sea, certain that someone must have heard a good report on the fish. It was two hours before someone told me there had been scores of over one hundred fish caught off Point Reyes the day before. Even four hours pounding the rough sea at night couldn't dampen a buildup of excitement. Those one hundred fish represented upwards of three thousand dollars.

One hour after dawn, only one hour away from the spot, a fisherman on the scene was yelling out the story line of things to come. "Yeah, Ron," he says to his buddy, "it sure looks like this place went to hell in a hurry, looks like we might have to make the move up to the rock pile." The rock pile, as Fish Rocks is affectionately known, was over ten hours up the line.

The boats were leaving Point Reyes like rats from a sinking ship. I stayed on hope, worked the middle grounds, then out to the north island, and back to the point. By the end of the day I had scratched out a total of five of the one hundred fish. That night in the whole expanse of the anchorage, it was only me and that big black buoy moaning out its fate as it fell off the crest of each passing wave. "Should I go or should I stay?" I argued with myself long into the night in perfect time with the buoy. If I go, I'll lose another day running, the fish might be gone by the time I get there, and besides, I didn't know the grounds; on the other hand, I'd sure feel like a fool hanging around here.

In the morning I figured to take a tack up in front of the bluffs, take one back, waste a few hours, and then leave. For the first half hour I stood poised and ready in the stern while the lines hung dead in the water just like I'd expected. So I went up to the cabin to eat my heart out and watch the cliff face go by.

The Point Reyes bluffs aren't just any old bluffs on the sea. For over two miles this naked, jagged stand of rock juts into the sea like the head of a hammer and hundreds of feet into the sky like a monolith. On days like that day with the sunshine and blue sky it looks a magnificent and bold assault on the sea. But on days of a gnarly grey fog it looks like evil faces in the dark rocks retreating back to the underworld, and except for the Farallon Islands, it's the creepiest place I've seen on earth. I reached the west end of the point, changed the old water-logged bait, and turned around to make the tack down and a little more on the inside. In a little closer to the bluffs you can see that not even the moss wants to live here. Only the hardy old seabirds, adamant sea lions, and the Yukon gang have the fortitude to call this place home.

Right now the Yukon gang was about twenty miles on the outside of me, trying to scratch out a day in the deep. As usual on a slow day, they were talking on the radio steady, ribbing each other about having their heads examined and maybe they'd lost their touch.

"Right, right, Governor, we're getting old, this gang used to be tough, now the fish leave us like dogs."

"Yeah, what are we gonna do, Charlie, run all the way up there so the next morning they give us a call from one hundred miles further up? Come on, them days are over."

The first time I'd ever heard of the gang, I was tied up in a string of boats in Bodega Bay when someone came yelling down the dock, "Lock your boats, lock your boats, the Yukon gang's coming into port!" And I remember my curiosity was piqued again whenever Hobo would tell me the first rule of the sea. He used to say, "It doesn't matter if a guy is your worst enemy on the coast, you always help the other guy out at sea," and as if to certify the rule as unbreakable, he added, "I'd even help the Yukon gang if they were in trouble." Naturally, I asked around about this gang, but the stories people told about them were of such legendary proportions that it was hard to know what was true. I did know that during the salmon season they lived in a building behind the fish dock at Point Reyes. In fact, the way a lot of people talked, Point Reyes was the gang's territory, and the tone of voice they used always left me wondering just how to interpret that. The one other thing I knew that distinguished them from the other fishermen was that they traveled in the tightest gang on the coast. Their boats at sea were always within yelling distance of each other, despite the invention of radios.

I had even met the gang during my first year of fishing, and I still didn't know much more about them except that they formed a very strong first impression. It was on the occasion of my first and only delivery of fish at the Point Reyes dock. It's a real outpost buying station tucked into the shelter created by the bluffs, mounted high on rotting pilings, eleven miles from the nearest grocery store, and forty-five miles from the city. A grey-haired, nice-looking old lady came out on the dock to buy the fish. We were smiling and delightfully surprised to see each other in this overwhelmingly male business, when steam started pouring out of my engine room. Nada's smile vanished immediately, and she yelled at me to get my boat out of there so I wouldn't block the others that wanted to offload. "But, Nada," I yelled back, "there's not another goddamned boat in sight; besides, I can't move anyway, the engine quit, it got so hot." In the midst of the screaming, she grabbed a knife and was about to cut the lines loose in the wind and coming dark when the Yukon gang came to the rescue.

"Don't worry about it, Nada, we'll take care of it," and five spry old fishermen and two younger guys all scrambled down the side of the dock onto my boat. All at once there was a guy up in the cabin, screaming to me in the engine room, "Hey, you got a pretty nice rig here," and a short, squat guy in the stern, yelling "How the hell do you expect fish to go for junk like this?" and an old guy on top of the cabin, asking if we wanted to hire a cook on the crew, while another one squeezed up between the engine and the pumps said, "Check the damn strainer first, Mario," and Mario, who was squeezed between me and the engine said, "Just shut up, Scheff, and get some gasket material." I wanted very much to ask them how come they were so sure without even checking that the problem was in the pump and not the heat exchanger, but I knew I had a better chance of pushing through the wall of a cyclone than trying to enter that conversation. "Come on," said another, his volume adjusted to cover everyone, "let's get this little maneuver over with and go eat."

Scheff came back with the front cover of *Playboy* magazine.

Mario held it up in front of his eyes, gave it one last adoring look, and said, "I sure hate to do this to you, honey." He grabbed the hammer, pounded out an impression of the casing on the lower half of the picture, cut it out with a knife, screwed it into place, and said, "You'll never blow that gasket, kid. Why don't you come up to the old shack-ala and eat while you're waiting for your engine to cool?"

"Thanks anyway," I said calmly, just barely covering my uncertainty, "another time."

I couldn't figure out if this gang was the Hell's Angels of the fishing fleet, the merry pranksters, the Mafia, or the radical fringe of the Grey Panthers, but I was dying to find out. Now, a year later, dragging in front of the bluffs with nothing doing and no one around would have been the perfect time. But with this gang I didn't know how to begin. What was I going to do? Get on the radio and say, "Hi, my name's Marie; the fishing's the pits in here, too," or "Gee! The weather's sure nice." Besides I was just about back at the other end of the bluff. I'd wasted enough of this day, and it was time to leave.

I walked to the back deck to pull the gear and stopped dead in my tracks just long enough to feel a rush of blood pound through my head. Jesus, there were fish pumping on every line. I leapt into the pit, made a dozen baits faster than if my life depended on it, hated myself for not having paid attention, grabbed the gaff, and started pulling fish. They were coming up big and sassy, swirling and slashing the surface of the sea with their massive tails. I was holding my breath and trying to control the shaking in my hands. That thin leader between me and the fish was only three fathoms long, but pulling them together is like trying to put two poles of a magnet in the same spot.

There were seven fish on the gear, but who knows how long I'd been dragging them. I made a quick back tack, hoping I'd caught them in the close vicinity, immediately picked up five more, lost two of them behind the boat, turned around, jabbed more hooks into the bait, replaced a couple of broken leaders, saw at least two more fish had gotten on the other line, when it hit me. Not only had I tripped over backward into a bucket of honey, but I'd also come upon the perfect bait for the bees, an offering of friendship that no fisherman on the coast could refuse. I ran to the microphone, "Hey, Mario, you pick me up?"

"Yeah, who's calling Mario?"

"Mario, it's Marie. I'm working on the reef by chimney rock; I just picked up ten fish. They're all big ones too."

"What size did you say they were?" he asked.

"They're all big ones," I answered assuredly.

"OK, kid, thanks for the call."

I ran back to the stern, and over the back deck speaker I heard the gang talking back and forth in Italian. I was sure they'd pick up their gear and come running in, and in a couple of hours they'd be throwing fish over both shoulders, and I'd be the hero. I was working like lightning, trying to keep the lines clean for the fish, and I missed the tone of their conversation. Then one of the gang said something in English, the tone of which was unmistakable. "Sure, sure, Charlie, and they're all big ones, too." I suddenly felt queasy, I'd branded myself; an amateur never catches ten fish, an amateur always catches ten big fish.

They called again in about an hour. "I've got eighteen fish now" was all I said. The gang argued in Italian for a little while and went back to their bantering. I called again at twenty-eight fish, then thirty-three and thirty-seven. Finally at five o'clock, seven Monterey fishing boats came running up to the buoy, and I thought for sure they'd drop their gear for the evening bite, but there wasn't even a wave. It didn't make any sense; how could they be fishermen and pass up numbers like that? Maybe this gang is just plain nuts!

I wasn't very good at fishing the rocky reefs with their unseen jagged edges and the currents swirling around them; I'd already tangled two lines and lost a couple of leads. And in between the blitz of baiting the hooks, cleaning the fish, and replacing the gear, I couldn't quite calm down enough when another leader came up to the surface, stretched tensely with the weight of a lively fish. I'd grab the leader a little too firmly and make the fish come to me. Too many times I was left with nothing but a surprised look on my face and a salmon tail disappearing into the wave.

But this evening the fish didn't seem to care that I was Jane Doe from Kokomo who couldn't run the show. They just kept biting, and if one got away, there was another there to fill its place. And they were all big ones, too, slabs or suitcases as they're often called, spilling out of the overfull boxes on the back deck, with the brilliant hues of sunset reflecting out of every silvery scale.

I was running into the dock in the last glow of day, and I couldn't take my eyes off the fish. The afternoon had passed in such frenzy that it was as if the fish had suddenly appeared out of nowhere. Seven hours ago I didn't know how I was going to pay for the next load of fuel; now coming out of the delirium of some manic fever, I had close to fifteen hundred dollars to my name. That kind of shift in the cosmos can have a pretty lasting effect on a person, like a bolt of lightning so hot that every time it strikes, it zaps a weld into the brain between fish and fast money. Staring at those fish, I never gave such concentrated thought in my life to improving my on the job skills. I had to be more prepared; even if I hadn't caught a fish for three days, there had to be at least forty fresh baits made up at all times, that was new rule number one, and two dozen extra leaders, and, God, I had to stop losing fish behind the boat and start paying attention. The taste on my tongue set me dreaming about everything I'd ever wanted to do. I'd have it made, work like a dog for six months out of the year and the other six months, bon voyage! Never mind that this was June, and the fifteen hundred dollars would barely cover my boat and insurance payment that was due in May.

I steered through the Yukon gang's boats, all moored quietly in front of the fish dock. One of the guys was apparently still on his boat as I went by. When my stern passed him, he yelled up to the dock, "Eat your heart out, Mario." I was a little more than embarrassed by the way this all worked out as I lay rocking against the tall wooden dock, loading the fish one by one into the bin. Nada worked the hoist without the slightest glance of recognition. The gang stood silently on the dock; I had sacked them in their own backyard, and there wasn't the slightest indication from them of how that would be dealt with. Finally Mario yelled down, "You did all right, kid, we'll give it a try in the morning," and walked away.

Nada handed down the fish tag on a long pole, and as I glanced at it, I couldn't believe my eyes. "Three hundred sixty pounds?" I yelled in anger. "What the hell are you trying to pull? I know damn well . . ." And I stopped myself; I knew damn well it was too late. I should have been up there on the dock, watching the scale, even though as I was alone on the boat, it was impossible to be two places at once. Every dock on the coast seems to have a little tariff system that operates faster than the eye—a fish thrown off to the side before it gets weighed or a cigar placed innocently on the weighing arm—but this was over 25 percent of the catch, and I felt like tearing the place apart. I tried real hard to remember Freckles's advice about such things. "Sicilian style, Maria, always wait till the tide turns before you make your move."

The next morning a sharp breeze from the northwest was stirring a nasty chop over the reef. My hands ached in the cold, and I braced my legs hard and wide against the coamings of the gaff hatch to keep from getting pitched by the boat's snappy roll. But the prospect of a whole day on these fish was enough to draw the harshness of the sea into the sphere of excitement. And the presence of seven mast lights scattered around me in the dark, and I figured all would be well with the world.

There was the normal twenty-minute radio silence as the sun rose while everyone was busy in the stern setting their gear. I was just barely getting the last line in the water when one of the gang yelled, "Maruchis! Let's get the hell out of here." It came out of the radio like a spit. Maruchi is Italian for hake, which in English is also pronounced like a spit, because of the strained nature of the relationships between the fishermen and the hake. Hake are a school fish that attack the salmon bait like piranhas. When they show up in large enough numbers, it doesn't matter how many salmon are down there with them, you can forget about it. But thinking about the money they cost you is only part of the story. Their personal appearance has as much to do with the fishermen's reaction as anything. These shit brown, jaundiced-eyed, bulging-bellied fish, which fall apart at the seams like mush whenever you handle them, had ended the show. My name with the gang, I was sure, would forever be pronounced like the hake.

Everything was pointing north but my compass. I piled the gear on the boat and gave the whole deal the broiling wake of my stern. Hardly did I know that one day I'd be the first honorary woman member of the gang, made official when my name went on the dishes list. Nor could I have possibly foreseen that the very strangeness of their behavior would be the spiritual salvation of my fishing.

For now, it just felt good to be moving on. Full bore, sea room, a sky bigger than the one that spans the Great Plains, and new territory; Fish Rocks was nine hours away but it was only six in the morning; there'd be plenty of time to look around along the way for another pot of gold with my name on it.

I had to trip fish now if I was going to make ends meet. Running into port every night had to fade into the realm of the good old days. And I had to travel and stay on top of a good bite of fish as much of the time as possible. The potential area that entailed off the California coast alone was over ten thousand square miles, to say nothing of the cubic dimensions. Since there's nothing to go on that means anything for sure, you take the color of the waters, what happened yesterday, what happened last year, who said what in what tone of voice, the weather, the suspicious look in the eye of a bird, the color of the starfish that came up on the anchor in the morning, and you put it all together in a big wad the size of your brain, mull it over, and update it for the rest of your fishing days. And never expect to germinate anything but a hunch.

Actually, I was thrilled by the prospect of it all. The freedom and challenge of a nomadic life at sea felt bigger than I ever could have imagined. That poetic metaphor I remember from high school about being captain of your soul was sure a raw pancake compared to the real thing. Why couldn't the fishermen understand why I didn't want to be a deckhand on my boyfriend's boat? Wasn't it obvious? Deckhand is cleaning fish, making baits and breaking ice. But captain was my chance to try out my own game plan on the universe.

The beauty of it was it didn't matter what the fishermen thought. The rules of the sea didn't take any regard to sex, and one of the most important of these rules is that one captain never tells another captain what to do. The freedom that gave me was beyond anything I'd ever experienced before. Add to that the rule that was taken just as seriously about helping anyone in trouble, and I felt I'd managed to find as utopian a community as existed anywhere, and I was certain the rest would eventually work out.

I was proud of my boat, too. Despite her limitations. *Angelina G.* was over fifty years old, and by now, even the jokes that were made about these little Montereys were getting old. "You know what's holding those planks in place, Maria? The teredo worms are so scared they're holding hands." Ha, ha. But in times of seriousness there was nothing but respect expressed for the unique seaworthiness of these old boats, and the craftsmanship that went into them was talked about as something that would never be seen again. There isn't an angle on the boat anywhere that you could lay a carpenter's square. Every surface is curved in every direction, and no two curves on the boat are the same. A flat surface on the boat stops the ocean and something's got to give; it's never the ocean. The ocean hits the hull of a Monterey from any direction and it keeps on rolling, which is all the ocean ever asks.

So perfectly did the old builders execute their wooden curves that the calculated swelling of the wood in the water is enough to hold her tight in the sea. The Monterey is probably the only wooden commercial vessel that doesn't depend on caulking between its seams.

Now if you happen to be a brain surgeon or a rocket man and you're still not too impressed, consider the Monterey was never laid out on a drawing board; there were never any plans. The builder merely stood back from the boat and eyed it into form. The names of those builders, like La Bruzzi and Pascanucchi, are spoken among the fleet with more reverence than the name da Vinci.

Angelina's biggest problem was spelled out clearly in the forecastle. All the Italian-built boats had a bronze plaque tacked in the forepeak with an engraving of the entire fisherman's prayer. "Oh, Lord, Thy sea is so great and my boat is so small." For *Angelina* that went double. To say that every function and maneuver on the boat was cramped is to belittle the predicament. But the worst consequence of her size was the fact that I couldn't have a crew. I had to fish alone. The extra work that generated went beyond a mere challenge.

Point Reyes was fast becoming an innocuous speck on the sea behind me. Since the weather permitted, I poured a cup of coffee and continued to look around for signs. Five hours bounced by and there wasn't a bird, a bait, or a boat. The water for miles was clear, light green. A lot of my friends from Hawaii see the North Pacific coast and they say, "Yuch, it's so dirty," and I forgive them for they know not what they say. The word that describes the usual condition of our sea is murky, not dirty, and that murk is the broth of life; plankton water, bait and salmon water, it's the closest thing on earth to holy water. These miles of clear water I was traveling through held no more promise of salmon than the floor of Death Valley. I wasn't much worried; I was beginning to pick up conversations from Fish Rocks, and it sounded like they still had fish.

The whole Nevada desert must have been baking like a blast furnace in the late afternoon sun, the hot air rising off its surface, leaving a vacuum that was inhaling so much air so fast through the Sierra and Central Valley that the sea in front of Fish Rocks was slamming my boat into the trough of every wave that passed. Damn that desert. I couldn't work the evening bite. So I stood about a quarter mile off land and looked in at the shore lined with twenty thousand rocks. "Hmmmm," I wondered, "which rocks is Fish Rocks?" If only I had a loran, it would tell me exactly where I was in latitude. The loran is a one-thousand-dollar black box of navigation that was fast coming to be standard equipment in the fleet; mine was at the bottom end of my shopping list.

"Is there anyone on the anchorage who can tell me how to get in this place?" I called.

"Is that you, Marie? This is Doug from Bodega. Fish Rocks is a cinch compared to the others. You see a rock that looks like a big sail on a sailfish? Look down the coast from there a little ways and you'll see a big rock that looks like a distorted pyramid about to fall down."

A real out and out cinch, I thought, as long as everyone agrees on the shape of a distorted pyramid about to fall down. Finally, after half an hour of trading surreal rock descriptions, I said, "Does it have a little rock beside it that looks like its baby?"

"Bingo," he said, "come in on it from the northeast, throw me a line when you see my boat, and come over for dinner."

I threw a big rope from my stern to Doug's. With the big swell running into the anchorage it was a tricky maneuver trying to pull the boats together without letting them smash each other to splinters while at the same time bringing them close enough so I could make a quick jump and shove the boats apart. The smell of hot, buttered fish wafting from his galley made it entirely possible.

Fresh filet of lingcod, just about every fisherman's favorite, a cup of red wine, a big galley table to sit at, the slow roll of a deep hull, and good company. Doug had been fishing most of his life and had distinguished himself by learning to take it all with a grain of salt. "How come you're in so early?" I asked.

"Didn't you hear them talking about tit-suckers and rags? Everyone's coming in. Right now you gotta go through ten small ones to get one legal size. When the babies move in like that, you don't keep working them over and call yourself a fisherman." I was always impressed that that was indeed true. Even though every fish under twenty-six inches is released, most of them eventually die because of blood loss or slime loss which inevitably leads to infection. So the area was being vacated, not exactly out of maternalism, but at least in regard to the future catch. "What are you doing here is the real question," he said. "Word was that you were knocking the shit out of the fish down at the point. A bunch of guys took off a couple of hours ago to find you.

"Oh, boy," I said, and told him the story.

"Ah, don't worry about them; I talked to Earl when he'd gotten in front of Fort Ross. He said he saw a few birds working; he was going to give it a try and then give me a call and let me know what happened. That's the last I heard from him all day." Doug was laughing at the game of it all, but I was serious.

"Doug, I just came from there and the water was like a swimming pool." He didn't stop laughing as he stretched his suspenders, got up from the table, and started digging to the bottom of a drawer full of small spare parts and rusty old lures.

"I'll show you something," he said and unfolded a couple of the charts over my plate. I was astonished. The charts were covered with thousands of tiny coded marks. For a period of many years, Doug had daily recorded the water temperature, sea conditions, feed conditions, location, and the number of fish caught. The obsession shown on these charts made Ahab's mapping of the whale look halfhearted. "You know what I found out?" he asked, pausing long enough to make sure I drooled. "You've got as much chance of finding them as I do, and that could be anywhere, under any conditions. Every year this salmon becomes more of a mystery to me than before." He folded up the charts and purposely put them back underneath the pile of tools in the drawer so they wouldn't get in his way.

"Ah, shut up," he yelled out the door to the barking sea lions on the rocks as if he were yelling at his neighbor's dog, and he was still smiling, like he was somehow amused by all the years of useless work that he'd put into those charts. But that smile was starting to look more and more like a shit-eating grin to me.

"Dammit, Doug, you do see things I don't, otherwise you wouldn't always catch more fish than I do." The most important question of my life, and he gave me the same old pablum that I got from every other fisherman: "Patience, experience, you're doing all right, and relax, there's nothing you can see." I gave up. "What are you going to do in the morning?" I asked.

"I dunno, maybe I'll run down and find Earl. If you don't want to go back that way, it sounds like there might be something doing around Fort Bragg. Don't just charge up there, though; keep your eyes open, you might see something along the way." I didn't ask him what.

I got back on my boat, thanked him for a great dinner, and he hollered over the wind, "If you do go up that way, you ought to leave early so you get around Point Arena before daylight. I don't think this wind wants to quit; it's got all the earmarks."

I threw the anchor behind a rock that would dwarf the buildings of New York, made fifty baits, and set the alarm for 2 A.M. Between the time I hit the sack and the time I fell asleep one word passed through my head: "Earmarks?"

It was rough all right as I came on to the point, so rough that I wondered at every steepening wave if I should turn around and go back. I wouldn't be foolish enough to climb Mount Everest because "it's there," but a lot of times I just kept going because I was already "here." I was always scared, though, pounding around in a mountainous shadowy sea by myself. The only indication that there was even one soul left in the universe was the eerie flash of the lighthouse five miles away and the nagging memory of the stories of two fishermen who had just recently met with tragedy here. Burt on the *Westwind* only a month before was rounding this point on a stormy night, had hit a wash rock, lost the boat and a crew member, and somehow managed himself to swim from the rock to the shore. And only a couple of weeks ago one of these rolling monsters smashed through Andy's windows, cut his face with the glass, ruined all the electronics, flooded the boat and kept her from rising to the next wave, which boarded the boat and flooded the engine. I don't know how he got out of that one. He was holed up in port for a long time after, and nowadays he doesn't want to talk about it.

I worked my way north with not a boat in sight, trying a couple of spots that Doug had suggested and a couple that he hadn't, hoping as always I'd hit a gigantic school. By the time I reached Fort Bragg at four o'clock, I had three whole fish. Luckily the port was deserted, too, and I didn't have to think of smart answers to smart ass questions like "How long have you been keeping that run of fish a secret?"

Fuel, bait, ice, and groceries and I finally got a chance to pull up to the only two boats around to find out what was going on.

I threw them my lines and they whipped them around the cleat in a one-handed knot without even saying hi, then they jumped back to the stern where they were pounding nails, tying rigging stays, fastening chains and springs and taglines on a brand new pole with a frenzied speed and glazed look in their eyes like they were doctors over a patient that had just stopped breathing. Rigging new poles is an all-day job, and I swear they were trying to do it in an hour.

"Hey, Charlie, what happened to your poles?" I asked out of sheer lack of diplomacy.

"I was scouting," he said with a sheepish grin, "and I discovered a new high spot off the Mendocino reef and it took everything."

"Yeah, sure," I said. "Somebody just put it there yesterday. Where's the fish you're so worried about missing?"

"The Tolo Banks," he mumbled, as if he didn't want to say.

"The Tolo Banks? That's over five hours away farther up the line."

"Well, it's starvation around here. For two days we looked everywhere as you can see. We're leaving at one o'clock in the morning if you want to come." With three of us working on the poles, the job was done two hours early, and we hit the sack at eleven.

Charlie, Mike, and I were three of about fifty boats that the old-timers called the "new breed," which they sometimes said in the same tone of voice that was reserved for the word maruchi. Refugees from the dying embers of the sixties who bailed for the sea in the seventies, a lot of these guys have gotten the word crazy permanently attached to the front of their names, Crazy Paul, Crazy Charlie, Crazy Frank; Marie seemed to speak for itself. In a very real sense we were crazy by the process of natural selection. We were all short on knowledge, equipment, and money; the only way to make it was to push hard and only crazy people work that hard.

One o'clock the next morning, with two hours' sleep, the fog was so socked in, the light on the dock was nothing but a haze. Getting out of there would be Russian roulette with the narrow entrance lined with rocks.

"I don't like it, Charlie," I said without hesitation.

"Fucking fog" was all he kept repeating as he stared out blindly in the direction of the black sea with an intensity that was weighing his life.

"Look," said Mike, who used to be a happy-go-lucky hippie,

"there's a lot of fish up there, they've already been working on them a day, and they aren't going to last forever. You snooze, you lose."

"I sure wish we could wait for light," I said.

"Come on, Marie, what difference does light make in this shit anyway? Besides then we get there at nine o'clock, just in time for the start of the midday drag. We gotta make the morning bite," and he started untying the lines.

The morning bite! I'm surprised the fishermen haven't erected an altar to the morning bite at every port so when the wind blows, everyone could sacrifice live anchovies and maybe an occasional fish buyer or even go so far as to sacrifice a bottle of wine. The morning bite, those sacred couple of hours at dawn when the salmon like to feed. The morning bite was at stake here, so I concentrated as hard as I could on conjuring up a firm image of the positions of the rocks, the jetty, and the buoys, the swell, the current, the timing, and the course because the thought of dying scared me to death.

I made it to the outside and as usual I swore it was the last time. Mike got on the air, "Everybody make it OK? Let's go." Running up the line was hardly less tense. All I could see in front of me was the little red indicator light of the radio reflecting back from the black windows; the gentleness of the swell felt sinister, and the only thing I knew for sure about the location of Charlie and Mike was that they were on Channel 4 on the radio. If you ever hit a log like some of those big telephone poles you see in the daytime or if another boat happened to be coming the other direction—Jesus.

For the next four hours, in between long silences, we jabbered back and forth, catching up on each other's lives, which consisted entirely of who caught how many fish, where, under what conditions. Having exhausted that subject, we got into the current war among the buyers over the price of salmon, how it looked like they might have pushed the price up to the point where we could make a living, which is the same price where the buyers get nervous, they pull the market orders, and the fleet goes on strike, and nobody makes anything. "I'm not tying this boat up for nothing; I'll market the fish myself if it comes to that bullshit again," said Charlie.

"Yeah, just like the last time," said Mike, "when it took you two whole hours just to get one thousand pounds of fish onto the dock

because the buyers wouldn't let you use their hoist, then you drove
them to the firm deal you had lined up in the city and the restaurant decided they only wanted five hundred pounds, then the ice
melted in the truck so you panicked and tried to hawk the rest of
the fish in the parking lot of the ferry terminal, and the cops busted
you. It's always something, man, bum checks, broken deals, rotting fish, and if nothing else, the association gets on your ass, and
they got a point, too, the price stinks. We're stuck with the damn
buyers any way you look at it."

There's kind of an unwritten rule on the radio at sea. You can
get as immersed as you want in the cries of despair, but you've got
to stop before someone jumps overboard. "Have you heard the one
about the millionaire and fisherman?" Charlie yelled out from the
darkness of three in the morn. "A millionaire wanted to give away
a million dollars to someone who'd put it to good use, so he started
asking different people what they'd do with it. The alcoholic said
he'd take the cure, the farmer said he'd develop a new crop to feed
the world, and you know what the fisherman said? He thought a
long while and said, 'Well, I guess I'll just keep fishing till it's
gone.' " Hell, I'd heard a better one than that.

"You guys know about the new brain bank? You can buy a brain
from an auto mechanic that goes for five hundred dollars, a brain
from a physicist goes for one thousand dollars, and the fishermen's
brains sell for no less than five thousand dollars apiece. You know
why? Because they've never been used." And all the time this is
going on, part of me is frozen, waiting, wondering just how long
we can get away with this game before our number comes up.

With dawn the fog went from black to grey and the visibility
opened wide to a breathtaking ten feet on either side of the boat.
There were lots of boats around; we could hear them talking steadily on three different channels on their way out from the anchorage. There were lots of fish, too. Now that everyone's gear was set,
the dead silence on the radio screamed out the news. Besides, I'd
heard Doug and Earl; they didn't run all the way up here for the
good visibility. And we couldn't find the fleet!

This was the Tolo Banks, and in the space of half a minute the
Fathometer would jump from fifty fathoms, up to nine, and back
to thirty. It must look like Pinnacles National Monument down
there, navigation by Fathometer was ruthless. We'd already lost
an hour and a half running around trying to locate ourselves in

this soup. I was tired, disgusted, and getting more uptight by the minute, sitting there staring into nothingness, trying to decide which way to look next, when Charlie blurts out, "Hey, gang, I think I hear Hawaiian music."

And Mike says, "Hey, Charlie, start throwing breadcrumbs over the stern and maybe somebody will find us." We were laughing harder and harder at the increasingly stupid comments, and someone finally asked us to please use another channel.

A couple of little partner birds darted out from my bow wake. They look like pint-sized penguins and their ability to fly is only slightly more advanced. Nonetheless, the whole fleet finds them lovable. The farther I went, the thicker they got. There must have been thousands of them in the area; by now their collective raspy squawk was drowning out my engine. Their book name is murre, but the fishermen don't call them partner birds for nothing. I slowed the boat to trolling speed and saw three of them sitting there with anchovies hanging out the sides of their mouths, their bellies too full to swallow. Everything left my mind but the mechanics of getting thirty-two hooks in the water immediately, if not sooner.

Bam! there was a fish on the first line down. And the second and the third. The salmon were mixed in with the rockfish, and I went through a case of bait in the first five hours. Trying to keep the gear from tangling on the pinnacles was itself a full-time job. And the fog meant that I couldn't let even fifteen seconds go by without checking in front of me for other boats. There's still a lot to cry about when you're in money country, but you never do. Instead, everything appears in a different light. The subtle boundaries of the grey white mist feel like a moist cocoon encasing a faraway universe where only the boat, the swell, and the birds are needed to make it complete. The rest is all the intensity of your imagination trying to visualize the fish below swimming in the deep green fluid among the rocks and reefs. Then, suddenly, one of the fish grabs out at the passing bait and gets hooked into your reality. There aren't too many thrills that can last as long as the sight of wet, iridescent-colored salmon breaking the surface of a grey, misty sea out in the middle of nowhere.

It was six o'clock. I couldn't hang around for an evening bite because I had to go through the nerve-racking task of finding the anchorage before dark. I was happy with my thirty-six fish even though I knew I'd be hearing of scores over one hundred among the guys who'd worked this all day. It was ten o'clock by the time I finished breaking the ice, bedding the fish, and making baits for the morning. I decided to call Charlie anyway. "Hey, you know what time it is?" was his immediate answer.

"Sure, Charlie, but Mike and I have been trying to get hold of you all day. We were worried, man, what happened?"

"I got into a hot pile of fish. I turned the music up full blast. You got to have the beat of some fast acid rock vibrating down the lines, it drives the fish crazy, don't you know that yet? It's the only thing that really works." I'd heard all this before, though some swore by rhythm and blues and others leaned more toward Muzac. But I was too tired to get into it.

"Next time tell somebody before you shut the radio down. Good night."

"Sorry," he said, "sure hope this damn fog lifts."

Three thirty the next morning every star in the sky was visible, and I could see at least seventy-five mast lights heading out to the grounds. I was at the Banks fifteen minutes early. The last shadows were just beginning to reveal a gentle sea and the morning soft lines of the cliffs five miles to the inside. In half an hour the first tack was over and the radio was jumping. There were a lot of hake mixed in with a lot less fish, and everybody at once was trying to decide what to do about it. The usual apocalyptic tone of these conversations was mitigated by the bins already full of fish in their holds. The reports of those off scouting and the news from other areas didn't seem to carry much more significance than the easy trading of recipes, jokes, and stories of the recent past. About thirty of us were completely satisfied to hang in the area and work with what we had. The only intensity of the day came at sunset when the entire sky screamed out its loss in blazing electric reds and purples. There wasn't a fisherman within radio range that wasn't moved to explain its beauty with a freshness of emotion that can dissolve every rough edge from this life.

Someone in our group suggested that tonight would be a good night to spend at Jackson Hole. We'd save a half hour running time each way. Jack knew the spot and we all followed him into the rocks. "Hey, Jack," yelled one of his friends, "where'd you get the nerve to call this place an anchorage?" There sure wasn't much protection in here, but the weather was good, and everyone seemed happy for the extra hour's sleep.

One o'clock that morning there wasn't a fisherman there who'd ever be back again. The wind blasted a stiff thirty knots, and the building sea and swell threatened to jerk every anchor out of its holding. I was OK, but there was no doubt the guy beside me was dragging. He had about a whole ten minutes to go before he hit the rocks and lost everything, and no one aboard was awake. People were calling him on the air and shooting shotguns into the sky, and still he didn't budge. Jack was about to pull his own anchor to go and save the guy, when his cabin lights finally went on. That was just the beginning of one of those long, aching, miserable, nasty, endless nights where you spend hours standing by the wheel with the engine in gear, trying to keep the strain off the anchor till it's time to go fishing, and life ain't worth a dime.

The next morning the group from the anchorage farther down wasted no time in asking everyone of us how we felt after all that extra sleep. No one found it particularly funny as the sea continued to beat us to death on the way to the grounds. Sometimes I like a riled up sea, a big, rolling, deep breathing rhythm from morning to night, pulsing the day with an intensity that invigorates and keeps you on your toes. Today wasn't one of those days. Everything was there but the liking it. I was too wrung out to respond. And when it got to the point where every other wave was exploding behind the stern and drenching me with fifty-degree ice water, I began looking for an excuse to end this trip early. As I was pulling a line, I came to the bottom leader and it was stretched taut, straight down into the sea. "Good," I thought, "that's all the excuse I need. If there's going to be blue sharks on top of bum weather and slow fishing, then God bless the ocean."

These six- to eight-foot, mean-tempered blues aren't supposed to come around till the water warms later in the season. But there isn't a creature in the sea that ever took a biology course. The way this leader was hanging straight down was all the proof I needed. I put on some heavy gloves that are too clumsy for use with salmon and started to pull hard against the dead weight of the shark. Most of the time I don't care enough about retrieving the hook and I cut the whole thing loose, but today I just felt ornery enough to find myself a good knife-wielding battle.

The shark was just about at the surface. I timed the next pull to coincide with the push of the big green wave that was rolling up to the stern. "Oh God." The fish head that came out of the wave was the biggest salmon I'd ever seen. It must have been over sixty pounds with a body longer than mine. It's probably the biggest fish I've hooked to this day. Ever so gently, I let the fish and the leader slide back into the sea so the both of us could have a moment to calm down. I dumped the gloves and tried to feel its mood in the thin line between my thumb and finger. "Oh, God, fish, please, don't mess me up," I said out loud. "Come on, fish, please don't get shook, please fish, please," I begged as I slowly, easily, with the most sensitive of touch pulled it toward me. Day could have become night and the seas could have doubled in size, and I wouldn't have noticed. The fish was coming like a sleeping baby and making me more uptight by the second. Too many times the big ones wait until the last moment at the side of the boat and explode to life. I felt every muscle coil and recoil in that old fish, but there was nothing to do but keep pulling. "Come on, fish, please don't fight me, you're so beautiful!" I raised its head slightly and at the same time I raised the gaff high and swung hard, ready to instantly release the grip on the leader and put a death grip with both hands on the gaff to keep the fish from twisting free.

The gaff slashed into the water and my fish was gone. I scared myself to death; there was a feeling in all my muscles like I was just a hair's breadth away from jumping in after it. I was left standing there with my mouth open and everything around me spinning. "Goddamned, rotten, ugly, no good fish!" I screamed at the top of my lungs. I took the gaff that was still locked in my grip and hurled it wildly into the sea. I was shaking all over as if I'd been cut in two.

I went up to the cabin and started some tea to try and cool off, but the water wouldn't boil fast enough. So I went back to the deck. I kicked everything in sight, but nothing would break but my foot. There was nowhere to lose that stunning image of the fish I wanted more than anything else in the world as it swam back to the sea. Some puny, rational voice inside of me was trying to say, "Look, all you got to do is hang around another couple of hours, run the gear up and down, and you'll catch enough to equal the weight of the one you just lost," but that just wasn't the point.

All the way home for five hours I couldn't lose the feeling. I never flipped out like that before in my life, and I was still shaking and sullen. This was getting out of hand. The way I'd always thought about it, I wanted to make my living on the water, and fishing was the best way to do it. A job! Pretty soon I find myself risking my life over and over for this fish, devoting my life to it, thinking about nothing but current changes, scores, weather and bird reports, and now this! I'm thrown into a bout of total insanity by the loss of one fish as if it had somehow leached the juices of my soul down through the leader and stolen them out to sea. These fish were the captain of my soul, not I, and that scared me as much as the sea.

Pete was standing on the dock when I arrived. He's one of the best fish buyers on the coast. He parties with the fishermen, and wines and dines them any time of the day or night. But this isn't the reason he's considered to be the best; it only makes it the more amazing he can do his job so well.

He could see I was tired and in a rush, so he sent one of his crew down to unload my fish. Within a half hour he arranged for a welder to come down to the boat to make a new bracket for the steering column which I'd just barely been able to hold together for the trip. After I took fuel and ice, he waited till after nine o'clock when I got back with the company truck from grocery shopping. He did everything he could to help you make a turn-around. At 11 P.M., finally, I walked into the forecastle, and the bunk came flying at my face. Only one quiet breath from sleep, and I remembered I forgot the bait. Pete wouldn't be back until seven o'clock, and I wanted to leave at three. I pried myself from the bunk, dressed, grabbed the bolt cutters, a flashlight, and wrote out a note. "Sorry, Pete, forgot my bait, had to break the lock." I got into the icehouse and slipped my way down the aisles between the rows of three-hundred-pound blocks of ice that looked like headstones glistening coldly in a cemetery, past the big bins of rock cod heads sticking out of the flaked ice, shined my light on the freezer door and haloed the sign that read, If It Stinks, Freeze It. "Oh, no," I said out loud when I first took a look inside, "who's responsible for this one?" Someone had taken an eight-foot-long octopus and wrapped the legs around the cases of bait so when it froze you couldn't budge even one case from the octopus's grip. It was zero degrees in the freezer, spookier than the bottom of the sea, and I was pooped. I wrestled that octopus for twenty minutes before I got the case of bait and beat a fast trail back to the boat. There was never any question of my determination to do whatever had to be done to make it.

But trip followed trip, week followed week, month followed

month, and it seemed like the pace would never let up. Every day, no, every hour on the ocean was a whole new set of conditions. I needed desperately to make some kind of sense of the relationships of winds, currents, feed, bottom barometer, sun, moon, and tides, etc.

It's asking quite a lot, I realize, but I was completely dependent on what began to feel like a tyranny of arbitrary forces, and I was ragged from flying around the ocean like a pinball; up to Eureka, back to Monterey, run all night to Bodega, only to reach the spot and have the fish turn hot behind me. It only got worse as time went on; the more I became aware of the possibilities, the more I was burdened with trying to solve the question that squawked at me like a drunken parrot in my brain—should I go or should I stay? At the end of every tack and the end of every day. But the universe ate my game plans, one after the other, until I felt I'd been stripped of every resource I thought I had. For the first time in my life, I felt like the dumbest kid on the block. What was it the other fishermen tapped into, what part of their being hooked them daily into more fish than my fish?

I had to figure it out before I went crazy and before I went broke. I needed a loran, a haul out, a new alternator, insurance money. At any one moment what I needed more than anything else was fish and sleep and never the twain shall meet.

And I needed to figure it out before I got hurt. I already had a reputation of fishing too tough, and it wasn't meant as a compliment. It meant I was fishing weather beyond the boat, and it was true. But until I could up my production, it was the only way I knew to keep fuel in the tank. The pressure of making those endless decisions about how far to risk my life was the worst pressure of all. At times I even wished there was someone who would invade my freedom to say, "No, you shouldn't go."

Instead, I'd be hanging on for dear life, trying not to break my teeth as the boat dropped off one watery cliff after another, and some fisherman would call on the radio and ask, "Hey, Marie, how's your social life?" Well, let's see now; one night after having worked all day for one big fish, I fell asleep and dreamed I took the fish to bed with me and spent the rest of the night with my arms wrapped around it. Where was I going to put a social life?

To be sure, Windy was fishing the same fish on the same ocean, but you have to keep in mind the size and scope of this place. We were lucky if we passed in the night.

Very few salmon boats work together as running partners because of the differences in timing on fuel, ice, and breakdowns. Once you're separated for any reason, you're caught in a different flow. Just the gap in size of our boats kept Windy and me from even considering it.

For some reason, that first year with *Angelina* we rarely even fell into the same port on a blow. But four or five times we spotted each other on the anchorage, tied the boats stern to stern, made an island to the wind and the waves, and the morning bite be damned.

There was one other event toward the end of the season that made the cyclone stop. While fishing off Bodega, I heard part of a faraway, garbled conversation. Lefty up north was trying to talk with someone just on the edge of his radio range farther up north. "Did you say they didn't find anything?" was all I heard, but the tone was dreadfully wrong.

"Lefty," I called, "can you pick me up? What happened?"

"We lost Nardo" was all he answered back. I stood for a long time with the microphone in front of me, unable to answer. How could I tell Lefty he was wrong, Nardo is my friend from the first year of fishing, he's my age, he knows more about the ocean than I'll probably ever know, I just saw him a few days ago, and he's as alive as you and me.

I hung up the mike and walked to the stern. I cast around the back deck, when the water caught my eye; it's movement made me shiver. My stomach turned. I looked away and baited six more hooks. The radio blasted through my daze. Nardo had been running in to Fort Bragg in rough weather with Martin on the *Annie C.* They stopped chattering over the radio for a minute while Martin went below to make a pot of coffee. And when he came back up, Nardo's boat was gone as if it had never been there in the first place. All that could be surmised was that a wave caught him wrong and he rolled. There was nothing else to go by, no drunk who crossed the center line, no patch of ice on the road, just an ocean stretched out far and wide that rolled on like before.

Again the water caught my eye, churning as if nothing had changed. I stared it down, and down, and down. I saw Nardo laughing, alive and light, and then I saw him drown.

A salmon swimming through the blasphemous depths of his grave bit my bait and shook me from the trance. I pulled it up, gaffed it to the deck, and the moment that fish was mine I remembered; it was Nardo, sitting in the restaurant at the Tides, who told me two years before, "You better watch it, Marie; that ocean that gives you the fish is the same ocean that takes your friends."

Nardo was only the first. I guess it hadn't sunk in before because I didn't know the people to make the stories real. But this year before the season was over, six people, whose faces and smiles and walks I knew, went down. Even my own close calls hadn't shaken the illusion from my bones. This fishing's not the game it seems from the vantage on top of the sea. It's reaching in on mysteries with lines that pull both ways.

I needed a break. I needed my six months off, my bon voyage! And what I got as my prize was herring fishing on San Francisco Bay.

6

Enter the Herring

LITTLE DID I know five years ago, anchored in the pristine security of Fish Rocks, that I was being recruited for a war. How could I know? It was one of my favorite days of summer, where I wake up all tense to pry myself from the warm bunk. But before moving a muscle, I hear the unmistakable, relentless howl of thirty-five-knot wind. Yippee, it's too rough to fish! What a soft, self-satisfied roll back into my pillow and dreams. It wasn't until hours later when something in the idle radio conversation caught my attention. Freckles was making a great, flamboyant deal about how refreshing it felt to take a hot bath surrounded by the cold, ruthless sea. I grabbed the microphone, "Do you really have a bathtub on your boat, Freckles?" My anchor would have come up immediately if I could have wrangled an invitation on that score.

"I knew I'd think of some way to get you out of the bunk, Maria." I should have known. Freckles was merely looking for a running partner with whom to shoot the breeze. Actually, I was beginning to realize it was more. Like a number of other fisher-men, whenever he crossed my path, Freckles would give me a call and ask how I was doing, warm and interested, as if he were gen-uinely glad to see me still hanging in there. I always tried to take advantage and ask a lot of pent-up questions about a mechanical problem, a baiting method, or a question about the fish. He'd answer me when he could, but like the rest of the fishermen, having to give advice seemed to be an embarrassment, an infringement on what should be a personal relationship between me, the boat, and the sea. What he really wanted to offer was encouragement in the form of a friendship, in the form of shooting the breeze.

Our chat progressed to all the crazy luxuries that fishermen could put aboard their boats, then suddenly regressed to the money it would take to do it, and how hard we work, and how little we get—the old "how tough it is" that normally can go on for hours. But fate was writing the script today, and Freckles said suddenly, "You know what you ought to do, Maria, if you're gonna make it in this business, you need a winter fishery and herring is just the one for you."

Freckles said he had been fishing on the bay for the fast-developing herring roe market in Japan. He ran down the advantages: I'd be working on the bay, my boat was the ideal size for gill netting, the fishery wasn't crowded, and the price was rising.

Little did I know, any more than Freckles or anyone else in the fleet, that the decision to apply would place me squarely center target for the full-scale invasion of the twentieth century into the fishing business. Until now, all the monstrous, tense forces of our time, the bureaucracies, the legal mumbo jumbo, the institutionalized greed and hatred—all these forces seemed barricaded safely behind the shoreline. To be sure, there were some ominous cracks in the wall. Recent laws were beginning to establish governmental jurisdiction over the fisheries, a wave of technology was sweeping over the back decks and into the pilothouses, and there were some nasty competitive dramas played out when the fleet got crowded on the fish. But for the most part, fishing was anchored firmly in the lee of a different era.

For some reason it was the herring roe fishery that burst the dam wide open. The flood that has ensued has reduced this fishery to the classic picture of twentieth century raging chaos without any of the subtleties of civilization.

Bay herring fishing itself wasn't new on the scene. In fact, forty years ago members of the Yukon gang were peacefully fishing herring on the bay, in front of Sausalito, down by the airport, in a little cove at Tiburon. But the human consumption market they were supplying had a low demand and a lower price. It's another example where the beefy American mentality has robbed the American palate of great tasting seafood and the highest quality protein. In the 1950s Freckles and a few others were supplying

Dr. Ross Petfood with herring. This market seemed to have potential, until it was found that the herring made the dogs constipated.
Freckles pleaded with them to add just a little castor oil to each
can. But, alas, Dr. Ross just quit buying. It was back to relying on
the human market.

It wasn't until the early 1970s that the Japanese roe market was
developed by a Monterey fish buyer. But the price he offered the
fishermen was so low, fifty dollars a ton, that only two lampara
net boats showed up to work the annual winter spawn. The second
year, two additional fish buyers were down from Washington
state, hustling fishermen to go for the herring. The price to the
fishermen remained the same, but the little flame was beginning
to generate some smoke. The old-time net fishermen knew there
had to be some money in this roe or the buyers wouldn't be pushing, and the fishermen wanted their cut. A little of the smoke
finally drifted all the way down to Fish and Game headquarters in
Menlo Park. They immediately tried to cool the situation by
devising a lottery system for doling out herring permits. The man
with no experience had as much chance of being picked for the
fishery as the man with fifty years' experience. The effect was anything but cooling. The third year, the fishermen were furious with
Fish and Game, with each other, and with the buyers. And the
third year was only the beginning.

When I filled out the application for the permit lottery, I was
completely oblivious to this history. When they pulled my name
out of the hat, it just seemed fitting that the first thing I'd ever won
in my life was a damn job.

I began asking around about the necessary gear, and in the
process I heard a lot of bitterness from the old-timers about the use
of this lottery. After all, many of them were hauling nets before I
was born, and now a Reno-style lottery was eliminating them from
the fishery. In their place were what they called "shoemakers"
and "outer space people." I was among the shoemakers, people
who didn't know a lead line from a cork line, who wouldn't know
which end of the net to pull first. The outer space people were the
fishermen from Washington who despite their own state's system
of limited entry were allowed to apply on an equal footing with
California fishermen for the California fishery.

When I brought my boat up from Santa Cruz to Sausalito on the
bay, I was surprised to see that the twenty-five gill netters picked

were indeed mostly shoemakers like myself. In fact, they were my age group friends from salmon fishing, and, for a while there, the Sausalito dock was turning into a big winter party. It wasn't but a day or two before the atmosphere snagged. We'd been going through all the standard preseason rumbles and rituals about price negotiation, and it quickly became obvious we were throwing toy jacks in a big game of craps.

The herring buyers literally laughed in our faces when we approached them to negotiate a price and get the market orders signed. "Price gets determined when you have the fish on the boat." Then they turned their backs and walked away. "Since when?" We laughed back, but they were already halfway down the dock.

That was for starters.

We didn't have proof and we weren't sure how to get it, but in our guts we were fast becoming certain that the buyers were reaping knockout profits on the Japanese market and offering us a mere sliver of the margin. What really cinched our dilemma was the fact that we were dealing with fish buyers from out of state. Carpetbaggers, with baggage claim stubs hanging freshly in their coat pockets and a plane ticket out of here in their billfolds.

Stories about these buyers from previous years were being passed around the dock like storm warnings. There was Tom who wouldn't dare show his face around here again because he left last year in such a hurry, he neglected to write out the checks. There was Ricardo who had gotten dragged out of his bed in the middle of the night when they discovered the water tanks in the bottom of his trucks that he was using to phony the weight. There was the heroic story about Paul (told mostly by Paul, but confirmed by others) who in middle of the night tied his boat off to a ten-thousand-dollar fish pump, put the boat full ahead, and yanked the fish pump into the water to remind the buyer that they wanted their checks. There were stories of missing bins of fish, sunken boat stories, forklift drivers on the rampage stories, stories that would fill a TV series that could run longer than "The Untouchables." That market order we were carrying around to the buyers might as well have been a Girl Scout petition.

We were baffled by the level of consciousness surrounding this fishery, but we were also so green that most of our energy got focused on learning to rig the boats and gear. Weeks before the season was to open, buyer Don, from the Idaho Fish Company (Idaho?), piled us all on the back deck of the *China Cat* and took us out on the bay for a fishing lesson. Most of us tentatively planned to sell to his company, so I guess he figured it would be worth his while to have us know how to set a net. It was a pretty intense session; he must have answered a hundred questions about the currents, the spawning behavior of the herring, how to move with the tide, how they mark on the Fathometer, how to lay out, when to lay out, the drift net laws, and the borderlines. You would think this skinny, wiry guy was our guru, so faithfully were we hanging on his every word.

It's not an atmosphere in which fishermen are particularly comfortable. So someone in the back had to stir the waters and ask a question about the price. "We won't be discussing price until you have the fish on the back decks. That's the way it's done." He said it like you would say, "A herring has a mouth in front and a tail in back." It brought a chill to the back deck as if the wind had suddenly shifted from off the Arctic ice cap. Before anyone could get into it, Rich, always the pacifier, quickly changed the subject and asked Don about the progress of the additional nets we needed. We had all been promised three nets by the company, and most of us had only received one. Poor Rich, in his haste to thaw the mood, had latched onto the tip of yet another iceberg. Don assured us more nets were on the way from Seattle and then added sarcastically, "You wouldn't be waiting now if some people in your group hadn't stolen over a dozen of the nets from the first shipment."

One thing was sure, fishing class was dismissed. People nervously busied themselves stacking the nets in the stern, Dave headed the boat toward Sausalito, and Don stood by the rail, staring uncomfortably out over the water.

My deckhand was Roger, the big husky guy you may remember whose designs on a love hot cruise with Molly were so rudely interrupted by the Columbia River. "I won't let a little thing like that stop me," said Roger, and as soon as Molly and I arrived at San Francisco, Roger had his thumb on the road from Seattle. Molly took up gardening terra firma, making certain the roots were deep in the soil; Roger took up carpentry, but never to this day has he been able to separate the wood from the salt. We had been friends for the intervening years, and as a great credit to his prevailing sense of humor, we are still good friends today.

On the day following the demonstration we had an afternoon free; it seemed like a good idea to make a trial set before the season opened. Surrounded by breathless sunshine, we pulled into the shallows in front of downtown Sausalito. Very carefully and methodically we let out the first buoy, put the boat in gear, and the net peeled off the stern perfectly, the lead line to one side and the cork line to the other. Without a tangle or a hitch we reached the harness at the other end of the net which stayed attached to the boat. We drifted for a few minutes as if waiting for fish, then proceeded to pull the net back in the boat. Roger coiled the lead line, and I coiled the corks as easily as rolling up a ball of yarn. Reaching the final buoy, we couldn't contain ourselves.

"Boy, what a snap!"

"No sweat."

"Yeah, this'll be a cinch."

For our next set, being as we had all this experience behind us, we moved around to the deeper waters in front of Yellow Bluff, a rocky point that juts out just this side of the Golden Gate. Once again, the net peeled off the boat like we'd been doing it for years. The current was moving a little, so I put the boat in gear to hold us into it. We weren't holding our spot exactly, but I presumed that moving a little with the tide was just going to be part of drifting a gill net.

I looked outside of me and saw with very different emotions what I had seen many times before. It was a tide rip, the border of a fast running river of tide, like a flash flood moving out the bay. These rivers have no banks to bind them; their course is as free as a snake's. The foamy, turbulent rip line was fast moving toward us. When it hit, I gave the boat full throttle to keep the boat and net from being swept away. A set of oars would have done us as much good. The net was like a parachute, dragging us backward. It was a toss-up whether we'd hit the rocks or get sucked out the Gate. Suddenly the buoy at the other end of the net disappeared below the water. From the strain on the rope at the boat you would think we were attached to the tail of a diving whale. Moments later, with a resounding crack that made us both jump, the rope broke. We never saw that net again, and for the time being that was just A-OK with us. At least now we had control of the boat. Our mood, however, was decidedly less cocky.

On the way home we discussed and studied the tide book (for

the first time, obviously) in humble recognition that it held more than a few hints for our survival in net fishing. We talked about the fact that when a four-hundred-square-mile bay dumps six feet of water in and out a one-mile gate twice a day, the tide is supreme, and we'd better learn all we can about this big watery cat. The tide tables gave us the good news that we had set the net at maximum ebb, the time in the cycle of the tide when the currents run most swiftly. Later we learned that our choice of location had been equally charmed. Precisely at Yellow Bluff, the water that has flowed off the flats suddenly surges down into a deep canyon that leads out the Gate. It would have made as much sense to set our nets on the edge of Niagara Falls.

This was only our first introduction to the complex tidal behavior that has continued to amaze me with every new encounter. Though I had traveled the bay for many years, it wasn't until I began throwing nets in the water that the awesome intricacies of this powerful cycle made themselves all too clear.

But enough hooray for the cosmic tide. We were behind two nets, the one that had been arriving "any day now" on the truck from Seattle and the one that went over Niagara Falls. We would have to figure out who had the stolen nets and go liberate one. Since we knew everyone pretty well, it took only our first guess to land on the right boat. After dark we climbed onto Tom's boat, laid out our predicament, and begged. Sure enough, he had an "extra" stowed away back in his ice hold.

The next morning we inspected the net and couldn't believe our eyes. This net was the only one in the load that was different. Every other net was two fathoms deep; this one was three fathoms. Not only was it a very recognizable freak, it was also illegal—a fact that could easily be seen by a game warden standing on the dock. We had to get rid of it.

Naturally we failed at our most persistent efforts to make a trade. We were forced to set out again in search of the other stolen nets. Yes, Virginia, it's all part of fishing. We could hardly comprehend it ourselves, but there seemed little else to do but play the scene out. Vic, the local lampara fisherman who always seemed to have the latest scoop on every form of mischief, told us that Crazy Paul had three extra nets stored in his garage, and, praise the Lord, he handed us the nice shiny key. All right, all we had to do now was get the big net onto the dock, into the truck, switch at the garage, and get the new net back on the boat—without attracting attention.

On the way back to the dock with the new net we were laughing like crazy people at our professional management of the most outrageous maneuvers. We even managed to straighten up our act as we opened the back of my truck. Suddenly a little red sports car was racing toward us, going over thirty miles an hour. He slammed on the brakes so hard when he reached us that the back began swerving into a side spin. Out stepped Skinny Don puffed up like a peacock, his face the color of his car, as he screamed through the stench of burning rubber. "I don't care what you guys have to say, I'm calling the sheriff immediately. I'm fed up with this crap." Oh, boy, it was time for fast thinking. I stammered and fumbled something about repairing a net we'd damaged. Roger, however, was still in top form.

"We're getting fed up with your company's insults. Everyone's thinking about selling their fish elsewhere if things don't start shaping up here." I couldn't believe it when Don suddenly changed his tune and reached out to shake Roger's hand, apologized, and expressed his "deepest hopes" that we'd continue to fish for his company.

Roger and I took off immediately for the anonymity of a cup of coffee at Howard Johnson's. We tried to stop laughing long enough to figure out what the hell was going on. Who was this Don character who was becoming a darker figure by the day, what the hell was going on with the price, why were Fish and Game wardens swarming the docks like cops on a load of cocaine, how the hell were we going to fish nets in these crazy tides without anchors, what happened to the nets, do these herring really come into the bay? Every day the situation looked shakier, and we were making pretty good progress in that direction ourselves.

It was only a few days before the season opened, and one of the deckhands found out that the Seattle bank where his brother worked was the same bank where the fish companies transacted business. It took a lot of persuasion, but we finally got the real numbers and figures we needed to show the incredible profits the buyers were making on these fish, and we found out that the Washington gill netters were being paid four times the price that California fishermen had gotten last year down here. Word spread quickly, but trying to corner Don on the subject was like chasing a squealing greased pig. We got nowhere.

Well, fishermen rarely stick together—on the ocean when someone's in danger, always, but on the dock it's usually everyone for themselves. But there were only twenty-five of us; couldn't we at least try? Seven o'clock, the morning after the season officially opened, everyone was up on the dock, milling around like cats in a canary shop, all pretty proud of ourselves that no one had gone fishing. Predictably Don walked up and asked why everyone was still tied to the dock. We made it clear we weren't fishing without a price, and we weren't dealing with him any more. We arranged a conference call to the head of the company in Idaho. It was like calling Las Vegas to discuss birth control with the pope. We got the price settled at $210 a ton, a mere $50 over the price of the year before. But at least we had a price.

Big deal! In 1980, the base price was $2,000 a ton, and even now the buyers are willing to jump through all kinds of hoops to ensure an unloading spot on the dock. One Washington buyer pays a local buyer's entire rent of $60,000 a year just so he can put two pumps and a couple of scales at the far end of the dock for two months out of the year.

There wasn't much time to worry about all this. Money was tight, and the price was wrong, but the fish beckoned. Besides, from the first moment, the chaos that unfolded on the water made the scene on the dock fade into the realm of the trivial. The trouble we had at Yellow Bluff was a meager sample of what developed when twenty-five gill netters tried to fish together in these washing machine tides. Each of us had two or three nets, each 390 feet long, off our sterns, like giant flags hoisted in a wind storm. The tides were infinitely more complex than any of us had imagined. Instead of regularly patterned currents, there were back eddies, swirls, currents, updrafts, downdrafts, currents running one way on the surface and another on the bottom. Much of this behavior was entirely unpredictable; even the faithful tide books and current tables would be off an hour or two without notice. Most of this savageness resulted from the irregular shape of the bay. The huge volumes of water from the north bay and south bay merged at the center where we fished and then exited out the narrow Gate. Even the inlets of the northwestern United States, where tides are double or triple the height of San Francisco's tides, don't create such merciless confusion in the water. The islands and deep water canyons of the bay add to the effect as do the varying runoffs from the rivers that feed it. The winter storms that bring pelting rains and winds up to sixty miles per hour were beginning to arrive, and the stage was appropriately set for the upcoming drama.

Enter the herring. The massive schools of herring, the spawners and the nonspawners, the young and the old, the whole family moves into the bay from the ocean to usher forth the next generation. They mill around in the deep holes for days and sometimes weeks until something triggers the spawners to break from the school and head for the most shallow area of the beach. Here in a frenzy they lay and fertilize their eggs. The problem for us stemmed from the fact that these fish only run to a small area of the beach at any one time. If we wanted to catch them, and more than anything else in the world that's what we wanted to do, we would have to pile on top of each other as earnestly as do the herring.

The drama that unfolded was as predictable as the tides are unpredictable. The tangles, the loss of gears and temper, the nets that got wound up in the props, our hands torn up in the strain of the thin nylon webbing, the perpetual state of emergency that had us so pumped up on our own adrenaline that no one knew when to stop. In the time it would take to shake a few fish from the net you could easily drift over a mile, through everyone else's gear or out the Gate or too close to the rocks or back over your own gear. It was impossible to control the boat with these nets off our stern. And if by chance you missed the visible obstacles, you'd probably catch one of the submerged objects as the net swept across the bottom. If nothing else, the tide would change abruptly and destroy the most carefully laid out strategy. There were so many screams into the night that Sausalito residents were steadily calling Fish and Game with complaints about the noise.

Probably many felt at the beginning as I did, that we just needed more experience and we'd soon learn the tricks of the trade. But by the end of the first couple of weeks there wasn't a lingering doubt in anyone's mind, drifting nets in this area of the bay was the height of insanity.

The pull of the moon was breaking our backs, but it was the California Department of Fish and Game that broke our mind. The solution to our pain was so obvious. You put an anchor at each end of the net and the net stays put. But anchors on a gill net were against the law, a law that was as much of an artifact in the Fish and Game books as the cohabitation laws of California. The law was passed in the days when salmon were gill netted in the rivers where the currents are decidedly more gentle. It prevented the fishermen from setting a net across the river and completely trapping the fish.

We talked together and individually to the dock wardens, the boat wardens, the brass, the commissioner. "We can't trap the fish in open water," we explained, "since we're working from a quota we can't overfish, it's suicide in this section of the bay without anchors on the net, using anchors would cut down on the loss of gear," etc., etc. We explained from every angle, trying desperately to find a pathway to their common sense. There wasn't any. The only response that echoed back from all these dead ends was it's the law, it's the law, it's the law. It was like standing under the Gate and talking to the outgoing tide.

Gill netting for herring

In the previous three years that I had spent on the ocean, I had only seen the Fish and Game twice. Only rarely from the far reaches of the grapevine, word would come of a bust, and then it was always for something like a few undersized fish. There were very few laws that governed the ocean fisheries, and Fish and Game ignored enforcement of the ones that did exist. Preferring to bust a kid on the dock for one shiner over his limit rather than patrol the harsh cold ocean for the seiners that took one hundred tons of anchovies from a restricted zone or the draggers that routinely tow inside the three-mile limit.

But now for the first time there was a major fishery in the protected waters of the bay where any donkey could maneuver. Overnight, after so many years of looking for an undersized crab in a crate, these wardens were full-flown cops like on TV, they were managers of big industry.

They were in their glory with all the multitude of new laws they had passed, the quotas, the lotteries, the gear restrictions, the borderlines, the papers, the documents. From the first day they hung around our necks like a leash. The thing they seemed to enjoy most was boarding us for paper checks at the most inappropriate times. The first month they got me three times; no matter what I was doing, I would have to climb down into the fo'c'sle and search out my fish license, the boat license, the boat documents, and the permit. And if you couldn't locate any one of them, you'd be busted. Another common bust was for drifting over the borderlines they had drawn on the chart. These borders were worse than speed traps, considering the close quarters and crazy tides that we worked in. By the time they got finished writing up Dave's ticket for drifting over the border, the tide had shifted and they were already back in the legal zone when it was time for him to sign his name. It was more than a pain in the ass, two busts and you were out of the fishery. The only glimmer of hope was that they'd carry this thing so far that they wouldn't have anyone left to play with.

The real tragedy though was in the laws they chose not to enforce, and the real victims were the fish. There was a law against purse seiners rolling fish. Very frequently a purse seiner, because they fish deeper water, makes a set and comes up with thirty or forty tons of immature fish. Because the price of the fish over and above the base price was determined by the percentage of roe, these immature fish were worth very little money. In addition, if the seine fisherman delivered these fish to the docks, those thirty or forty tons would be subtracted from the overall quota, so naturally the skipper wants to throw the fish (roll them) back in water. But these fish are dead or will die because of the damage that's been done to their scales by the webbing of the net. Daily we saw seiners rolling their fish, but the Fish and Game's eyesight always seemed to go into acute failure whenever they were looking at the seiners. There was never one bust for rolling fish. Then there were the gross violations of the weigh-in laws. Twenty-ton trucks of herring were being driven out of town in broad daylight— unweighed. Then there was that dock in Richmond where the only scales present were the herring scales. But so far the ugliest part of this whole fishery was the violation of the food waste law. The buyers were interested in roe only, which was purchased as a delicacy for the Japanese rich. The herring themselves were referred to as carcasses. Every year four thousand tons of high quality protein were relegated to garbage. The margin of profit on attempting to utilize these fish was so low it was ignored by the buyers. You couldn't even get Fish and Game to discuss this issue, let alone enforce the utilization.

So it's the middle of night, the nets are peeling off my stern into the swift moving waters of Paradise Cove, and this big grey steel bow pulls up to within feet of my bow, and the megaphone blares into my ear. "Prepare to be boarded."

"Stand by!" I screamed. "You'll have to wait." I couldn't believe it; they could obviously see the nets flying off the stern under the big deck lights, and they could see my boat moving forward.

"We're boarding you now, we want to check your papers." I yelled back that they could go to hell and a few other appropriate comments. They picked up the megaphone again even though we were barely feet from each other. "Do you know who you are talking to? This is the Fish and Game, and you'd better clean up your language." And Fish and Game wondered at our growing contempt!

By the end of January we gill netters barely made a dent in the quota for all our trouble. Tempers were short, winter storms were unyielding, and our gear and nets were damaged and torn. I was exhausted, and Roger quit with back troubles that even now serve him well whenever he gets tempted to go back to the sea.

One day, jumbled in there amidst the confusion of time, the semi arrived with Don's shipment of nets from Washington, nets that we all needed twice as desperately as before. We waited around the truck like a band of starved vultures. Finally the forklift unloaded the first bin. It was full of cement! As was the second bin and the third and the fourth. The few nets in the shipment were nothing but torn rags. Don turned the color of the cement. Man, did he look sick. It was so pathetic, we all kind of sneaked away without saying a word. Who knows what he had done to deserve this. That was the last time any of us saw Don; who knows where they shipped him. Who knows, maybe he's still en route. The guy who replaced him came up with a load of nets in one week.

February was worse; I nearly lost the boat and net in a freak snowstorm, my new deckhand had to be fired because he refused to work without sleep, and I went swimming in the cold, miserable, murky bay at night to cut a net out of the prop before the boat drifted into the rocks. But instead of deluging you with all of the details, I'll tell you the stories of the *Sea Mount* and the *Sea Bird*, which illustrate a whole other dimension of this whole crazy business.

The *Sea Mount* was a fifty-foot troller, a new, hometown boat from Sausalito. Russ, the skipper, got a seine permit, and because he'd never seined before, he hired a northern "we got bigger tides than you" skipper to rig and fish the boat. The fish were showing heavily in the deep water off Sausalito, and in one set at the top of the tide they loaded the boat to 80 percent capacity. She was sitting pretty low in the water, and the swollen bay was beginning to empty. But the fish were still holding in big, black, tempting balls below. "Let her go," said the captain to the crew, and with those words the boat was doomed. In twenty minutes they had the net hauled in tight to the boat, full of fish. In the same twenty minutes the boat had drifted out the Gate. There was a southwest wind, and the tide by now was pumping heavily underneath the chop. The drag of the current against the sack of fish was pulling the boat heavily on its side. It took only the wake of a passing ship to finish the job and push her over. The *Sea Mount* sunk in five minutes, and the crew barely escaped with their lives.

On the same day and the same outgoing tide and with the same greed, the *Sea Bird* made a set in front of Sausalito. The net was loaded with fish, and the boat was lying broadside to the tide. The

Sea Bird, too, lay heavily on her side with the weight of the fish off the boom. Suddenly something in the rigging let go, and the boat snapped back. An older man on the bridge was thrown into the water. They couldn't go after him with the net flowing around the boat. Somehow, this old fisherman pushed against the tide, the cold, and his age and swam three hundred yards to a rock off Yellow Bluff. By now the *Sea Bird* had gathered the net aboard. Is there anyone in the world who can explain what they did next? Instead of picking up the old man, they took the boat in directly to unload so that they could get back quickly, make the next tide, and catch more fish. The old man was finally rescued by another skipper who had the strange idea that life was worth more than fish.

At the dock, people were pretty shaken by the dual catastrophies of the day. It was as if we had all gotten a good look at ourselves in a mirror. With everyone competing from the same quota, the fish one boat gets another boat has no chance of getting. It was bringing out the ugliest side of everyone.

By the end of February, we barely had ten tons for the season. Joe was with me now. He was a young San Francisco Bay fisherman and a distinguished poacher. We worked well together. But he was getting pretty depressed over the lack of fish. In fact, I think he was about to quit, when we got into the biggest, lushest run of herring on the bay I've ever seen before or since.

First, I have to explain a little bit about the lampara net boats, for it was they who led us to the fish and then finally left us like a flotilla of defenseless duckies in the pack of wolves. The lampara boats were having their own nasty run-in with the Fish and Game. The law said that lampara boats and seine boats were limited to work in the waters in front of Sausalito. It was difficult enough for everyone because this area was so small. But the real bone of contention was that the lampara net, as opposed to a seine, is a surface net and fishes best only in shallow water. The prescribed area was 95 percent deep water. The lampara fishermen did their full share of trying to educate the Fish and Game to the differences in the two types of nets. But naturally they collided with the same brick-walled ignorance we had encountered on the issue of anchors. The law is the law is the law. To this day you would have a hard time trying to find even one game warden who could look at one of these big nets and be able to tell you whether it was a seine or a lampara net, so carefully have they guarded their ignorance with this wall of arrogance. So while the gill netters were tying nets to pilings and moorings, or throwing in double lead lines in a desperate attempt to get around the no anchor law, the lampara fishermen were sneaking around the bay at night with no lights, playing a fancy hide-and-seek with the Fish and Game while looking for shallow water and a few fish.

The first day of March three lampara boats made a midnight maneuver through Richmond Harbor, a protected little out-of-the-way cove on the other side of the bay from Sausalito. The Fathometer paper was black with fish from top to bottom, and the boats loaded to the brim in no time. The next morning Vic, one of the lampara skippers, went into the fish buyer's office. "Come on down to the dock, Tommy, we've got 150 ton of fish on three boats, all for you." There hadn't been many fish for weeks, and there hadn't been that many fish all season. Tommy knew that Vic wasn't beyond a bad joke, so he slipped right into his well-polished cry, "Hey, Vic, I can't take that now; I'm losing money on this herring right and left, and you want to torment me at 7:00 A.M.?" They just about had to drag him down to the boats. What he saw made his eyes pop out of his head in the shape of dollar signs. The three boats had fish spilling out of the tops of their hatches, the weighted sterns were barely above the water, and the boats sat there with the same bloated look a person gets after an orgy banquet. Tommy couldn't contain himself, and word of Richmond Inner Harbor would not have spread faster had it been carried by light.

For the next couple of nights Richmond Inner Harbor was buzzing with gill netters, lamparas, and seiners. It was alive with the carefree spontaneous energy of a gypsy carnival. And what a spot! The currents were tame like little lambs by the time they reached this secluded area. The narrow channels were like a big, brimming salad bowl for the lampara nets to dip into; the fish couldn't escape out the sides of the net. For the gill netters there were endless pilings and navigational aids on which to tie the nets and make them totally secure. And our friends from the Fish and Game weren't anywhere in sight.

Unanimously, gill netters, seiners, and lampara boats threw all precautions to the wind; we turned our backs on the troubles of the past, and we went for it wide open. We literally ignored the ships and tugs that regularly travel up and down this narrow channel, the radio talk was bold and open, the nets were spread out everywhere, at night even the lampara boats worked under the full, bold glare of all spotlights on; everyone shared the same big smiles, and the fleet of boats looked great with their sterns buried and their bows high under the sudden weight of success. It was the land of milk and honey.

On the morning of March 4, the lampara boats were all back at the dock unloading. Some say it was luck, and some say they had had word of what was coming. After a couple of hours of fishing, Joe and I had two tons of fish on the boat. We were all psyched for a full day of some serious banking, when someone on the radio said simply and clearly, "Fish and Game." I looked up and saw at least five little speedboats buzzing out from behind the shadows in the docks. I wondered how many nights some bureaucrat had lain awake before arriving at this creative event. Not a moment later one of the boats buzzed right up to my stern. At the same time I could see all the neighboring boats being boarded. We were busted, for tying a gill net to a navigational aid, anchoring the boat while tied to the net, and for having an anchor attached to a net. Joe got cited for "assisting in the setting of a set gill net in San Francisco Bay."

"Why now?" I kept saying. "Why now?" Foolishly I argued with the fish cops. For a whole month they had seen us using all these little tricks to hold the nets; they had plenty of opportunity to enforce the law, but they led us to believe they were going to ignore it. When they boarded us, they only checked our papers. "Why now at the first sign of fish?"

"The law is the law, sister; if we saw you robbing a bank, we'd have to arrest you, too." God that made me mad.

"There's no way we can safely fish with a drifting net. The law is stupid and you are stupid for enforcing it." And as my voice was rising, the warden on the stern opened his jacket and put his hand threateningly on the gun. I felt my arms begin to rise as if hypnotized by my own rage. I came so close to shoving him backward into the water, gun, badge, smirk, and all. I guess what stopped me was Joe saying I'd better cool it. Up to this point he'd been pacing around the back deck, kicking the gunwales and swearing under his breath. He was very, very, very disgusted. For a minute everyone was very quiet as if shocked by the intensity of the feelings. The back deck speaker of the radio broke the silence. It was Tom on the *Pisces*.

"You know what those stupid assholes busted me for? They busted me for having a lead line on a drift net. These fools don't know anything." Joe and I laughed at Tom's timing. It just made the wardens angrier.

"OK," I said, "what the hell happens now?" As if to prove Tom's point, the warden said they were confiscating the nets. He told us to pull them from the water and then put them in his skiff. I looked at Joe and Joe looked at the skiff. There was no way in the world that three gill nets would fit in their skiff and not sink it. It was obvious they had never seen a gill net. With not a whole lot of sympathy in our voices we explained that they had better think of something better than that. They scurried to their radios for a quick conference call. They came back with a decision that now they were going to seize the fish we had already caught. "That's out, there's no way you're getting those fish. You have to see us taking the fish illegally before you can confiscate them, and you didn't see us taking these fish." But there was no arguing. They left and we sat down right where we were, in the dumps. The idea of pulling our gear and taking these fish back across the bay and unloading them by hand for the Fish and Game was making us sick. I walked to the stern where the net was tied and pulled a few corks until I reached where I could see the webbing. You could actually watch the fish swimming into the net.

That weekend there was a lot of debate on the dock as to whether we should play it safe and go look for some fish elsewhere on Monday or whether we should return to the same spot. Come Monday, no one was surprised that we all found each other back over at Richmond Inner Harbor. We began setting nets almost as if the bust had never occurred. Fish and Game must have been off celebrating the bust. That night the moonlit shallow waters of the harbor were like a pond. The air was breathless and warm, and the completely full moon seemed to be no higher than fifty feet over our heads. It gave this incredible silvery glow to the little ripples on the water created by the masses of teeming fish barely below the surface. The night was charmed, and once again the only worry we had was how much fish we dared pack on the boat before going in to unload. Though Fish and Game eventually showed up, they were without their hired hands. It became obvious they were on a nine to five schedule, and we had no trouble working around them. In two and one-half days we made the season.

On the third day when we went to pull our nets, we got our final fishing lesson of the season. The nets weighed a ton. But there wasn't a fish in them. They had been spawned on. The eggs had somehow gotten on the net without catching a fish. No one seems to agree on the explanation for this, but one thing is for sure, your heart just isn't in it to pull all that weight when it's not worth a cent. The season was over, and the herring had returned to the sea. We couldn't help but wonder if they'd ever come back.

Two weeks later the Fish and Game called a meeting at the Marin Rod and Gun Club so we could all air some of our feelings. It was obvious we needed a space more like the Astrodome. At least during the season, our main core of energy was drained by the cold, the tides, the boats, and the fish. But the day of the meeting we were all too rested, and our only task was to express our discontent. It started off normally enough, like most other fishermen's meetings; all the coffee and doughnuts were gone before half the people had arrived. Then Mr. Rolland from the Fish and Game lost the first round when he attempted to formally call the meeting to order. It was actually Joe, a much admired fish pirate from Alaska to Monterey, who got things really rolling when he yelled from the back of the room, "Number one, the Fish and Game has to stop its Gestapo tactics." There was a big roar of "Yeah, right."

And Rolland yelled through the din, "We've got to stick to real issues if we're going to accomplish anything." This was followed by another chorus that this was the real issue.

One of the gill netters jumped in, "We've got to get rid of the seiners; they're destroying the bay and the fish."

And then one of the seiners yelled, "We've got to stick together if we're going to get things settled with the Fish and Game." Another seiner yelled that the gill netters should be eliminated. And then someone yelled that it's the Fish and Game that should be eliminated, and round and round we went like the tide at Yellow Bluff. There was a question of the anchors, the border disputes, the mentality of Fish and Game, the length of the nets, then back to the anchors.

Rolland tried to take the focus off this confusion for a while. He held up a big chart on which they had marked in pretty colors the areas of the bay where the fish had spawned during the season and had a big number printed there that was supposed to represent the number of fish they had calculated to have come in the bay. Out of the restless sea in front of him came "What about the San Pablo spawn? How could you miss the spawn at Red Rock?"

"Yeah, and your biologist never even knew about the Richmond Inner Harbor spawn until somebody ran into him at the fuel dock and told him that it had been going on for three days, and even then he had to give your biologist directions because he couldn't find the place on the chart."

Then Freckles stood up. Freckles, who preached all the time to us younger members of the fleet that it was time for us to carry the ball for the old-timers like himself. But he could bear to watch us fumble for only so long. He stood up very calm in contrast, and as a result he had the attention of everyone. "I think we ought to talk about that number you have up there, that number that's supposed to be the number of fish that came into the bay." Then without warning he thrust his voice to full volume as if screaming from his flying bridge to a crew that had just lost a good set of fish, "Who are you, God, that you know this number or did you stand under the bridge and count the fish as they came in?"

With a glazed stare out over the tops of everyone's heads, the biologist began to outline his methods: "We counted the eggs in a square foot of beach where a spawn had occurred, multiplied by the area of the beach, and then multiplied by a surface correction factor, and figured out to the low tide line how many fish it had required to spawn these eggs."

Freckles went right into top volume. "You keep saying these fish only spawn at the tide line, and we keep showing you crab-pot line from ten to twenty fathoms covered with herring eggs, and you keep saying these fish only spawn at the tide line. I am so sick of dancing to that same old music."

You could tell Fish and Game was looking for a moment to put that big chart back under the table and the questioning along with it. But every time they reached to put it away, Freckles would refer to it again. The fourth or fifth time we all started laughing. Having gotten the desired effect, Freckles said to Fish and Game, "OK, you can put it away now." Without time for a breath the free-for-all resumed. I think almost every topic got covered: the question of lampara net territory, the question of the lottery, whether or not more gill netters should be allowed in, whether quotas should be individual or whether there should be group quotas, did the Golden Gate Ferry have a right to demand a throughway through our fishing, can't we keep the out-of-state buyers out, can't we keep out the out-of-state fishermen, can't we call on the constitution of the United States, etc., etc., etc. Quite clearly nothing was accomplished. A few weeks later we received a notice in the mail that Fish and Game had called another meeting to formulate changes for next year. The meeting was set very conveniently for May 4. All the fishermen would be safely out on the ocean, trying to make a living at salmon.

Marie anchored at Cuffey's Cove on the Angelina G.

"No bread today." Riding out a blow, anchored in the lee of Point Reyes.

The bait, a salmon, and an opah—a rare fish that swam here from another sea.

The sea off Double Point, in one of its brighter moods.

Moss Landing Jim, in a mood to pay some bills.

Freckles, the old man of the northern sea.

Jerry, delighted to be sewing on the net again, after another "little mistake" at sea.

St. Herman *Dave with that sinking feeling behind a swell at Pt. Delgada.*

Forty-five tons of herring hold the Lorinda *of Moss Landing on the brink of fortune or losing it all.*

An unexpected gill net full of herring. The net had been thrown to locate a missing six-pack.

Talking it over after the work is done.

7

Sundog

THANK GOD FOR salmon and the open sea. The relief is immediate. The horizon works its magic and disperses your thoughts
across the sea to air in the infinite breeze. The rolling swell rocks
you into its trance, and the setting sun makes the change complete.

When that searing ball of the sun's fire sets itself into the open
ocean, it isn't anything like the sunsets you see on land. At sea, all
day long amidst the changing rhythms of the waves, the wind, and
the fish, only the sun has roots in its arc across the sky, only the
sun is anchored in time. At sea, only the cycle of the sun is true.

To watch it then hover precariously on the horizon like a far-off
ship aflame and sink into the waters pulling in its vortex all the
light of the sky, no matter how much you know of tomorrow, that
moment stirs some primitive fear in a soul left deserted to uncertain motion on an uncertain sea.

Try to imagine the planetary sweep of the sea, a vastness that
scales down the Himalayas to the size of a snowcone or Texas to a
handful of dust. A few thousand fishermen aren't even specks
upon it. With everyone moving around as randomly as the whims
of their hunches and the demands of their boats, there are days
when you don't even see another boat; you're alone, face to face
with the space. During the day, at least, the sun keeps it from being
nothing but a shimmering eternity. Nighttime, and there's nothing
but the soul to fill the void.

And when the fishermen are around, when ten or twenty mast
lights dance against the infinite black, even if you have no idea of

their names, the bonds you feel are an ancient comfort and security in the human race, reasserted in the uncertain motion on the uncertain sea. There was no better way to heal the wounds of herring than to meet out here again.

Politics at sea is illusory, a "now you see it, now you don't" proposition. The issues don't hang in the air like they do on land, but more like a wave, they pass under the boat and get cleared from your mind by the shape of the next wave, the fish on the lines, the course through the fog, the setting of the sun; things that so urgently engage the raw energy of instinct that even the greatest effort of human will cannot turn your back or your mind from the sea. Politics, even the politics of fish, is unheeded by the fishermen as carelessly as the politician dismisses the fish.

Besides, ever since commercial fishing began on the West Coast, there were very few laws that governed the ocean fishery. The limits of fishing were set mostly by the market and the sea. And the few laws that did exist, such as a prohibition against nets in the salmon fishery and the twenty-six-inch size limit, made sense, and the fishermen were glad to comply. They were more aware than anyone of the connection between next year's crop and the care of this year's young. There were exceptions, of course, but most of the fishermen took a great deal of pride in the little things, like the way you release a small fish from the hook without ever touching it with your hand so as not to remove any protective slime. Certainly, there were a few issues that riled the fleet, like the dams that were choking the spawning grounds in one river after the other, and the lumber companies that with sloppy logging techniques silted the streams and killed the fry. But on the rare occasions when the fishermen talked about fighting any of it, their tone had about as much expectation of success as if they were talking about calming a ten-foot sea.

Even the fishermen's associations, one in each port, were shaped more by the life of the sea than by the issues. They were hardly models of political mobilization. Most of them didn't have a telephone, and for six or seven months of the year, with people scattered all over the ocean, they didn't even meet. Even desert nomads have better coordination because they, at least, travel in a band. The state of the fishermen's readiness was all too evident when you'd hear one association director get on the radio, desperately trying to track down the whereabouts of another director so they could pull together a quick conference call on what to do about a bill that had already passed.

During the winter, in an unheated hall that's nestled in amongst the buying stations, the associations meet three or four times. Naturally, since it almost never happens that everyone gets together like this, there's a lot of "Hey, how are you?" and it takes a while to get business under way. Then slam, bang goes the coffee cup on the table. "Okay, everybody," Mack starts out before everyone is seated, "let's get this stuff out of the way. We got this letter from the Coast Guard dated last, let's see here," he pauses while checking the letter for the date, "last August, and they say they're going to turn off the fog horn on the jetty because the campers in the state park have been complaining about the noise." Normally the elected secretary would write the response, but he's fishing crab in Eureka. It takes a good fifteen minutes, but after a few unusable suggestions and some good laughs, they've whipped off the final letter. "With all due respect, we don't think the fishermen should be lost in the fog so the campers can sleep. Sincerely, . . ."

The agenda usually handles three or four such letters and then moves on to the inevitable status of the ever fluctuating price negotiations with the buyers, and then there's usually arrangements to be made for donating fish to a fisherman's family who has met with disaster. This is a painful and perennial problem because when a fisherman goes down, there's rarely a body to prove the death, and the insurance takes seven years to come through. Another grinding issue that comes up over and over are the problems at the local hatcheries which are supposed to supplement the loss due to dams; despite their college degrees, Fish and Game has not been very successful at duplicating Mother Nature. The fish are always dying of something or other. Nine thirty at night and enough is enough; no matter how far away from the date, there has to be time put aside to discuss plans for this year's annual fishermen's picnic. There wasn't much in these meetings to keep you in touch with the fact that commercial fishing is a major industry functioning in the modern world.

Still there was always someone at some point in every meeting who got up and gave an emotional rendering of what we all knew on some level. "We've got to do a whole lot more than we're doing or we're going to lose the whole fishery in no time."

The discussions that followed had little chance of going any-where. Free-for-all arguments about making political maneuvers nobody knew anything about on a budget of less than two thou-sand dollars a year were dizzying, to say the least. But the real nix on progress was the attitude of who wanted to argue in the first place.

At sea, you're captain of your boat and I'm captain of mine; I don't tell you what to do and you don't tell me. We come together because the ocean's huge; and whether it's trying to kill you, awe you, or feed you, going through it one more time with another fish-erman is the only cure for the sheer intensity of it all. Just being together, crowded around the galley table of the boat tied next to you, huddled around the stubborn embers of a barbecue on a windy dock, pulling your tables together at the fanciest restaurant in town; just being together with the other fishermen always had the excitement of an unexpected reunion and the ardor of a secret religion—bread and wine consecrated by the tales of the sea. Poli-tics is as welcome as sobriety.

It was a full four years since I had blithely pointed the bow of the *Donna Lou* out to the open sea in search of adventure. And still, even now, every trip was giving me more overwhelming action than I desired for a lifetime. But this one surprise, this unex-pected way that the sea had shaped the spirit of its people, was so pronounced that it tempered all the rest.

I guess I had early on braced myself for some shitkickin', brawl-ing, wave-riding broncobusters out to tame the sea like the West-erners of old. I was surprised over and over—when I'd hear the old-timers get on the air and exclaim like delighted kids, "You'll never believe what I just saw"; when I'd hear young guys turning tail to a roughed up sea, unashamed of their fear; when I saw how matter of routine was the fisherman's willingness to risk his life for another; how, even after long days in port, alcohol just brought out more stories instead of the fights. More than any of this I was surprised by an underlying gentleness among the fishermen, a gentleness that was unmarred by their rough-weathered exteriors or the tough physical demands of the sea. A gentleness toward their boats, to the sea, and with their friends.

I absolutely couldn't have made it without the fishermen. I'm not talking about the help with dockside mechanics, though there's no question I got more than my share. And I'm certainly not talking about being put on fish because that didn't happen much at all. I could never resist passing the news on to my friends, who would in turn call their friends, and it tended to dry up my sources.

What helped me more than anything was early on getting unceremoniously accepted into the fleet. And completely to my surprise, the fishermen truly seemed delighted to see me making it.

Strange because, at this point, I bet three-quarters of them wouldn't think of hiring me as crew. Superstition is as important to the fisherman's life as bait, and, of course, the most unquestionable superstition of them all is that women are bad luck on a boat. Because the sea is a jealous woman who will withhold her fishy favors, because women aren't strong enough, because the mast will come down, because of the temptations, because men have to pee over the side? The rationale, of course, defies analysis. But the fact was that some of the same guys who were delighted to have me in the fleet didn't want me walking across their decks.

Perhaps I was accepted because with all the space on the sea, what difference does it make what's going on on another boat when each captain has complete sovereignty of his own? Maybe this is what promoted tolerance among the fleet for all kinds of idiosyncracies and included was mine, the fact that I was a woman.

Or perhaps the respect was automatic, part of the pride everyone took in each other just from knowing they all lived with something so much greater than themselves.

Or maybe it had more to do with the way the ocean whets the fishermen's appetite for surprises. Whether it's a fish from the Indian Ocean that suddenly shows up in the North Pacific or a whale that leaps beside his boat—it's "Well, I'll be goddamned," with a smile of delight, a love of the magic and almost a pride in having seen it. And when this woman who couldn't possibly make it turns around and makes it, it was "Well, I'll be goddamned," with a smile like they were glad to have me around, proof that the magic knows no bounds.

Whatever the reason, it turned out that what I had expected to be my biggest problem venturing onto the male world of the sea became my biggest advantage. I was very happy in this tight family of fiercely independent people. Whatever it was that the ocean lent to the kinship of the fishermen, it was there for me, too.

A kinship as strong as the fearsomeness of the sea that forged it. Even alone on the darkest night, miles from another boat, I never felt lonely at sea.

And all this, the tightly woven mesh of the fishermen on the sea, made for a strange new uneasiness in the fleet on these evenings of late when we'd look out to the darkening horizons and see a tiny pool of lights arise in the direction the sun had set. They'd been with us this salmon season more boldly than ever before. When the main body of salmon was off Monterey, they were visible on the night horizon off Monterey. When the main body of fish was off the Cordell Banks, they were there off the Cordell. Whenever our fishermen reported the heaviest body of fish from California to Washington, they were there, invisible in the glare of the day and glaring in the dark of the night. Over three hundred foreign ships —Russian, Korean, Japanese, Polish—ships that in one tow of their gigantic trawls can take more tonnage of fish than any one of us could catch in a year.

The foreign ships weren't coming here from all over the world because fuel is cheap. They come because their own coastal waters are already fished out and because there's nothing much in between. The Pacific Ocean, you see, is not a fertile field of fish; it's more like Siberia without the land. Fish need plants, and for the most part plants need shallow bottom where the light can reach them. They also need oxygen which the warm surface of much of the Pacific cannot hold. Only perfect conditions of continental shelf and massive upwellings of cold water can turn the blue desert into teeming life, and we have one of the few great marine oases of the earth right in our own backyard.

Nobody likes these ships lurking on the horizon; they were as unsettling to the fleet as any band of strangers milling furtively around your unprotected home. But what the hell were we going to do? These were international waters, and when they have three-hundred-foot boats and you have a thirty-foot-boat, joking about it seemed like the wisest strategy of all.

It wasn't long, though, before a new event turned the nervous joking to rage. The National Marine Fisheries Service began trying to pacify the fishermen with reports that the foreign ships were only taking the hake. If there was one thing the fishermen couldn't stand, it was being treated like a fool. Freckles was no exception.

"Maria," he hollered one day when I asked him about these ships, "even our own drag boats get salmon in their nets, and the speed of our drag boats is nothing compared to those ships. And they're going to make me believe they don't catch salmon and rock cod and every other thing that swims in the water? Sometime taste the water after one of those ships has passed and you'll see even the salt is gone. They drag a deep net on the bottom and a shallow net on the surface. What do you think the shallow net is for, to catch the seagulls?" It wasn't all conjecture either; at one time or another most of the fishermen have been close enough to see what was in the nets as they hauled up the stern of the ships. In fact, a few of the fishermen had submitted photographs showing the catch of every fish the government denied they took. So strong were the fishermen's feelings about this that it became the impetus behind their first lobbying effort, an effort to push for passage of the two-hundred-mile-limit bill. Freckles had the bumper sticker on his truck, too, like everyone else, but long before its passage he was warning, "That two-hundred-mile-limit bill is going to be the ruination of the fishermen. Mark my word!"

The more I got to know Freckles, the more I liked him, not just as a salty old fisherman who mirrored the moods of the sea, but especially as someone who never stopped taking delight in filtering it all through some prism of his mind and reading it out the other end like a crystal ball.

But just how Freckles was able to foresee the long-term outcome of this development, I can't even hazard a guess. Freckles doesn't read or write, and he attends about as many meetings as any other fisherman. I doubt he could have known about the United States' push for ocean mining or the billions' worth of manganese nodules that were recently discovered on the ocean floor, two events of the early 1970s that had more to do with the shaping of ocean policy than any concern for the fish. When I asked him where he came up with this prediction, he would only say it came from the same place as his other ideas—he got it from his eyes and ears.

One thing for sure, I know he didn't get it from the other fishermen. When I say the fleet got involved in this issue, it only means I'm talking relative to how they got involved in other issues. During the whole season I heard no more than half a dozen discussions on the two-hundred-mile-limit bill, and all of these were of the tone that people should go to their local associations and support this thing. I doubt if any of it would be on my mind now if it weren't for Freckles's strange remark and the light of current events.

The fleet moved through this salmon season no differently than before, tuned to the rhythms of fish checks, weatherchecks, upwellings, water temps, gossip, and recipes. Friendships and events were shaped by the conditions of the sea. And the sea was still a vast territory where even the most customary intrusion of politics as occurs on land was received with disbelief.

That's how it was the afternoon that year when Michael got news of Valerie. It had been two months since anyone from Oregon to Mexico had heard any word of Valerie's whereabouts. And though the news was pretty much what everyone had by now surmised, it was a long time before the radio resumed the normal chatter.

Valerie was an officer on one of the Russian fishing ships and one of the few who could speak English. Valerie's boat was a 307-foot processor and fishing boat. He'd been fishing in the Russian fleet out of Vladivostok for the past ten years. Michael is a lanky, energetic fisherman from Half Moon Bay who, before the age of forty, had made a name for himself along the full length of the coast not just as one of the best salmon fishermen in Oregon and California but also as president of the Z Squad, a gang of younger fishermen who left a trail of stories in their wake as legendary and infamous as those left by the Yukoners.

Michael and Valerie had been friends for quite some time, filling in the slack hours of fishing with traded tales of the sea, gripings about the weather, and musings about the fish, the standard chitchat of sea-going friendships spiced with the peppery sense of mischief which brought them together in the first place. It was inevitable that they would try and meet.

One day the Z Squad was tied up in the slips of Newport, Oregon. The Russians were using Hecata Banks, about forty miles offshore, as a kind of base where they were waiting for their supply ship.

Michael called Valerie and the fated meeting was set. So the whole Z Squad gathered up their gunnysacks and went on a shopping spree from one end of the town of Newport to the other. They loaded the gunnysacks full of plums and oranges, every kind of magazine they could find, clothes, hats, postcards, booze, cigarettes, everything they could think of that might amuse their sea-locked friend.

Seven guys hopped aboard Michael's boat with as many gunny-sacks. Michael got hold of Valerie and told him they were on their way. They talked with Valerie for four hours, the whole time going out. The buildup was something else.

Valerie told them how to locate him out of the other forty ships. When they got there, they all went up on the flying bridge. Michael ran the boat right up to the ship, bow right up to the side of the ship. Valerie was standing up there with a couple of his friends, and everyone was waving and shouting and laughing, and they could see this was going to be a party to remember.

Finally, Valerie threw a line down, and Michael tied three gunnysacks together for the first haul. The line was strong enough, but it was too small for the three of them to pull on, and they couldn't lift it up the side of the ship. They threw a second line over the side, a bigger line, and Valerie went down the other line, right down the side of the ship like a monkey, tied the bigger line onto the gunnysacks and then back up the forty feet like a cat. Then they hoisted it aboard.

As soon as the bags were aboard, Valerie looked forward and gave Michael a forward moving hand signal. They threw that big boat in gear and away they went. They moved to another spot. Something must have happened, thought Michael; the old man must have caught them in the act or somebody must have dis-approved. Valerie got on the air and told them to drift there over-night, that their supply ship was coming, and the next day he would try to get away and come and visit on Michael's boat and meet Michael personally; plus he wanted to get together some stuff from their supply ship as a return offering.

The problem was that one of the gang's mechanics was supposed to be in Newport the next morning, and he couldn't miss him because he was driving all the way up from Eureka. So they had to get back, but it was like pulling teeth to get everyone to leave.

Michael and the squad kept trying to get hold of Valerie for two months after that deal, and all they'd get was a long empty silence. Finally, after two months of calling constantly, day and night, some guy came on the air who was a friend of Valerie's. He could barely speak English. He said very slowly and carefully, "Valerie is no longer with us, he was sent back home with the supply ship."

Into the silence that followed the news, another fisherman came on the air. "Jesus," he said, "a couple fishermen meet on the water to break a little bread and some official on the other side of the world plucks him out of the sea. Valerie's probably in the salt mines now, and we'll never see him again."

In 1976 the two-hundred-mile-limit bill was passed. The United States, like most other countries with a coastline, had written up a deed to the sea. Officials in the United States alone, in one fell swoop, had claimed two million square miles of the ocean for their exclusive domain, from the mud on the bottom all the way up to the people on top of the waves. And hardly a word was heard in response. Out at sea, nothing much had changed at all. The foreign ships certainly didn't go away. Instead, our government gave them permits, and now the ships could come even closer than before. They didn't even have to buy the permits! The permits were gifts; the rich field of fish along our coast became no more than a trading chip on the international tables.

Nor did there seem much consequence in the fact that the Department of Commerce took over jurisdiction of coastal fisheries. Fish and Game had never done a whole lot about the ocean fisheries, and it seemed obvious that Washington would care even less.

About the only thing that changed on the ocean was the Coast Guard. In a way it was nothing more than a giant nuisance; looking back, it was the entry point of a gaff aimed hard at pulling the fishermen from the sea.

Until the two-hundred-mile-limit bill, relationships between the fishermen and Coast Guard were pretty good. Though it was a military organization of many inexperienced men who made a lot of mistakes on the water, they held the respect of the fishermen for one important reason. No matter how treacherous the conditions, these kids would hop in their small boats and risk their lives for yours.

But now they were cops.

Until now, the territory we worked was international water, ruled only by the wind. People had dominion over only one thing, their boats. Here the power was complete. Captain at sea is as a head of state with absolute control over every aspect of life in a country the size of his boat. It's a relationship so extreme and unique in human experience that it's not surprising that many of the novels most revealing of the human soul have taken place at sea.

Now, for the first time in the history of the earth, the sea was owned, all the way out to two hundred miles. It was United States territory. And the Coast Guard wanted to make swift and certain that every fisherman got educated to the meaning of colonialism. After all, what good is a colony if the natives don't know their place.

That summer, the Coast Guard began regular patrols of the fleet at sea, launching their zodiacs from the big cutter and randomly boarding the boats. Stumbling over everything, tangling lines, stepping into bait traps, endangering fishing operations they knew nothing about, endangering lives, especially their own, to issue five-hundred-dollar fines for such things as missing letters on the boat's identification. Until the two-hundred-mile-limit bill, such acts constituted piracy on the high seas.

In the grossest possible manner, the Coast Guard drove a wedge between the fisherman, his boat, and the sea. So gross, in fact, that when fishermen's reports of the boardings filtered up to the top brass, the maneuvers were stopped. But not before something very ancient and strong had been broken.

It was plain amazing how fast we forgot about all this and returned to business as usual. The shape of the next wave, the mood of the fish, a course through the fog, the arc of the sun, at any moment, demanded the full attention of your senses; that's what kept you alive. Politics at sea seemed illusory. It was at once the beauty and the downfall of the fishermen.

"Hey, Dick, oh, Dick, you pick me up, Dick?" Freckles's big, amplitude-modulated voice boomed into the radio one afternoon on a beautiful, beautiful day.

"Yeah, Freckles, I got you, Freckles, what's going on?"

"Didn't mean to startle you, Dick, but I just got to thinking you're probably one of the few guys here that was paying attention to what just happened in the sky."

"I seen it, Frecks," said Dick, as pleased with himself for catching Freckles's drift as he would have been pulling a forty-pound salmon from the sea. "That was the sundog, and I haven't seen that sight since those years in Alaska. Two suns in the same sky and you can't tell which one's real, one's just as bright as the other. Most of these guys don't know what they're in for. We'd see that old dog up in the north and the whole fleet would head for the beach. But I *never* seen him here."

I could tell by the easy, measured, rhythmic phrasing in Dick's voice that these guys had found a topic worthy of their lengthy deliberation, and I mean lengthy. These two could literally go on for hours.

"That's right, Dick," said Freckles, "he was only up there a few minutes. You don't see them things unless you're watching everywhere, all the time. That's yours and my experience," he said, knowing full well that everyone was listening. "You know, Dick, there was one time in Bristol Bay . . ."

What the hell these two were doing getting into it right now was beyond me. There'd been less than eight fish for everyone all day, and now with evening they're coming up like grapes. Pick one, pick two, pick three . . . salmon as easy as grapes. On a sea that was as oily slick calm as a Sunday pond. Maybe five times a year it happens like this, and they're up there in their wheelhouses, chewin' the fat about sundogs and Alaska.

Everybody was getting the fish, that was obvious. Came 9:00 P.M. and not one boat out of thirty was heading toward the beach, despite the fact we were way out here at the Cordell Banks with a three-and-a-half-hour run just to get to the closest anchorage. Everybody was squeezing the last drop of light out of a sun that had already set.

Pretty soon, I couldn't see one end of the herring from the other; I ran up to the cabin to flip on the deck lights and dashed back to the stern so as not to miss a fish. But the action had died just that fast. Salmon will not feed in the dark.

I doubt if even Freckles or Dick knew what was coming next. In the time it took to put the first line on the boat, the winds had already carved a sharp, foamy chop across the sea. Before I got the second line aboard, an eight-foot swell had moved in underneath the chop. A loud, wood-splitting crack exploded behind my back as a 250-pound box of salmon literally fell from one side of the deck to the other. In less than the twenty minutes it takes to get the gear on the boat, the ocean had changed under my feet from a duck pond to a sharp, thrashing twelve-foot sea with winds at fifty knots. It was a long, terrifying ride to the anchorage.

Usually in weather like this there's a little bit of talking to ease the tension. But not tonight. Two guys were already in bad trouble. One of them was my friend John, who had a boat that was just a little smaller than mine. He had caught a wave that tore open the side of his cabin. He couldn't afford even one more wave to board his boat, but in a sea like this they were all coming aboard. A bigger boat was trying to run next to John on the weather side in hopes of breaking the tops. But in the dark, in weather like this, one wave could just as easily have put the big boat on top of him. Times like this and nobody talks.

By 1:00 A.M. everybody had made it into the hole. All boats accounted for. Thirty mast lights tucked in behind the tall, black bluffs of Point Reyes. And the radio was making up for lost time: who had what damages, people getting lined up for the morning to exchange parts and help each other make repairs. I was lucky; it would only take an hour or two to clean up the certain mess of hooks, leaders, and fish. For now, I was too cold and tired to even look.

I crashed into my bunk and listened to the ebbing conversations give way to the howl of the wind. One long breath and I was drifting out, one more and I'd be gone.

"Hey, Dick, oh, Dick, you pick me up, Dick?"

Dick answered with a big laugh into the mike, "Yeah, I got you, Freckles. Man, that was something else. I ain't never seen that old sundog, but he wasn't trying to tell me something."

"Right," said Freckles. "That dog's all bite and no bark. Good thing nobody was hurt. John sure had me worried there for a while but he did the right things. I'll bet it's a long time before he stops staring at the sun."

"You know, Freckles, I saw it one time . . ."

My God! Laying at anchor, you can't turn off the radio at night, especially in weather like this; you can't even turn the volume down because what good is an emergency call if it doesn't wake you up. They were into this conversation now fifteen minutes, and it sounded like their memories were just getting warmed up to the topic.

God bless Ray! He must have had to stand by the mike who knows how long, waiting for a break. "Freckles," he jumped in when he got his chance.

Ray was anchored way on the other side of the fleet from Freckles, but from the tone in his voice I could picture him with his arm draped around Freckles's broad shoulders, gently steering him to a quiet part of a room. "What do you say we get some sleep, old man, time to get some sleep."

8

The Yukon Connection

THE RELIEF OF dropping the hook at the end of the day, turning off the engine, finishing up a few chores, and finally sinking into my bunk was the most exquisite pleasure of my life. I'd try to hold myself awake long enough just to enjoy a few minutes of floating free. But with one breath, gravity would lose its grip; one more and I'd sink into a bottomless sea. And the next thing I knew was the piercing rage of the alarm. Unless perchance I dreamed.

Sometimes I was so tired that I'd actually dream about sleeping. No kidding, I'd be lying there sound asleep on the anchor and dream about lying down and going to sleep, I guess the same way a starving person dreams about food.

Then there were the dreams I had over and over about the anchor breaking loose or the boat taking water. Sometimes it was heavenly, drifting free as a cloud or soaking luxuriously in the waters that lapped around me. Other times, I'd jump up in such panic to save my life, I'd crash my head into the top of the forecastle. But mostly, I dreamed about fish. I could see way down into the water, ten or twenty fathoms, clear as a crystal. And salmon as big as boats, beautiful dream salmon, would swim slowly in the sparkling light of the depths. Mythic salmon, full of silvery colors, powerful, majestic salmon that moved like they knew everything there was to know. Sometimes I'd just hang over the stern, watching them for the whole dream, and sometimes I'd load the boat. Man, could I catch fish in my dreams!

Fishing and the ocean had become the entire focus of my life, day and night, around the calendar; it had awakened and re-aligned every sense of my being, consumed the full spectrum of my emotions, taken all my energy, and now it had my dreams. And even with all that, the complete rendering of my soul to the sea, the sea was not yet rendering to me.

To be sure I was learning some things along the way that were beginning to make my life a little easier. Obvious things like getting to know the territory so I didn't have to consult a chart on every change of tack, or recognizing the individual subtleties of different fishermen's voices on the radio. My own strategy, too, was picking up a glimmer of sophistication. For one thing, when a crazy gang of boats pulled their anchors in the middle of a windy night because they'd just received news of a bite at the other end of the world, I'd take the pillow and wrap it around my ears and roll over. Rare anymore were the all-night runs to the morning bite of fish that were already iced in somebody else's hold.

The mechanics, too; the mechanics of rigging, of pumps, engines, winches, steering gear, propellers, rudders, the mechanics of baiting a hundred hooks in the dark with one hand on the helm, the mechanics of making repairs upside down in the engine room with a sea tossing the boat from bulwark to bulwark, the mechanics of jury-rigging, the mechanics of staying alive—the mechanics that every land friend thought would be the Waterloo of my fishing. These things over the years had begun to fall into my command. It's the kind of knowledge that day by day adds to itself, that builds on what went before; the same "If this, then that" kind of logic that is the ever faithful basis of modern civilization. And though the application of it at sea was endlessly more complex and required the nth degree of ingenuity, I could always take pride by looking back and seeing the progress I had made. To all outward appearances, I was becoming a certified regulation fisherwoman!

But look out over the sea that from horizon to horizon breeds waves to the north that are identical to the waves at every other point of the compass and tell me, for the sake of food on the table, which wave is the wave that's hiding the fish? And when the boat is trolling over a fat bonanza school, and sometimes you know this for sure because every boat in sight is throwing salmon over both shoulders, tell me for the sake of sanity, with what prayer, in what language, can I make them bite? And I'll recite that prayer 'til I mouth the words in my sleep. Because four years in this business and I still couldn't fathom the fish or the sea!

Tack for tack, day for day, I was doubled, tripled, quadrupled by fishermen using the same hooks, lines, and bait, the same boats, hands, and brain as me. Aha, except for maybe the brain! That's actually what I started thinking on those long maddening tacks with nothing to do but change the baits and listen to the radio scores. Maybe all these years being brought up in a civilization that refuses to deal with things that by their very nature can never be solved, that part of my brain that's supposed to deal with such things had atrophied like the thighs of a paraplegic. The modern ego seems only to thrive in the cocoon woven tight with the illusions of control, and I'd been in there so damn long, I didn't have a clue to the logic of the universe beyond. I was aware, to be sure, that I had found myself in the sparkling foam of a big wave of life, and I knew, without doubt, I didn't want to wipe out no matter what the cost; but I was also so damn mad at the end of every day down in the ice hold counting fish—no—at the end of every tack, that I felt like biting the planks that bore me over the sea.

Now I wasn't unaware that these ragings at the sea were a common occupational hazard. Deckhands from other boats had given me plenty of scoop on that score. Freckles's deckhand told me that when the fish wouldn't bite, Freckles would storm up to the flying bridge, the highest spot on the boat, shake his gaff to the sky, and spit into the sea, cussing everything from the salt on up to the creator.

Then there was the guy who for three days was tripled by his running partner. He went on a rampage and took the fish he already had and threw them back into the sea. I knew everyone occasionally had the same problem, but I was certain the universe had singled me out for long-term, intensive treatment.

There wasn't a fisherman on the coast I didn't ask for his tricks, and there wasn't a trick I didn't try: speed changes, curved hooks, sound muffling on the drive gear, electrical insulation on the gear, special stern bearings, positive mental attitude, visualizations of fish on the hooks, anchovies soaked in milk. My perseverance was admirable. Believe me, I would have put a dog turd on the end of the hook if I thought it would have caught a fish. In the end, it was the Yukon gang that did the trick.

It was late August, the water was hot and clear blue, there were a few stragglers in seventy fathoms right on the bottom in a cool layer of water four hours out from Bodega. Not my scene at all; lines tangle in the current at those depths, it takes extra leads to get them down there in the first place, and it takes so damn long for them to come up that you forget about the extra lead and run it through the sheave and lose everything. At least that's how I felt about it. Freckles loves this fishing; the deeper he could reach in the sea, the happier he'd get. He'd pull the sun down out there every day, even when it meant getting to anchor at midnight and leaving again at two in the morning. So I was surprised when he called me at 6:00 P.M. "Maria, pack your bags, we're going to see *Bubbly Ann*."

I always have trouble deciphering information from Freckles, mainly because it isn't necessarily information that he's putting out. "Bubbly Ann" was no problem, just Freckles's affectionate twist on *Barbara Ann*, Mario's boat. Fishermen refer to each other by the boat's name as frequently as they use a first name. What I wanted to know was how many fish. However, it's worse than useless to call Freckles back for elaboration. If it is real scoop he'll play it down, and if it's bullshit he plays it up. What the hell, it wouldn't break my heart to change scenery. Besides, Freckles is one of the sharpest fishermen I know. Like he says, he sleeps with one eye open, and if a bird passes his boat in the night, he knows if its belly is empty or full. His keen observation of the ocean environment over the years has given him a store of knowledge that's unmatched. And he catches a hell of a lot of fish. I never used to turn down an invitation to get on his tail till I realized at times he's just a mover.

Five hours later, I pulled up to his boat in the Point Reyes anchorage. Freckles came striding out of his cabin toward the stern with the proud carriage of a man who knew he could take ten steps and cover the length of the universe. "Hey, Freckles, I sure hope I didn't come here just to keep you company."

"Maria, Maria, Maria, did I ever steer you wrong?" Without giving me time to answer, he got right to the point. "The gang got nine hundred pounds a boat on the outside of the Islands today. You see all the mast lights here? I don't think these other salamies know what's going on. So lights out and no radio, two o'clock we leave."

The complete darkness and complete silence, save for the hum of the engine, only served to intensify the purity of my one thought. Fish. By the time the first glow shimmered over the land twenty miles behind us, I was completely psyched, the back deck was thoroughly organized in my mind, and every move precisely rehearsed for the morning kill. The jagged, bare rocks of the North Island looked soft and castlelike in the predawn light; the sea was oily slick calm. The Yukon gang was now visible ahead of us, and I knew it wasn't bullshit. Maybe three times a year they get up that early, and it's not for their health. It was perfect; we were the only boats, and no one was likely to find us out here. The sun wasn't quite up, all my lines were in the water, and every bait was as carefully balanced and juicy as I could make it.

The first ten minutes nothing happened. I looked around and no one else was making a back tack either. I could see Freckles make a turn in toward the Islands, I kept working down and out, and the gang fanned out to the north. Within forty-five minutes we'd lost sight of each other; the radio was still silent, but I could just about feel everybody standing by waiting for someone to find where these fish had moved and issue a telling "Come my way" before we lost the morning.

Ten more minutes and the back deck speaker actually vibrated on its mounts with a voice that flexed the human vocal cords like the biceps of Mr. America. "It sure looks like a shitty one to me, boys!" screamed Mario in his first proclamation of the day. Freckles must have come to the same conclusion and was standing with his finger on the transmit button. Without a split second he was unleashing his disgust on the air like a morning constitutional. "Giusto, *Bubbly Ann*, I was nice and peaceful up there and look what I've come to, the death of a thousand cuts. Ah, what's the matter with me? I know better, I know better . . ." and he slipped into a long singsong, mournful Sicilian cry.

"Giusto, Captain Ole," said Mario in refrain, "it's a bad one. Maybe you pissed off the wrong side of the boat this morning. You better check and see if maybe your mast ain't coming down. Something's got to explain it, Captain Ole; there was a big school of fish here yesterday, you would have made a lot of loot, enough to retire, and now look at the mess we're in." Freckles started in worse than ever.

There's a little trick when someone else is talking. You push the transmit button simultaneously and almost invariably the other boats hear your quick comments over his strained battery. "We're in for a good hour of this," said Vaughn without hiding any displeasure.

Then it was the Governor, whose voice always carried the air of energized persecution, "What'd you go and stir him up for, Mario, ain't things bad enough as it is?"

Mario always had an answer. "Come on, Governor, if we all work together, we'd get him to burn up that antenna in a day." Freckles was still singing as if he had the audience hanging on every note. He went to grab a breath and Mario grabbed his chance.

"I sure wish Maria was here; she works too hard, that crazy kid. One day we're going to get a postcard from Alaska saying what a big school of salmon she found." Mario knew I was there; we'd waved hello just before setting the gear.

"Hello, kid," I said, and everyone was accounted for. With only three or four fish on everybody's deck the radio, without exaggerating, had less than a total of three seconds' silence for the next four hours.

"Ah, Maria, you've come to the right spot," said Mario.

I had indeed come to just the right spot. I don't remember exactly how it started. I must have accepted a dinner invitation with the gang at one point and was immediately taken by them. Every September since I had the *Angelina G.*, I joined up with the gang in a style of fishing that defies all natural law. I could never have made it through September without them.

Mario was president, minister of internal and external affairs, master of ceremonies, bartender, fleet captain, fisheries director, and chief of predicaments. At age fifty-two he ranked fifth in age with the gang, and he ranked sixth on the list of alternate chef for good reason.

"It sure looks like an early barbecue today, boys!" he screamed over the ocean around one o'clock in the afternoon. And finally no one answered. Everyone was taking a break. Such a lull never phased Mario; in fact, it was a favorite opportunity to create characters and proceed to answer himself in soul searching dialogue that would challenge the inspection of Socrates.

"Yes, Mario," he said to himself, "there's no doubt you're right about that. You've been fishing this area for quite a few years now, and by now you ought to know a flat tire when you see one."

"Yeah, Ray, I remember a long time ago when your dad was alive and we were fishing the North Island. It was a long time ago because I remember blowing into the sail because the wind quit, and we had jellyfish smothering the bait, and blue sharks were tangling the lines, and the hake were climbing up the mast, and the wind threatened to come up any day; it was one o'clock and your dear old dad had one lousy salmon for the day. He said something to me I've never forgotten."

"Yes, Mario," said Mario, "I sure would like to know what my father would say in a situation like that."

"I'll tell you what he said, son; he pulled over to my boat and yelled, 'It sure looks like an early barbecue today, son.' "

As president of the gang, when Mario said "Roll 'em up," the gang picked up the gear and went in. But as minister of internal affairs he never said "Roll 'em up" until he knew by telepathy that everyone was ready. Never before in history had a group mind managed such loyal unity from a thing that by all laws of social cohesion should at any moment be blowing apart like a bomb. For twenty years they've been together, for twenty years the fuse is always lit.

Two o'clock and everyone had had enough. It was silent the first half hour of running in while everyone cleaned up the back decks. But inevitably the entertainment resumed. The gang had their own private radio channel, channel 7 on the mickey. Other boats didn't use the channel unless they wanted to listen a lot or try to discern the whereabouts or fish conditions of the gang. The latter was impossible because, except for days like this, there's no way the gang lets slip a clue to their goings on.

Besides, with the gang, whether fishing's good or bad is pretty much irrelevant. Life revolves around the higher things, and for much of the ride in the Governor was trying to figure out whose fault it was that the deer wasn't taken out of the freezer to thaw for tonight's dinner. By the time they got to the dock, Mario and Vaughn were ready to go up on the bluffs and bag another one just to get his blood pressure down. I pulled up to unload, then secured the boat on one of the moorings the gang laid every springtime in the anchorage; Candy picked me up in the skiff and rowed me to the dock.

Before I even made my way through the fishhouse, the din from the old shack-ala behind it was deafening. I opened the door and walked in just as Mario raised a tray of ice cubes over his head and slammed it on the table, sending ice flying everywhere. No one would have said anything because Mario never runs water over the tray, but this time one of the cubes went flying into the Governor's soup. The Governor is number one cook in the gang; there are few chefs in all of San Francisco to compare. His lusty gastronomic specialties are matched only by the heat of his temperament. More than one meal has been untimely ripped from the stove, rushed out the door, across the dock, and dumped over the rail because someone had breathed too close. "For Christ sakes, Mario, you ruined my soup," the Governor's hands gesturing in front of him and his voice carrying the burden of artistic despair. "You don't even have to get near it and you ruin it. Can't you ever learn to do things right?" His face was red and excited.

Vaughn was quickly prompted to make a big exaggerated reach for the first aid box to pull out a Kotex. "Ah, Governor, it must be the wrong time of the month."

Mario saw me; "Maria!" he screamed and gave me a big hug.

"The lost sheep," laughed Pabst. "Come on, Mario, get the kid a drink," and Mario poured me one all over the table.

"Hey, brother, we gonna play this game or not," said brother Scheff.

Mario picked up his cards, looked through the hand, yelling, "You know, boys, Joe Ricci's getting out of line again. I think he's going to have a little trouble with his crab boats this season."

The Governor was yelling at Candy for the second time to dice the onion into smaller pieces. "Hey, Governor," answered the youngest, mild mannered member of the gang, "how about if I run over these things with the truck, would that make you happy?" Three people at once were asking me about my season, and that ignited Mario to rise up out of his seat.

"Did we," louder, "did we," louder, "did we ever tell you about the last time we were ever in Fort Bragg and Candy and Vaughn disgraced the gang when—Rummy!" And he slammed his hand on the table.

"No, no, no, no," said Pabst, the seventy-two-year-old, healthy looking, intellectual and philosopher of the gang who watched over the card games. You would never believe it could happen; six conversations at once layered and enmeshed with the others, crossfiring, misfiring, spit firing, and never is a thread left to dangle but someone doesn't pick it up and hang themselves. It's not only possible, it's unstoppable. There are only seven people in the world God hot-wired on 440 volts, and He must have put them all together like this to ensure He wouldn't get bored with the human race.

Carlos, number seven member of the gang, was barging in the door with four big abalone in his arms he'd gathered from the cliffs on the low tide. "That's all you got?" screamed Mario in amazement.

"Sure," said Carlos, "this is over a thousand dollars' worth of fines right here . . ."

Point Reyes had just been declared a national park, to the complete and utter puzzlement of the gang. What was even more to their amusement was the new law saying that no wildlife could be taken from the park. "What are we supposed to do," said the Governor, "eat out of a can? For Christ's sake, the whole ecology of this place would break down in no time."

Way before he was through, Scheff was yelling, "After all these years, we're not going to start worrying now about the game wardens."

"Yeah," said Vaughn, "we'll get Sam to defend us like the time he had the judge in tears because of his blind sister and all the fish he was donating to St. Anthony's Orphanage."

And all the time the table was getting spread with big bowls of steaming rock cod pasta soup, a pan of fried abalone, cut loaves of French bread, a big pan of deer basted with coffee to remove the wild taste, a big salad, milk that Candy had just picked up from the big fresh vatful on George's farm, a pan full of potatoes—every night without fail, a feast, the evening bite, sacred rite of the gang.

The gang and guests. Every night there was an open invitation to any fisherman on the anchorage who wanted to chuck it for the evening, touch land, and have a home-cooked meal. Whatever else the gang may have done in their lifetime, and from what I've seen I have to believe most of what I hear, the gang has never turned anyone away from their table. Tonight it was Sal on the *Priscilla G.*, a long-time friend of the gang. But we were just about through eating, and he still wasn't off the phone with Joe Ricci, arguing with him back and forth that he'd never put another fish over this dock if he didn't pay the same price as Bodega and the city. He hadn't noticed the low price on the ticket until his fish were already mixed with the others, and he was hot. "For Christ's sake, Sal," said Mario after listening to enough of this, "don't you know how to deal with that guy yet? Give me the phone! . . . Joe Ricci?" screamed Mario into the phone in the same volume as he'd yell from boat to boat. "Go fuck yourself!" and slammed the receiver down. "Come on, Sal, *mangia*, don't you know the leopard don't change its spots? You talk too much to them guys and they'll have you believing the sun rises from the west."

It was getting late; the first night you're always a guest; the second night and thereafter, you're part of the organization and duties, dishes, and hassles. I decided to get back to the boat early. Out of habit, I started to ask what they'd thought of the day's fishing, had they heard any dope? Everyone kind of mumbled and left the duty to Mario. "You been away too long, kid. You forget the number one rule." Number one strict rule of the gang, you leave your troubles and your fish on the boat, no comparing fish scores; stories, yes, but talk of the day's fishing, no! "It takes the flavor out of the food," and "makes for bad feeling; it makes it so you can't enjoy life."

Most of the time I ended up with the skiff behind my boat unless someone else had rowed me out. Five o'clock sharp I had to be at the dock to pick up the gang, their bait, and their gear and ferry them out to their boats. The wind was already blowing a bitter cold, nasty fog through however many layers of clothes you had on, a dirty northwester that didn't bode well for the conditions we'd find on the outside. September's supposed to be the best month of the year on the North Pacific. A lot of times that means it's just barely fishable on days where you otherwise would have stayed in.

I don't think the gang knows that for most seventy-two-year-old men even one day being pounded by this kind of freezing slop would be the last day of their life. As far as everyone of this gang is concerned, they're living the life of luxury. The morning bite starts when they get there, the evening bite's around the big wooden table with friends. And for the long hours in between they figure they've found a way to transcend the pain.

The radios are switched on before the engines are started. I just dropped Mario off on his boat, and already I see him checking the oil with one hand and keying the mike with the other. "Hey, Sal," he yells, "Joe Ricci called last night after you left. He says tell Sal I sure hate to lose a good producing boat. He says to bring him another load, and he'll fix you up with a steak and a bottle of wine. That way, Sal, when you look at the tag and see it cost you $300, you'll really make sure you chew every bite."

"Yeah, Mario," says Sal, "I sure hope you never change your spots. There's an eight-foot sea out here, and you could choke on this fog, and somehow you got me to laugh."

I never once heard the gang discuss water temperature, current patterns, fish conditions, let alone get in an argument about which way to go for the day. It was uncanny. Seven boats got to the buoy on the outside of the anchorage, and seven boats all turned the same way. They didn't miss very often, and the best boats on the coast would be hard put to beat them in their own backyard.

The gang, with all their scams, feats of organization, and wit, has kept me on the edge of astonishment since the first day I met them. But there was one day that topped it all. It was three thirty and everyone without doubt had close to two thousand dollars' worth of fish on their decks for the day. The fish were beginning to show signs of a good evening show. In all likelihood we would come close to doubling the take before the day was done. The jackpot was spilling into our laps, that one day in hundreds that is suddenly born right out of the stuff of your dreams. Even channel 7 was silenced for many hours by the bounty of it all.

Three thirty and Mario got on the air and said, "Roll 'em up, boys."

He's out of his mind, I thought. It'll take us the whole month of September to make what we're going to make in the next three hours, if we're lucky, and he says, "Roll 'em up, boys." I just can't do it, so what if I eat at their table; if you've got to be a dumb idiot, stupid to qualify, forget it.

I'd just worked my main line and was replacing all the baits on the hooks as fast as I could. I was about to throw the first one over when I gritted my teeth, closed my eyes, and put the lead in the holder. In the process of putting the gear on the boat, I'd picked up eleven fish. I was nauseous as we drove away. At cocktail hour, no one even made reference to what had happened. The closest they got was when Mario turned to me a little puzzled. "What's the matter, kid, you don't look like you feel too hot." I couldn't even answer, it took all the energy I had to hold back the tears.

I'd bet every cent I've ever made that no other fisherman on the whole United States coast has ever voluntarily made that move. The gang, above all, trusted the ocean to feed them; they trusted the heart of its depth no matter how irregular its beat. For their part of the deal they were more than happy to daily toast its gift with dinner and laughter and friends. That's why the gang passed me up those years ago when I tried to win their friendship with fish, and that's why they left these fish today. Celebrating the sea and their life came first.

To be sure, I wasn't singing the praises of this philosophy this night. In fact, I went back to the boat early to pout. But later, whenever the frustrations of fishing got beyond tolerance, that alternative was always there in the back of my mind like a pressure relief valve. I could pack up my gear, turn my back on the fish, and leave.

There was something else the gang taught me that would put a lot of money in my pocket in the years to come.

The Farallon Islands is a lonely chain of three rock islands about twenty-three miles southwest of San Francisco and eighteen miles south of the point. It's the heartland of the gang's territory and over the years has probably produced 50 percent of the gang's fish. The Governor, in particular, harbors a special fondness for his memories of the nights they spent anchored in its lee.

"I used to get up in the morning out there," he says, "and I was more tired than when I went to bed. All the beautiful islands down in southern California and they made us a pile of junk up here. We've got a rotten rock that should have stayed under the water and we'd all be a lot better off. Those rocks are out there for no other reason than the misery of the fishermen. That rock is bad enough but somebody had to put a foghorn on top, and you gotta listen to that and five hundred sea lions singing through the night. Anchorage? The waves coming down the islands curl around either side and meet under the boat. I've spent more miserable nights out there, for two cents I would have thrown my boots overboard and quit fishing. And when the wind turns and comes from the south, you've got big trouble as well as the misery. You have to get up in the middle of the night and leave."

"But, Governor, what about all the fish out there?"

"Ah, Maria, the fish too, they cost us a lot more than they were worth."

There's about fifty boats on the coast that have the knowledge and the nerve to fish the Farallons. Not on the outside an eighth of a mile out and beyond, anybody could work there, but on the inside where the irregular jagged rocks are swirled by the currents coming up over the continental shelf behind and meeting with the tidal waves coming from San Francisco Bay, and where the fish liked to lay in wait for the bait. No one in the gang had loran or radar, but they never gave it a second thought if they figured they could pull a couple of extra fish from the rock, even if it was thick fog and you couldn't see the hand in front of your face. One foggy day we were in so close to the edge of the North Island that I could hear the swells exploding on the rocks. I didn't worry, though. I'd followed the gang on some very hairy tacks in and around the islands, dragging the gear between slots that would make you believe the camel could fit through the eye of the needle. "Don't give it a thought," said Mario, "your old dad's been plowing this field since before you were born." I only had to work the gear, keep an eye on the Governor's stern, and try to remember the courses and timing in case someday I was crazy enough to try this on my own.

The guys just outside of us were crying the blues, and we were making a day of it. The fog lifted around eleven o'clock. I looked around at the gang and saw it wasn't just these few fish that had been keeping them off the radio. Every one of them was grappling with major damage, whose pole was broken in half with wire and stays tangled all over the boat, whose big steel davit was bent to the deck, whose mast was cracked. I was the only one whose boat came out of there like it went in.

Running back to the dock, the gang was in prime form. Mario began by comparing themselves to the big naval disaster that took place at Point Arguello when seven destroyers followed the fleet captain onto the rocks and every ship was lost.

The ocean just couldn't bring them down! It's a good thing I met this gang. They gave me more than they'll ever know.

9

Frenzy

EVERY YEAR AROUND the month of August a separate body of hot blue water from offshore begins pushing toward the beach. Summer begins on the Pacific coast. The screaming northwesterlies of May and June have simmered down. The massive, cold upwellings of water from the deep ocean canyons no longer have the strength to keep the rivers and swirls of hot water from penetrating the coast. One morning you reach the salmon grounds and instead of the murky green water of yesterday, you stare into a soothing emerald blue ocean, the same color blue that lures from dreamy postcards of the South Pacific.

The color is only a clue to a much vaster change that has taken place. One climate has literally replaced another, as if you went to sleep on a snow-peaked mountain and awoke in the meadows below; a whole new breed of plants and animals has arrived. With them is the golden promise of albacore, the high-grade, high-priced, long-finned tuna that annually migrates in these sixty- to seventy-degree waters and blinds the fishermen with its glow.

Salmon don't like the hot water; they leave, they go out in the deep, or to the bottom, or out the canyons, or off the bite, or who really knows where they go. Many of us would give an ice hold full of fish for the answer. But one thing is unmistakable, the catch of salmon isn't what it used to be, sometimes shutting off like a faucet, and sometimes worse, trickling out to just a slow death. Insult is added to injury, and the newly arrived blue shark begin attacking and tangling the gear. Increasingly huge swarms of jellyfish severely sting the enthusiasm of even the most devoted salmon fishermen. But nowhere is the change more dramatic than on the radios, as the fishermen begin relentlessly, mischievously, and mercilessly baiting each other for a run to the albacore.

Sometimes as early as June, they begin keeping serious contact with the boats that are two to three hundred miles offshore, a thousand miles up and down the coast, passing news through so many radios and interpreters that oftentimes, if it weren't for the boat names, you could barely recognize the same story on the second go-around. Soon the speculations take hours from every day as friends talk each other up and down, trying to arrive at the optimum time and place to make the "switch."

Jack says the recent satellite photo shows a warm water edge sixty miles off the Columbia. Rick says he talked to Dan last night, who is up there, who says he didn't hit sixty-degree water until he was 120 miles out, and Jerry says he never saw a satellite catch an albacore yet. Jack reminds everyone how long the fish held in that area last year. Rich reminds everyone that ten years ago when the weather pattern was similar to this year's, the run off the Columbia fizzled in one week. Jerry has just got a hunch. He thinks it is too early and he wants to make another salmon trip. Tune into their conversation that afternoon and Jerry has just talked to an old buddy off Morro Bay and the latest scoop is 150-fish score, so let's go. But Jack has since caught five hundred dollars' worth of salmon and wants to hold off, and Rich thinks it's gonna "blow." Sometimes you just wish the wind would blow, and blow so hard that there wouldn't be a radio antenna left on the masts!

Nonetheless, every nuance is crucial in this business of extracting a livelihood from the elusive movements of the albacore. A wrong move at this point could easily cost a fisherman twenty to thirty thousand dollars. What if the gang went to Morro Bay and the fish died when they got there? They argue for a few hours; did the fish move or did they go off the bite? They decide to hang around for a couple of days to check it out, when word comes that the fish began snapping like wild dogs off the Washington coast. The pressure gets too great; they run one thousand miles north, arrive for the tail end of the bite, and their friend from Morro Bay calls and says you left too soon. It happens all the time and it's called "too bad!"

Nor do I want to leave you the impression that all this brain-storming involves hard-nosed technicalities alone. Amidst consideration of sea temperatures and fish scores, you hear a weighty tribute to the fact that Morro Bay is just about the right distance from the old lady. For some, Bandon, Oregon's annual cranberry festival can counteract any fish score to the south. And, believe it or not, one of the strongest magnets on the coast is the Playland and Boardwalk of Santa Cruz, located conveniently within rowing distance of the anchorage.

The inroads of warm water are weak at first, advancing and retreating as fluidly as the fishermen's indecisions. Many of the larger boats who can tough the unsettled weather take the early gamble and shoot three, four hundred miles offshore in search of a jackpot uncluttered by a large fleet. But the smaller boats, who depend primarily on salmon, tend to beat the dead horse to a pulp before yielding to the switch. Finally, the combination of radio, fish, the boredom, the sharks, the jellyfish, some good weather, and all of the small boat agonies of the albacore fishery are erased from the mind. There is only the vision of albacore as the paradise of the fisheries; and truly in its moments, it is.

The farther out you go, the more it feels like you have slipped the boundaries of a weight more powerful than gravity. It's a strangely hypnotizing forever, heading farther and farther west, pulled through the blue, unchanging space by an imagined vision of fish, circled by a constant, unreachable horizon. And at night, drifting in the winds and the waves, there isn't even the tug of the anchor to remind you of the firmness of earth. The freedom from even the reminders of land is euphoric.

The fishing itself is elegant and simple. Unlike the complexity and constant attention required by salmon gear, albacore requires just eleven lines trailing behind the boat with feather jigs bouncing along the surface as you run nearly full speed around the wide open ocean. There is no baiting, no running lines, no cleaning fish. In fact, as memory always recalls it, there is no work at all until the fish jump on the gear. You put the boat into a circle, and it is just the primal thrill of pulling fish arm over arm into the boat as the infinite blue horizon sweeps past your eyes. That's the moment that sears the memory, that rages through the fleet like a fever.

There wasn't a year since I began fishing that I'd been able to resist the suction. The radio would start jumping with people's plans to run into port, blow ice, take fuel, strip the salmon gear, tie on the jigs, and leave at midnight for the tuna that were reported only sixty miles off the beach. The next thing I knew, I'd be coming out of a delirious frenzy of activity to find myself standing on the stern, staring at the silky, blue water boiling in the wake, waiting for that sound of the line when it suddenly pulls tight with the weight of a long-finned tuna that magically pops into view on the surface where before there was only blue.

This year was going to be different. I set my mind like an anchor in the rocks—*no more albacore!* I knew the pattern all too well. No matter how far out you go, the albacore are always just another 20 miles out. What are you going to do? Run eight hours back into

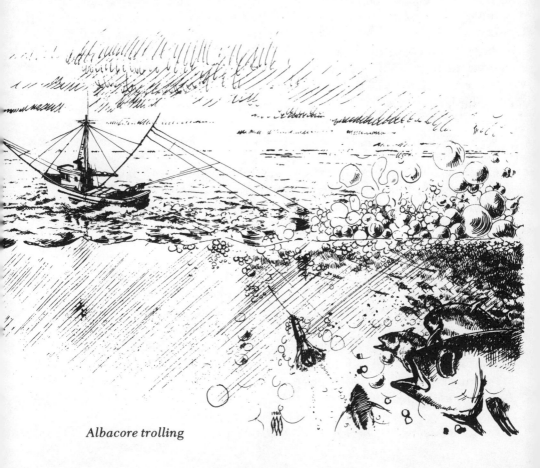

Albacore trolling

port, tear off the jigs and put back the salmon gear? Or run two more hours to get the albacore? And so it goes, as long as the weather's good, until the weather gets bad. And now you're what, 100, 125, 150 miles offshore? Who knows? The Fathometer doesn't reach bottom out here, the loran even if I had one doesn't give an in and out reading, and the drift alone has taken you anywhere within 100 miles of yourself. And here come da wind!

A lot of times you don't dare try the run for the beach; a four-teen-hour ride broadside to an angry sea is asking for it. So you head the bow into the crashing seas, slow the engine, and jog in place. And there you are, baby, a helpless molecule to anything the ocean will brew, days and nights of terror, every wave a battle-field, an infinite train of them, and not one can afford to be lost, marking time with cups of coffee and radio calls of fishermen whose windows are blown out, sprung planks, water over the engine, searing, feverish call to a friend to "please take care of my family," because he knows that no one can move to help, and radio calls to a friend, carving out time with an answer that never comes. Commercial fishing, according to the Department of Labor, is more dangerous than the most dangerous job on the industrial index, and albacore is one of the reasons: albacore, the paradise of the fisheries! With a twenty-six-foot boat, I knew it was only a matter of time.

This year as I fished a slow scratch of salmon in the Fort Bragg area, Mario's words came frequently and easily to mind, "He who lives pays the bills."

It didn't phase me a bit when the albacore scores came rolling in like a bull market ticker tape. Three hundred fish a day in the Gorda Sea Valley. I certainly wasn't dumb enough to be caught in that treacherous stretch of waters. Two hundred fish days fifty miles straight out of Fort Bragg. Christ, if the wind comes up out there, you're forced to slide all the way to Bodega before turning into port. Then the fish were being reported only twenty miles off the beach. Well, learned as I was, I knew what that meant. Twenty miles by the radio, at least forty miles by boat. For long periods of time I even shut the radios off to reduce the temptation to chase the elusive dream.

When I pulled into Fort Bragg to unload from the trip, my heart dropped into the bilge. Little sport skiffs were lined up under the hoist with albacore tails sticking out of every corner of the boats, their catch of the day! Refrigerated semis were lined up six deep behind every buying station. The thirty- and forty-foot boats all had deck loads that meant the ice holds were already plugged and they couldn't stop themselves. I could see the intoxication of big money in the broad smiles and bouncing walks of everyone. I couldn't swallow my tears. When people started yelling, "Hey, Marie, what the hell are you doing with the salmon gear on?" I knew I had to get out of there fast, somehow, but the unloading list was two days long. On the dock, conveyors of albacore were noisily filling one truck after another. Temporary crews had been spelling each other for the last three days and nights. It was fat city; I smelled money everywhere. I walked into Rick's office and there was a casual poker game among a few of the fishermen. I counted over fifteen hundred on the top of the pile. Rick and his bookkeeper were in a frenzy of fatigue and adrenalin and probably a few other chemicals. Tally sheets, Fish and Game books, checks were getting shuffled from one desk to another, with half of this shit falling on the floor unnoticed. Rick had one phone to his ear and the other was ringing.

Somebody ran up to the door yelling, "Hey, Rick, number two truck is loaded; where is the damn bill of lading?" He took off without waiting for any answer.

And another yellow slicker came yelling, "Hey, Rick, that guy Jeff we hired for the night crew quit in the middle of unloading a boat. Don't give him his last check because he took off with over five hundred pounds of albacore in his pickup truck."

I grabbed Rick by the arm and took my chances anyway. "Hey, Rick, I got a thousand pounds of salmon aboard and . . ."

"Salmon?" He looked at me like what's that and who are you?

"No, Rick, I'm the Avon lady." At least he laughed. "Christ, Rick, I've got to get them off my boat. My ice has melted. Mainly, Rick, I blew it. I need to get out there." I'll never forget him for cutting me in. I unloaded, went to the fuel dock, switched my gear, and split. Forget about groceries, I could eat canned goods and albacore for a few days. Forget about the weather, forget about a running partner, or rest.

I cried all the way out the jetty and past the red buoy, I was still crying at the black buoy, and for the next two hours I cried. When you try so hard to do the right thing, how the hell can it turn out so wrong?

The combination of blue water, wide open space, and complete exhaustion was finally relaxing. I threw the jigs, straightened up the boat, and put on a pot of tea. The fish started coming right away, but I'd go to the back deck and pull them mechanically, as if I resented their presence. My head was still at the dock. It wasn't until sundown that I snapped into place. I looked around my back deck and realized that since four o'clock I had picked fifty-six fish, more than I had ever caught before in that amount of time. The piles of shiny, fresh albacore in the sunset light, the beauty of the sunset colors shimmering in the water, and the promise of tomorrow completely turned the tide inside of me.

Darkness set in, but I didn't feel tired and decided to run up the line another thirty miles where it sounded like there were better scores. The next morning I pulled twenty fish right off the bat, as if they had been waiting there under the boat for me to get up. But the boats thirty miles up and out on the Gorda Sea Valley were already reporting over one hundred fish scores. It didn't require a decision. The power of greed set my course. Along the way I managed to get another thirty fish, in between bouts in the ice hold and a healthy breakfast of Coca-Cola and Twinkies.

I could see the fleet on the horizon when every line on the boat pulled tight with fish. What a rush! I put the boat in a circle and hardly touched the wheel for the next three hours. I was all by myself in a fisherman's dream, pulling fish after fish after fish, as if they were being propagated by an infinite wellspring below that fed right into my lap. It was all magic and transcendence; I no longer thought about bills, fuel, people, docks, or tomorrow. I even stopped counting the fish. It was just the moments of fish splashing on the water and pulling them arm over arm into the boat. The light blue wake of my boat circled a world more perfect than I had ever imagined. Each time around I was drawn deeper into its vortex.

The fisherman, while at sea, becomes one of its creatures, as subject to its moods and cycles as the fish he pursues. When the fish and the bait, the currents and temperatures, the moon and tides, and all the unknowns come together, the ocean breeds feeding frenzies like the land has never known. The fish start biting and snapping at anything. Big balls of bait boil on the surface for miles, and the birds dive voraciously into them. The sharks slash through it all like living machetes in a field of ripe wheat. The sight of the lines going down as fast as you can pull them and going down again before you completely get them back on the water and the fish hitting the decks and kicking their way out of the overflowing bins and more fish flying on the water, more than you could ever pull, and the feel on your shoulders gliding over the aches and the pains: all this locks the fisherman as securely into the frenzy as the creatures around him.

If you have wondered about the sanity of people who choose to beat against the ocean for a living and to tempt its fate, or if you wonder about the equilibrium of someone who spends nights upside-down in the engine room just to race the morning sun to the fish, you must keep this vision of the frenzy in mind. It is the vision that occupies the base of every fisherman's mind.

The circle died as mysteriously as it began. The birds and fish had disappeared, and I was left circling with jig lines hanging loosely in the breeze and a back deck that looked like a banquet room after a drunken bash. I didn't know how many albacore were there, but it was well over a hundred. Nothing spectacular to a seasoned fisherman, but a bonanza for me. There was no more room in the hold, so I began stacking the fish in the side bins, hosing them down and blanketing them with wet gunnysacks. I took off for the fleet, my mind still buzzing from the excitement and wanting more, more, more. The fish kept coming until sunset. The evening was soft and warm in the last light, and the boats spaced themselves closely in the gentle breeze. I sensed a rare contentment and satisfaction as playful good nights bounced around the fleet over the radios: "Good night, Mark; good night, Jack; good night, fish; good night, fish buyers; good night, Production Credit." I wonder if I'd get tired of this if it happened every day?

Naturally it's a pointless question out here on the misnamed Pacific. Around one o'clock the wind came up as quickly as if someone had let it out of a jar. When I felt the deep, sharp lurches of the boat and saw the sea of mast lights waving in the blackness, I knew immediately I was going home. I called Mike with whom I had been working and told him I was leaving. Didn't he want to come along and we could stick together for mutual protection? Mike's boat was fifty feet long. Probably mostly out of concern for me, he decided to come along. I was pretty spooked, the waves were invisible in the black. Normally I could judge the sea at night by the motion of my boat, but I had never carried two tons of fish and a full load of ice before, and it was sickeningly slow coming out of a roll. Actually, making things completely secure in this situation is a very simple matter. All you have to do is throw the fish overboard. If you think conflict of interest has something to do with politics, think of the poor soul who at the end of a long, successful trip is running in with a big sea. And the sea gets bigger. And the boat takes longer and longer to come out of a roll. How do you figure the odds? When do you go to the stern and rob the fish from the belly of your own boat and throw them back into the sea? How do you reach in your rib cage and pull your heart out? Or consider Vince on the *Lanida* who waited too long. He was still throwing fish over the side when the boat went down and took him with it. I didn't feel this was my predicament at all, but the conditions sure gave me a feel for what an impossible decision this was for a human.

I was busy and intent trying to hold the boat on course, weaving in and out of the fleet in the big fishtailing seas that were trying to climb aboard my back deck because the stern was too weighed down to do that quick, cork-bobbing lift that makes the little Monterey such a classy sea boat. It was all a familiar feel, the tension and concentration, but the seasickness was brand new. I had seen a few people go through it; I knew it was horrible. But after four years at sea without one trip to the rail, I also knew I was immune. I don't remember which came first, the waves of nausea or the first waves of rotten, sour albacore smell from the bilge, the most gut-renching smell in the world. It seemed impossible that this could be happening with fish that weren't even two days old. When I cleared the fleet, I checked the ice hold and bins, but there was only the sweet smell of fresh fish. As soon as I reentered the cabin though, it reeked. The deck heaved over a passing wave and I followed, for the rest of the night. Yesterday I had been captain of a dream, tonight I was a slave to the rail. The ups and downs of this business are humbling to say the least.

As many have noted before, the cure was instant when the boat held still in the harbor at Fort Bragg. Lines secured to the dock, I went below to cut the engine, and there lay the culprit stretched out on the floorboards next to the hot block of the engine, like a pig roasting at a luau. In the mayhem of the day before an albacore had kicked off the top of the pile and slid into the engine room and made like a tear gas cannister for the rest of the night.

The dock was jumping at the same feverish pace as when I left it. But now I was riding the train instead of trying to walk through its full head of steam. I doubt if the Gold Rush days could top the action of a fleet hot off a bonanza catch for the simple reason that in fishing most everyone hits the main vein at the same time. And everyone wants to buy the house a round on the same night, and everyone at once is swollen with the bravado and ego that always gets substituted for gratitude at good luck, and everyone has a story that tops the story that went before. And round and round the bars and barbecues until the centrifical force seems to lift the little town right off the earthly map. And the next morning at breakfast the fisherman realizes that he spent all his cash and he's flat broke and all he's got for the day's upcoming performance is a fifteen-thousand-dollar check that he put in his back pocket, or was it his jacket pocket, or, oh shit, where'd he put that damn thing now? And like the thirties, there is a massive run on the local banks; a fleet of tattered tee shirts, jeans, and fish boots moves up to the teller's windows and lays the clean, fat checks in front of her, and she asks for I.D., and all he has is an unshaven beard and black, borax-proof lines in the deep ridges of his hands, and she accepts and cashes the checks and fuels the fire that throbs the heart of this quiet little fishing town in the hills of Mendocino County.

But there is more than the drinking and the flight testing of expensive new lids of grass and the earthy, heavenly barbecues and wild dancing and chips falling like the albacore that overflow from the bins. Because for one more year you yourself beat the odds on the ocean. And once again you held back the predatory creditor who looks at you like an alien from outer space when you have to tell him month after month that the wind blew for twenty-three days or the warm water hasn't moved in yet. And then you blow his mind with a fifty-knot full force ten and hand him a check for the boat payment—paid in full!

10

Nets on Top of Nets

THREE MONTHS BEFORE the opening of my second herring season, I arrived in Sausalito with a little time on my hands and the jingle of change in my jeans. I'd always wanted to take pictures of other fishing methods aside from the ones I knew, and now was my chance. Someone suggested I ask Vic, a local lampara net fisherman who made day trips to Bolinas to fish for live bait. "You'll like lampara, Marie, it's the fastest, most skilled, and exciting fishery there is."

I talked to Vic briefly and he said, "Sure, why not tomorrow?"

When I got to the boat, Vic and one of his crew were sewing last minute repairs in the beautiful purple webbing stacked high in a pile on the stern. Their hands worked fast and precisely, while the two of them joked and jived over some crazy story, and Vic burst into a big, open laugh like a kid who didn't have a worry in the world.

I threw my stuff on the bridge. They finished their work; Vic made a quick scanning check around the deck and flew up the ladder to the bridge as if his heavy, muscular frame was just a feather to some raw driving power from inside. Already, I felt something shifting so precariously far off balance that it might never be able to come back the same if I didn't act now. It was too late; Jerry had cast the lines from the dock and we were headed out to sea.

By the time we reached the ocean swell at the Gate, all Vic had to do was turn from the wheel to talk to me and I'd sink deep into his soft sea blue eyes; his playful smile rolled over me like a hot, giant wave that tumbled me over and over whichever way it wanted, pushed from behind by some sea of raw energy that pulsed from every move he made. Raw, hot, soft, fiery, beautiful man.

A lone pelican was circling overhead without the slightest flap of its broad, three-foot wing span. Vic's stare was locked to the bird as intently as the bird's was locked in the sea. It pulled in its wings for a dive. Before the bird hit the water, Vic had the boat pointed on the spot. "Hit the deck!" he hollered, so loud the fish could hear. He looked back to the crew scrambling to their positions around the net, then back to the bird, then back to the crew. "Let her go!" The net whipped off the stern, he circled, picked up the first end of the net, pull, pull, pulling the huge net back to the boat, fast, yelling, pulling, watching, turning, in timing as perfect as a powerful, primitive dance.

In minutes they were scooping into millions of silver anchovies that flashed and flipped in the bag of the net that lay open at the side of the boat. Brimming brailfuls of water and fish onto the boat, into the eight-foot-deep tanks on the deck, where the fish again began to circle instinctively in the perfect galaxy pattern they have in the sea.

Before the crew finished restacking the net, Vic flew up the ladder to the bridge, stopped in front of me, looking right into my eyes, the ocean dripping from his hair, his eyes dancing like sunlight on the water, and a mischievous, proud smile bursting out of his whole being like "Well, what do you think of that?" and he turned back to the wheel. Well, I thought, you sure changed my life in a hurry!

Two days later I saw Freckles painting on the stern of his boat. I stood behind him and spoke a little uncertainly. "Freckles," I said, "I met someone the other day like no one I've ever met before."

Freckles didn't seem too impressed, and without even turning around he asked, "Oh, yeah? Who did you meet?"

"Do you know Vic who fishes lampara from Sausalito?"

His paintbrush stopped right in its tracks; he turned around, his eyes wide with surprised delight. "Jesus, Maria, you got yourself a whale."

I had indeed got myself a whale, instinctive, raw, playful soul from the sea. For the next two months our boats stayed tied to the dock while we dipped in a different sea. December had the nerve to jump on us like a tarantula, and along with it came my November bank statement. If I wanted to keep my boat, I had to keep fishing; and if I wanted to keep fishing, I had to take care of the boat; and in order to take care of the boat, I at least had to go down to the dock. It was that complicated!

The scene at the dock didn't help my motivation a bit. One look at all the net work strewn in every direction and in a flash I relived every tangle and trouble of the previous year. It's very likely I would have made a quick U-turn, but one thing prompted me on.

This year the gill netters would fish before the lampara boats. That meant Vic and his deckhand, Jerry, could crew for me, and I could crew for Vic. Herring season might even be fun. I knew for them it was a big laugh; they were used to putting upwards of twenty tons of herring on the boat in less than an hour, so this was like "Hey, what a kick, a chance to slide on back to the Stone Age and see how the primitives work."

We arrived off the waterfront restaurants of Sausalito on an evening that was so breathlessly still and calm, we could hear the conversations of sunset strollers on the walkway. It seemed as strange as it had the year before to be fishing only yards from the hustle and bustle of downtown, with a cement shoreline, and traffic, and crowds gathering with cameras and binoculars and telescopes. The two worlds were so close to their opposites, it seemed like any minute a spark might jump from one to the other, short out the works, and permanently blow the fuse. No doubt this herring fishery could supply the amps.

Last year there were twenty-five gill netters; this year there were one hundred. Last year the gill net quota was divided among the boats equally; this year the quota was overall, dog eat dog style, and the effect was evident before even one little herring had been caught. The season officially opened at sunset, but before the last light of day, the area was already so crosshatched with so many nets, you could walk on water in any direction just by stepping on the buoys at either end. There wasn't that much fish showing, but nobody wanted to let even a second slip past their nets. Just maybe it would be all right. Fish and Game had seen the light on the anchor situation and changed the law. This year we could anchor the nets at either end. It should make all the difference in the world.

I'd hoped that by the time we had finished setting the nets, the crew would have wrung the last bit of humor out their endless stream of gill net jokes; Vic poking Jerry while the net was flying off the stern, "Now, I remember, I saw them do this on the "Flintstones" when Fred broke his club."

And Jerry poking Vic, "I sure hope that don't mean we get paid in pebbles."

They'd had their fun and now they were bored. Now that the nets were set, we should be watching the gear, the tides, and listening in case fish suddenly showed up in another area. But it wasn't to be. Didn't I think that it would be a good idea if we let the nets soak for a while, go back to the dock and down to the Sausalito Food Company, that way we could get soaked ourselves and harmonize with the nets? "Aye, aye," said the captain to the crew.

Three hours later, I was somehow able to drag them from the watering trough back to the dock and make it back to the nets in time for slack water. Pulling the first fathom of net onto the boat took the full strength of all three of us, the fish were that thick. There was a herring hanging out of every mesh, a face in every window, the universal cure for whatever ails you. There had to be at least four tons in this net alone. With all the fooling around and monkey business, this is the last thing any of us was prepared for.

It had been a couple of handfuls of years since Vic shook a gill net, and it was Jerry's first time. This eighteen-year-old, cocky, spirited kid had a real uncertain look on his face as he tried to follow our example, stretching the net between us, lifting the heavy sides, shake down hard, lift again, shake again, unroll the web from the lead line, heave, pull more net onto the boat, lift, shake, lift, shake, pull. "Come on, Jerry, faster."

"Uh, oh," said Jerry, as he grabbed a moment to look out to the other end of net sixty-five fathoms away. "I think I got the picture."

"You got it, chump," said Vic.

And they were off again, Jerry answering, "Hey, chump, who's the real chump, the one that knew about this ahead of time, or the one who trusted his good friend when he said he was taking him for some fun?" Just then a fish whipped out of the net and smacked Jerry in the face so hard that he grabbed his hands to his face.

Said Vic, "There's your answer, chump." I tilted my head back to gaze in the heavens for guidance.

We shook the fish from fathom after fathom of web for an hour and a half until our clothes were soggy cold even under the wet gear, and our hands were all cut by the thin monofilament webbing, and the silver fish gorged the full length of the boat up to our knees, and our faces were dripping with scales, eggs, and slime. We were a beautiful sight to see. Vic and I reached across the net and kissed the wettest, slipperiest, most fertilized kiss since the sea lions' mating last fall.

We had two more nets to go, but the boat was already loaded beyond capacity. Unfortunately, I was obligated to a buyer all the way over in San Francisco; this meant a forty-five-minute run across the rough waters in front of the Golden Gate with a stern-rail that was only inches above the waterline. Don't think there wasn't a long, soul-searching discussion about delivering to Sausalito, the gist of which was "Fuck Vito, he's probably home dreaming up ways to screw the fishermen."

I was tempted, believe me. I figured our earnings were coming out to about five hundred dollars an hour, and I knew the quota was disappearing faster than a hunk of raw meat in a cage of hungry cats. The competitive pressure of this system was incredible, and I could sense every boat peaking to the frenzy. The thought of dumping two hours just to keep my word with a fish buyer was actually a little nauseating. But my ethics prevailed.

We got all the way over to the city, and the door of the fishhouse was locked. Vito was home, tucked away, sound asleep, when his telephone started to ring off the hook and some female maniac on the other end started screaming into his ear, cursing him up and down, telling him he'd better get to the dock in an awful big hurry, or Rome was gonna fall. He dresses like a madman and burns up the pavement on his way to Fishermen's Wharf. Herring money, he's thinking. How many boats have I missed already, herring money; oh, God, what are you up there for if not to warn me when the fish are going to hit. I was pacing the dock, adrenalin and numbers pounding through my brain, thinking about the nets back there, imagining them all tangled up in somebody else's prop, pacing and calculating the money that could be lost.

Finally, the buyer arrived with his shirt buttoned wrong and his hair sticking out in every direction. I was just about to forgive him when he informed me that the fish pump that was supposed to be there for unloading the boats hadn't yet arrived. "Hey," I said, staring at him in disbelief, "you wouldn't put me on about a thing like that at a time like this?'' I was about to say some things that I could easily regret when I was distracted by the thought that walking down to the boat with three shovels in my hands and seeing the expressions on those guys' faces the moment they figured out why I was walking down to the boat with three shovels in my hands—that moment would be worth it all.

Four tons of fish and three shovels meant we'd better get shoveling and stop for nothing till it's done. With the three of us grinding in fifth gear, those fish were off the boat in just one hour, and with them my entire sense of obligation.

The trip back was the hard part. As soon as you stop working like a machine, you start feeling like a human being, shivering in the wet clothes, fingers throbbing all the way up to your armpits; a cup of hot chocolate in my stomach and the hour of the night sent waves of fatigue sloshing through the cotton fibers of my brain.

When we got back to the nets, I had to look real hard into the cold, black waters for that insane something to give me the guts to start pulling the anchor chain with a grip that squashes open every wound and stretches every sore muscle. The tide was roaring past the boats but, given the quota system, that wasn't stopping anyone.

So pull, pull, pull the net onto the boat out of the grip of the tide. Lift the lead line over your head, shake down fast and lift again; fast, so the fish are always flying in the deck light like silver money snow falling at your feet. A wall of pain in my back, my neck, my chest, legs, and worst of all the hands. And I couldn't have been happier. Everything I ever wanted was on this boat: true love, a twist of moonlight, and so much fish you'd think it could never end.

It was a very lucky night for us; we didn't have to look far into the darkness to see that. The black stage around us was dotted with dramas under the deck lights of other boats that were more pathetic than a Greek tragedy. There was no way that one hundred boats, each armed with twelve hundred feet of net and a fierce winter hunger, could stay out of each other's faces when the fish hit like this. Anchors or no anchors was only a matter of degree!

Just downtide from us were the sterns of three boats all wrapped up in each other's nets, nets that led out into the water in every direction; there were nets in the props and nets stretched dangerously tight across the stern of the boats, with knives flashing and crews jumping from one boat to the other, and one captain screaming, "Don't cut there, you idiot! That's the wrong fucking net, the one on your right." I could tell he wanted to point at it with his hand, but both arms were locked in a strained grip around the legs of his deckhand, and his deckhand was hanging full body over the stern, reaching at the nets, his knife splashing and slashing, trying as hard not to make a mistake as he was trying to make his next breath be air. Downtide from them were two other boats with their crews standing on the stern yelling angrily at the tops of their lungs, "You guys are going to drift through our gear, goddamnit, do something!" They might as well have been whispering. Somehow we managed to weave our way around every tragic act without once having to perform.

I was three times lucky that night. Without Vic and Jerry things would be very different now. A green herring crew in this situation and I'd be using half my energy issuing instructions, and with the other half I'd be saying over and over, "You're not tired, your hands aren't cut, the wind's not blowing, it's not time to eat, and we can't finish this tomorrow. And the reason is that these fish that you see don't come like this every day, believe me, and they can split any minute; a meal can cost us hundreds and sleep will cost us everything." Jerry understood this fact of life or he wouldn't have been Vic's deckhand. And Vic? Are you kidding? If I'd have gone for it, he would have picked up six more nets from the buyer while we were in the city and had them set all over Sausalito and worked them till the fish went dry.

Vic had grown up with a tough bunch of kids on the East Berkeley Flats. By the time they were seven years old, they were already a long ways along on the path to trouble. Half of those kids never veered and today they're dead, drugged, or jailed. The other five kids, including Vic, took to hanging around the Berkeley Marina where they discovered that they could scrape pile worms from the pilings and sell them to the party boat skippers. By the time they reached their teens, they had their own small boats and striped bass nets they made under the tutelage of old man Spenger; and when the striped bass weren't running they made perch traps, animal shelters as they called them, which they ran all night and had their deliveries made to Chinatown before seven o'clock the next morning. By their late teens, they also had Fish and Game records, fifty fathoms long, and jail time, and a real good chance of going one step too far. But they also had a skill and money and a chance to clean up their acts (sufficiently) and step easily across and far up the line on the path to success. All five of them saved themselves, bought bigger boats, picked a fishery of their choice, and today are among the most respected fishermen in the fleet.

This good fishing tonight certainly wasn't going to make or break Vic now. It was just that a sudden rush of fish to him was like a flash of inspiration to a mad artist who knew instinctively that if you had to think about that inspiration or weigh its value or consider your tools, you'd kill it. But if you are truly addicted to its raw energy, that's exactly what you get. Vic was truly addicted. After all, being able to match his psyche and skill to the frenzy of the fish had saved his life.

Aside from the feelings we had for each other, aside from the fun we were having, working with this crew as they skillfully, quickly responded to every shift of the night, I saw what an art this fishing could be.

The boat was full again at dawn. So many hundreds of sea gulls gave us a squawking escort back to the dock that someone had to always stand guard over the fish or they'd easily eat us out of a ton before we got there. The pulse at the dock was pounding and racing on the verge of fibrilating. The only people not in the dead heat of the activity were the seiners and lampara fishermen who were waiting for their turn to fish, drooling all over the totes of fish, watching painfully as the boats unloaded, but unable to take themselves away. When a gang of them got a view of our operation, they took all that pent-up restlessness and couldn't contain themselves. "Captain Cunt and her two grunts," said one to the other, and they laughed and laughed till the phrase had echoed across the fleet and stuck to us for months.

The last tote from the third load of fish wasn't weighed until three that afternoon. Fish and Game announced that almost the entire quota had been caught in less than twenty-four hours; the season was essentially over in a night, a blitz. I put five thousand dollars in the bank that afternoon and soaked Jerry for every last ounce of his pride as I slowly, teasingly made out his check for seven hundred dollars.

The next part is what I was really looking forward to. Lampara net fishing for herring to me is the fisherman's ultimate fix. You search and search for minutes, hours, or days, you never know

Fishing lampara for herring

when it will happen; it could be in the middle of a good meal or a midnight snooze when suddenly there's a demanding urgent holler accompanied by a foot pounding through the bridge that will flip you from the bunk if you haven't heard the words, "Hit the deck!" You have fifteen seconds to get into your wet gear and out to your position on the stern. And you'd better be there because if a school of fish slips away while you're caught in your pant leg, relationships can freeze up awful quick.

The captain, meanwhile, is glued to the Fathometer, trying to judge the motion and the shape of the school. You couldn't move his concentration with a bomb. He puts the boat in a fast circle about thirty yards wide, turns to the crew on the back and yells, "Let her go!" and he means now. The buoy attached to the end of the net is thrown overboard, and that starts a wheel of events in motion that cannot stop, come hell or high water, until the entire net and catch are back on the boat.

The first wing of the net is flying off the boat, pulled by the drag of the buoy and the boat that's speeding out from underneath it. And you'd better stand clear; if a finger or a boot gets caught in the web, you'd be flung overboard before you knew what hit you, and under these conditions it's just about good-bye. At the same time, you'd better stand close enough because if the net suddenly snags and starts ripping in half before you reach in and clear it, it ain't never the captain's fault.

Next, a five-foot-high mountain of web, the bag of the net, has to be pushed off the stern in one pile at precisely the right moment. As the last wing then flies off and fairleads are put in place, you stand ready to pick up the buoy as the circle is completed and start pulling both ends of the net over the drum back onto the boat, evenly, evenly, damn it, so the bag won't collapse, while stomping hard on the deck with your feet to scare the fish back into the bag because until the bag gets back to the boat, the fish are still swimming free. The bag reaches the stern and is immediately swung to the side and pursed. The heavy webbing has to be pulled from under the fish until they are concentrated in one spot, then scooped onto the boat at eight hundred pounds a crack with a big dip net called a brail. Finally, the rest of the net is brought aboard, and you can breathe one deep breath of relief and immediately start restacking the bag and wings perfectly so they won't foul on the next set, and fast, faster! because in this supercharged game of chance, lightning frequently hits twice in the same spot.

Throughout the set, every member of the crew has a series of specific jobs that have to be performed with the precision of a dance, the brute energy of madmen, and the flawless concentration of cool cucumbers. That's the theory of lampara; the practice deviates wildly, routinely, and inconceivably. Anything can happen, and when it does, it's fast, it's an emergency, and it's always a biggie; the winds and tides don't stand by when you stop to fix something, and within seconds of any problem you've got bigger problems, and in seconds more you can find yourself in the middle of as much chaotic activity as you'll find anywhere on earth.

The speed, the skill required, and the stakes make this game mind-altering on the human scale of things; nets and boats are lost, sets of up to one hundred thousand dollars can be made, the water always deals, and the whole game is played and decided in less than half an hour. Watching a good crew lampara fish never loses its thrill, being part of one often does.

Vic is indisputably one of the best. For the past eight years he's made his living with this net, fishing anchovies in the bay and near part of the ocean. But experience is only one of his aces. Vic and this net were obviously made for each other. He can come up with the madness most people can't muster in a lifetime and breathe it into every set of the net. His severely overdeveloped sense of mischief and daring takes this game and stretches it to its most foolhardy. But Vic would be dead many times over if it weren't for whole decks of aces that seem to fall out of the sky the moment he needs them. Luck, so much damn luck that the other fishermen have long since stopped predicting his demise and just shake their heads in amazement at the boldness this man can get away with in the sea. There are about a dozen fishermen I know who have the stars on their side to the point that time itself seems to stop in its path and give them that one extra second to save their necks, rocks seem to suck in their bellies to let them pass—fishermen who endlessly are falling into shit and come out smelling like a rose. It's always fascinated me that the one thing they all seem to have in common is the refusal to let reason or common sense in any way interfere with their fishing.

The excitement and chaos of herring fishing for Vic was like a thick layer of icing on his favorite cake. The season opened and thirty lampara boats and thirty seiners set out to fish in the same little playpen area that had been outlined for them by Fish and

Game the year before. The lampara boats had not been able to make their point heard; the lampara net is a shallow water net, it cannot very successfully work in this area which is 95 percent deep water, and when a school of fish does come to the surface, and one boat jumps on top of the other to grab a bite, the chaos and tangles that result are downright dangerous.

The solution seemed simple to Vic. Fish and Game wouldn't open the line, so somebody else had to do the job. Big deal, what's so hard about working with lights out when you've got a crewful of pirates, when Fish and Game isn't even capable of keeping the game interesting, and when your whole childhood was a lights out operation to begin with.

For a lot of days we had the whole bay to ourselves. In between intense bursts of activity on the back deck and some awesome big loads of fish, most of the time was spent on the bridge; Vic always at the wheel, eyes glued to the meter, then out to the water, back to the meter, and out to the water. No matter how bleak the signs, he was always tensed like there was twenty-ton set fifty feet ahead of the boat, which he never allowed to get in the way of his role as chief shit disturber among the crew and on the radio all at the same time. The rest of the crew sat in ever shifting uncomfortable positions behind him, waiting, waiting, waiting, endlessly cranking out the latest theories on anything that could lend itself to misinterpretation or the progressive stages of retardation.

There was Jerry, his cool cocky eighteen-year-old prodigy deckhand; Walle, a fisherman friend from Alaska; myself; and Mark. As a kid, Mark was Vic's partner; he built the fish traps and nets, took his turn running the gear, and Vic, for his part, endlessly pushed the limits of their potential, physically, financially, and legally.

Mark was the only one of the Berkeley gang who made it through high school. He then went on to engineering school and built himself the *San Pablo*, a beautifully designed steel boat which he uses to fish albacore and salmon along the full length of the coast. None of this kept Vic and Mark from continuing to be like two halves of a whole. Mark is the cautious, cynical intellectual. He still designs and builds the equipment that comes out of their mutual ideas, and Vic, for his part, still finds new ways to destroy it. That's been the stated nature of their relationship since the beginning and seems somehow to have fostered the most unshakable mutual respect.

Though we'd already delivered over fifty tons of fish in a season that wasn't going at all well for the others, it had been a stretch of over two weeks since we'd seen our last fish. More and more of the lampara boats were crossing the line, the heat was on, and the whole crew was bored witless, grumbly, tired, and disgusted. It was getting so bad sometimes that a full day's communication consisted entirely of animal sounds.

We'd reached our limits. Vic was running the boat through Racoon Straits on our way back to Sausalito to take a break. High water slack was over two hours ago, and the tide rip was boiling, spitting, and churning in full fury; it's the only way all the water can push through this narrow, deep gorge. Setting any kind of net in this would be like pushing your car over a cliff.

Suddenly we were surrounded by birds and sea lions everywhere. "Hit the deck!" hollered Vic, intoxicated by the sight.

"That guy's crazy," said Mark for the millionth time, as he stood ready with the buoy in one hand, struggling to get his other hand into the jacket.

"Let her go!" Faster than the boat could complete the circle, the tide was collapsing the net into a straight line. By the time we got back to the buoy, clouds of fish were swimming over the sides of the net as it was sucked under by the rip. When the bag got to the stern, the only thing we could see were fourteen pissed off, hollering, thrashing sea lions. They're used to jumping in and out of the net for a free meal, but this time it had closed over their heads. We were no less vocal in our disgust than they were, leaning over the side, trying to open the net and drop the cork, getting splashed and slashed every time they took their fifteen hundred pounds and thrashed. To top it off, once the net was open, the lions made a game of it. You're working on getting one of them out, and the others are jumping back in. And there, underneath the lions, was a lousy two tons of herring waiting to be scooped aboard while the boat drifted only yards from the rocks.

By the time this performance was over, you knew that if this boat ever passed within twenty feet of the dock, the crew would be gone. Except for Vic. The way he was staring into the Fathometer, chewing nervously on the tide books, you knew that the chances of this boat going anywhere near the dock were just about zero. We were just about to cross the Mason-Dixon line and reenter legal territory.

"Hit the deck! Hit the deck!" he screams again into our disbelief.

In seconds the first wing was flying off the deck in the darkness.
All you can see is its shadow blurring by your feet, making the
sound of the chain and corks cracking against the stern seem more
like gunshot. Jerry was standing on one side of the net, watching
for snags, and the rest of us were poised against the big pile of
web, ready to shove it overboard as soon as the wing finished.
Freckles's voice blared unexpectedly over the speakers, "Take a
dixie, Vic, your mother's coming."

"Jesus," said Mark in instantaneous recognition of our plight.
One bust in this game and if you're a good guy, they revoke your
herring permit; for this gang, jail without bail seemed a more
likely outcome. Vic threw the engine into full bore reverse and the
boat heaved. It takes forever to stop a boat this size, and the net
was still whipping off the deck.

"Stop the net!" screamed Vic from the bridge. In the panic, all
hands reached into the dark webbing. Mark immediately caught
his hand and ripped it out; I grabbed some web and tried to hold
on, but it just cut its way out of my hands in a second. Wally
jumped back in pain as the cork line whipped against his leg.

"Forget it, before somebody gets killed!" he yelled.

How undeservedly lucky can one guy get? The boat came to a
stop with two feet of wing left before the bag would have been
pulled overboard, which would have left us with a ton of tangled
web hanging off the stern and a boat out of control in the tide. Not
only that, the Fish and Game boat arrived only a cool couple of
seconds after we'd gotten the wing back onto the deck.

"What are you doing over here?" called the warden to Vic.

"Ah, we just stopped the boat to fix a little trouble and, wouldn't
you know, it looks like we must have drifted over the line."

"OK," said the warden, and I couldn't believe my ears. It wasn't
so amazing that the game warden took Vic at his word; Vic could
be more convincing in his bullshit than was good for him. It's just
that the goddamned tide was going the wrong way for us to have
drifted in that direction. I just kept staring at this guy, waiting for
him to laugh and call Vic's bluff, but nothing clicked. Now if you
were speeding down the street at ninety-five miles per hour and a
cop stopped you, and you said, "No, officer, I was only going five
miles per hour; the earth was rotating at ninety miles per hour
underneath me and made it seem that way," and if the cop believed you, should that guy be a cop?

Herring season was just about over, and the lampara boats had barely been able to fill half their quota. Those that fished legally had almost no fish at all. The fishermen, gill netters, lampara, and seiners alike were angrier than ever about the mess that had been created in this fishery. They were determined to make things right. It didn't seem that it should be so difficult. Just a few changes in the regulations and we wouldn't have to work like animals, we could have a good winter fishery, still protect the herring, and hopefully ensure that the fish we did catch got used for more than just eggs.

For once the fishermen did their homework; people were polled, suggestions were typed up, Vic and I made up instructional drawings that showed the workings of the net in different stages of a set with arrows showing the tide and little figures with eyes and tails to denote the fish, meetings were attended, and for a while the fishermen even stayed in their seats when they talked. It wasn't long, though, and the whole thing seemed to break down to the same old arguments and brick walls.

It would have been a complete loss if it weren't for one important agreement. At the final meeting with Fish and Game, fishermen, the fish buyers, and representatives of the powerful sportsmen's groups, it was agreed that there should be a moratorium on the number of boats in the fishery for at least one year until the other issues could be worked out. It was unanimous!

The Meatball, *in the middle of a lampara set on San Francisco Bay.*

The boys from Monterey brailing herring with a cho-cho brail.

Vic and Jerry dipping into the bounty of it all—a twenty-ton set of herring right in front of Sausalito.

*San Francisco's net man,
Sam Tarantino.*

The Yukon Gang on the dock behind the old Shack-a-la at Point Reyes.
Standing from left to right: *Scheff, Hans, Pabst, the Governor, Candy,
Carlo;* seated: *a friend, Mario, and Vaughn.*

The Eileen D., *waiting for ice, bait, and fuel at the Sausalito dock.*

"Come on, Cindy, faster!" Another albacore goes into the hold.

Carlo, unloading at the Point Reyes dock.

The Eileen D. *scores— $22,000 of herring in one night.*

One for the barbecue.

11

The Herring War of 1978

I WENT SALMON fishing a believer and never gave that meeting another thought. After all, unanimous means that everybody's happy. Besides my full concentration was taken with trying to coordinate a boat, a home, and a lover. Vic's unique niche in the anchovy business allowed him to be home almost every night, and I wanted to be there, too.

The energy it took just to get together every couple of weeks finally hit the limit. I had gotten caught in Fort Bragg on a blow, found a safe slip for the boat, hitched a life-defying, two-hour ride on a fish truck to the city—a ride that should have taken four hours—took a bath, snuggled up, and the phone rang like a wood rasp over my skin. "Hey, Marie, you better get back up here."

"Oh shit," I said enthusiastically, "goddamn . . ."

"Hey, what's the matter with you? You ask me to do you a favor and give you a holler, so now you're gonna listen. Junior and Earl came in late, unloaded, took ice, took off, and didn't say hello, good-by or 'where's my check?' Nicky's under the ice chute, and he's been on the radio for two weeks about his daughter's wedding tomorrow. He wouldn't say anything specific when I talked to him except 'We're leaving at one.' "

"I'll get up there about five, give you a call, and let me know where you're at." We set up a quick code, I hung up the phone, took one look at Vic, and knew instantly that all was not well.

Driving back up to Fort Bragg that night was one misery on top of another. No sleep, the car heater didn't work, that bumpy, winding road with the cliff falling off on one side and deer jumping out the other, and I was trying to concentrate on how to resolve he, me, and the sea. And it just kept coming out impossible.

Much to my surprise, that phone call was the solution to my problem. It was such a big run of fish that I made enough money to drive the boat to Point Reyes and fish most of the rest of the season with the gang. I'd put my boat on the mooring at the end of the day, drive home for the night, get up at two, drive an hour and a half to the Point, fish with the gang, and sometimes make it home for a late dinner; and sometimes Vic would meet me at the Point Reyes dock. Dinners with the eight of them were worth every fish I didn't catch.

I wasn't unaware, however, that this solution was only temporary, a luxury made possible by an unusually fast catch. I certainly knew by now that you don't bank on a thing like that repeating itself.

More than ever, I knew I needed a bigger boat; a heavier-built, faster, tougher, catch-more boat, bigger ice hold, better engine, radar, and room for crew. That fall, while Vic finished up his anchovy season, I combed the ports from Crescent City to Monterey, but everything I saw that I could afford was too small, and everything I liked, I couldn't afford. I'd come back home pretty much resigned to another herring season on the *Angelina G*. I hadn't done anything but mope around the house for three days when Vic came bursting into the house. "Get your coat. I found just the boat for you." We went right down to Jerry's boat yard two blocks away, and what I saw from a distance flashed me right back to the *Donna Lou*; ten layers of paint blistering off the hull, chewed up guardrails, and rigging that looked like it would crumble in your hand. Vic was always proud of my fishing, he encouraged me all the way, but he was also never beyond a joke. I was about to say something, but he was already aboard, saying, "Come on, take a look inside." Inside, the spider webs nearly concealed what must have been the remnants of the first Fathometer and radio ever made. Vic pulled up the floorboards, and I began to see. The hull was superbly built and in prime condition, the layout was exactly what I wanted, and the 371 Gimmie was the ideal engine.

"But, Vic," I said, voicing my only concern, "there's no way in the world I can put this all together in the eight weeks before herring."

Vic looked puzzled. "Why not?" He really believed I could do it.

The first hurdle was Production Credit Association. It was 1978, and by now PCA had been in the fish boat loan business a few years, long enough to have tallied their accounting and to see that the drag boats showed the biggest profits. So naturally, being good loan officers, that's where they played their money. They had pulled way back on their loans for trollers, and at the same time they had about sixty draggers under construction for California. Never mind that the markets couldn't handle any more volume, never mind that the ports were too small to handle the draggers that already existed; and of course, on their tally sheets of plus and minus, there wasn't any room for the fact that dragging was ruinous to the ocean floor. Not surprisingly, today, as I write, PCA can't even afford to repossess these boats.

The few troll loans they did approve were often going to doctors, lawyers, and real estate brokers, people who had collateral safely tucked away on terra firma. PCA needed to start making good on some of their loans, and the professionals needed a tax write-off. One hand washed the other, and PCA all but ignored its own guidelines that the recipient of a loan should be a full-time fisherman with at least three years of good fishing records, and thus, some of the most beautiful boats of the fleet were left to deteriorate at the dock.

I guess I was just plain lucky one more time. My loan application seemed to be moving through the slots quickly and smoothly. And when the loan officer came down to the boat I intended to buy and said, "That's a beautiful hydraulic system on that boat," I said, "Yup, it sure is," even though there wasn't a hydraulic hose in sight. And when the surveyor looked into the bare wooden bins in the ice hold of the *Angelina G.* and asked, standing with pencil in hand, ready to fill out his form, "Is that a coil or brine refrigeration system you have in there?" I said, "It's coil." Sure, I saw my opportunity to mouth off and make them look stupid, but for once I easily kept my cool in light of the opportunity that waited for me on the ways. In just three days the *Eileen D.* was mine, and then it got really insane.

I had to start from scratch with hydraulic systems, wiring, electronics, pumps, deck machinery, ground tackle, the works! It was the biggest job of my life to try and make this boat fishable in the span of just eight weeks.

Katy, a twenty-eight-year-old woman acquaintance, was going to be my deckhand for the season and, as is usual in such arrangements, she agreed to "help me get the boat ready." I sure owe her a big debt. When Katy started with me, she knew less about mechanics than I did when I started fishing. She was a Sausalito newlywed with one week's experience on a boat, but something made me think she'd be a natural. I was right. Between the two of us, we were solving problems one after the other for twelve hours a day, seven days a week. There was no money from this work, but the satisfaction of every day doing things we'd thought were beyond our skill kept us going. There was nothing that interrupted our concentration until the bomb went off at the dock.

Fish and Game made an announcement that they were issuing an additional 125 gill net permits. Word zipped around the boats, and in no time everyone had left work and was up on the docks, standing around in stunned conversations. The timing was so obvious; it was too late for us to organize and do anything about it except possibly to file an injunction. And we didn't have to kick that idea around for very long to realize it was a lead balloon. The fishermen's lobbyist and, at the time, our only legal counsel, is also the son of one of the major fish buyers, the same fish buyer who, it turned out, had initiated this legislation in the first place. And the reason this fish buyer went out of his way to maneuver this deal was because, although his fishhouse was located in Sausalito, only two or three boats had sold him their herring the previous year. And the reason for that was because nobody likes a bounced check. Add to that the fact that his was the dock we were standing on, and his was the only dock in the area we could tie our boats to for the winter, and the case was closed. How's that for a well-wrapped package?

"Well," said Jack, who had stood quietly throughout the discussion, "I've got a lot more work to do than I thought. I've got to take off the anchor winch and mount a cannon in its place, I gotta put some steel armor on the bow, and then I gotta go over to the city and find myself a couple of goons to work the back deck." There was no doubt in anyone's mind about what this meant for the season to come. With 225 gill netters armed with three shackles of gear, the starvation of winter, the competition of the quotas, and the tyranny of the tides, the fires of hell couldn't have been better fueled. Still, I doubt if anyone that day was able to imagine the catastrophe that would be.

Opening night and there were only three little jobs left on the list. I kept putting off rigging the mast light because I hate it up there, being whipped around with the roll of the boat and looking down at all the sharp corners all over the deck. Now that it was now or never, the wind was blowing thirty miles an hour and a cattle prod couldn't get me up that mast. I rigged a "temporary" pipestand light on the bridge, Katy finished lashing the last harness onto the net, and we took off toward Angel Island. In twenty minutes, it was blowing forty, then fifty, then sixty miles per hour, a full-on winter southerly, hurling rain and sea water sideways through a mean, grey, blackening sky. It was a hard, hard decision thinking about last year, how the quota got gobbled up overnight. From the radio I could tell that a lot of guys had already set their gear. But finally I said, "It's no good, Katy," and she gave me that familiar crew member look that says, "With all due respect, you'd better not be blowing it." The first night of the worst herring season in history we anchored behind the island and played cards in the forecastle by candlelight and the cadence of the storm.

The next morning, I was relieved to hear that no one had caught a fish; in fact, many of them had completely lost their gear to the storm. I was also more than a little surprised and disgusted at my relief. The way things were set up, it's to your advantage when your friends go belly up. It doesn't take long for that reality to gnaw its way into the fleet.

All day long we didn't find a sign of fish until late afternoon, and then it was only a couple of scratches on the meter that you wouldn't even notice unless you were starving. We easily set the three nets in the company of only a handful of other boats, set the anchor, and fried some chicken. Our last supper. I only called one friend and told him to come over but "don't tell anyone else." Undoubtedly the other boats here did the same thing because, in a matter of two hours, the swarms descended, and the tiny cove was fused with hundreds of nets where there shouldn't have been more than twenty. The volume of screaming rose by the minute, and it didn't stop rising for a week and a half. I even heard Pabst and the Governor from the Yukon gang screaming at each other from one hundred yards away on the other side of the cove, and they were both on the same boat. "Sure, sure," said Pabst to his brother at top volume, "every year we say we're not coming back to this mess, so what's the use of saying it now?"

I looked their way and suddenly saw we were about to join the chorus. The two blinkers on the buoys of our inside net were touching, which meant that the six-hundred-dollar net and how much worth of fish were sitting on the bottom, tangled up in a ball. By now the tide was running like a freight train. In the time between breaking the boat anchor loose and pulling it aboard, we barely skimmed past five nets. We tried from every direction to get into our net to try and save it, but the shallow water was plugged with too many nets and every one of them with their cork lines strung barely below the surface like World War II propeller bait. We went out to another one of our nets in deeper water and hauled despite the tide. Five hundred pounds, a sign.

Sunrise was just on the verge of bursting out of the Berkeley hills as we pulled the buoy on our next net. It was plugged. A full net of herring is spectacular any time, but the first light of day on a full net of my first day fishing on my new boat, that was an omen to behold. Katy immediately saw the future in this and began shaking the net so fast and hard that I had to tell her to be careful not to rip the web from its hangings.

A fisherman in a forty-five-foot steel boat was passing by way on the outside. He must have looked in the binoculars because the boat took a sudden hard right at full speed. He was coming straight for us and never slowed until he was fifteen feet away, then he threw it in full bore reverse so fast it never hit neutral, turned the boat a quarter, exposing the deckhand standing on the sternrail with an anchor in his hands; and the captain yelled, "Let her go!" kicked it in gear, and took off setting like he was on the open sea.

"You're over my net!" I yelled; I know he heard me because he said, "Fuck you," and kept on setting. Apparently his anchor wasn't holding and he'd been dragging it behind him, because the net at our feet pulled so tight so quick that if we'd been in the way, it could cut an arm off. He didn't give a damn and continued to set. "Katy!" I screamed as I saw the tension building in the net and started a dive to the cabin. And finally the bastard stopped when he saw he had screwed himself up, too. He picked his net back up, but not before he'd torn out twenty-five fathoms of our webbing and probably two thousand dollars' worth of fish, loosened our anchor at the other end of the net, and left us dragging tangled up gear through the fleet, making enemies on each boat we passed. That was only a two-hour mess, just practice.

Before the season I had searched my vocabulary trying to describe this part of herring season to Katy. Now, toward the end of a dayful of emergencies, one on top of the other, I could see from her state of outraged shock that words could never tell this tale. We also had four tons of fish on the deck, which that year were worth forty-five hundred dollars. The price had nearly doubled over the previous year, and neither Katy nor I were any more immune to its lure than anyone else.

Dennis on the *Ruth*, a good fisherman friend of mine, was forty miles away at his home in Inverness. His wife had asked him why he wasn't fishing and he said, "Don't worry, honey, the weather's been bad. I called the boys this morning and there's nothing doing." Dennis was a dedicated practitioner of what most fishermen believed in theory only. You have to be in the mood or you don't catch the fish. So he and his wife snuggled up on the couch and turned on the TV.

Katy and I were the first boat to unload for the season, but still we didn't expect the news crew. Dennis was just about to switch from the news when the *Eileen D.* came sailing across the screen with her stern deep in the water and fish covering the deck. His wife leaned toward the set as two women blabbed into the microphones about covering all their bouncing checks. I was making enemies I didn't even know about.

We sold the fish, picked up a new net, ran back out, but the fish had moved, and nobody knew where. We ran into Joe, my old deckhand, on his new boat and immediately started working together, checking different spots along the way. The straits, nothing; the point, nothing; California City, nothing. I was running around the corner to Paradise Cove. "Hey, Joe," I called.

"Right," he said. I set our nets on the inside of Joe, and on the way out to deeper water we were instantly put out of commission as my prop wound up in Joe's net so bad that the engine quit. Joe was not at all pleased. The divers would take forever to get here. Twenty-five percent of the quota was taken yesterday, and the pressure was on so intense that I wrenched my mind against the cold, the murk, and forced myself over the stern into the bay. God, it was cold, my body was like a rock, but I forced myself under again and again, down to the prop for ten seconds of cutting and back to the surface again because that was the most I could hold my breath in this icy shock. Katy sharpened knife after knife, and I dulled them as quickly with only a few cuts into the ball of lead line, corks, and web. Twenty minutes in the water and I still wasn't halfway through the job, and suddenly, without any warning, every ounce of strength drained from my body. I didn't believe it could happen like that; aside from the grip of one hand on the hull, I was completely paralyzed.

Katy couldn't lift me over the stern so she called Joe. Not only did he save my ass, but he then offered to tow us back to the dock, with his net in our prop, and risking the gear he left behind. A touch of class. It was a bad time to be leaving the nets, too; not only had the herd descended, but a new storm started blasting monsoon winds and rains so hard, we didn't know if Joe's small boat was going to make the tow around the turbulence of Belvedere Point. We just plain prayed as the boats were swept within twenty-five feet of the rock by the southerly winds and incoming tide.

It was one o'clock when I finally got to a telephone to try and coax a diver out of a warm bed down into the cold wet blustering winter storm. Guess what kind of money you got to talk to do that kind of coaxing? And, even so, he arrived without his underwater light. So we hustled in the rain to rig wiring so our searchlight would reach the stern and sat on the back deck, gobbling chicken left over from our last meal thirty-six hours ago, drinking coffee, shivering, handing the diver hacksaws and knives, and each time his head came above water, we're yelling, "Come on, man, hurry up, do you think we have all night?"

It was daylight as we arrived back at the cove. Despite the warm ride in the cabin and the dry clothes, my insides could not seem to thaw. The light of day was making my ears ring, and the drone of the engine sometimes would get deafeningly loud and then it would fade off to nothing. At the same time I'd catch my mind racing around one thought and then getting hopelessly stuck on the next. The symptoms of no sleep and too much work were certainly familiar to me by this time in my career. In fact, I'd learned to function in this state just like a lifetime alcoholic finds his way home at three in the morning. What I wasn't familiar with in these circumstances was having to deal with the surfacings of blind, uncontrollable rage.

The radio had been throbbing all night with the angry fights and threats. Still, I was shocked as we turned into the cove and the first thing we saw was one very insane skipper on the flying bridge, ramming the bow of his boat into the midships of another. Everywhere we looked was disaster. It was hard to believe that I was voluntarily pointing my bow at the center of it. But I had to save my nets and make the season or I'd lose the boat. The fact was making me and everyone else do things I couldn't believe.

One of our nets was missing completely. We pulled the anchor on the second and found two clean knife cuts on the harness and no net. We went to the other end and found the same thing. Somebody had stolen it, fish and all, and I could feel the anger consume my whole being and radiate from my skin like searing heat rises off the desert. Fish and Game, as had become their pattern, were hovering on the outside of the mess, afraid to enter for fear of getting a net on the prop. Everywhere I looked and everything I saw was fueling this rage. I thank God I didn't have a gun on the boat. The rage had grown so out of control, it seemed the only way to release it was to blow the first person on the nearest boat back to Sicily. It had already happened to others that night, and though nobody was shot, boats and equipment were.

I don't know how long old man Vince had been hollering at me for help. He was only fifty feet away on the boat nearest me, and when I got there, he said he'd been calling at me for five minutes. I felt like a complete ass. Somehow we got a rope to him to hold him out of the tangled mass of nets behind his stern. I had to talk to myself out loud to figure out the simplest mechanics of maneuvering the boat against the tide. Fifteen minutes later he came to the bow to untie my line. "Maria," he said, his eyes lost in a gaze of confusion, "this ain't fishing." He didn't know if he was asking me or telling me.

"Hey, Vince," I said, as he seemed to just stand there trying to remember why he'd come to the bow, "what's your deckhand's name?"

Tom couldn't have been over fifteen, but the numb, frozen expression on his face carried the weight of fifteen lifetimes in hell. "Hey, Tom," I yelled to the back deck, "the old man cut the back of his hand pretty bad; why don't you go in the cabin and see if you can find something for it. We'll hold onto the boat so you don't drift." In the few minutes of peace that followed, Katy and I tried to figure out what day it was.

This didn't stop for a week, not for sleep, or storm, or common sense. To tell you the honest truth, I can't remember what happened in the last two days. I just know we ended the week with two fish tags for three tons of fish and a bill for two more nets we had lost.

In the middle of all this the big chiefs of Fish and Game had come down to the dock to pay a visit to the grass roots and watch the boats unload. "Looks like everything's going smoothly," said Mr. Watson to Walt, the buyer. Walt nodded in agreement. It was true. The boats were bringing in the fish, the fishpumps were working without a hitch, the forklifts loaded the bins onto the trucks, twenty tons a load, one driver pulled out and the next one moved in. It was very smooth indeed.

Friday noon to Sunday sunset the season was closed because otherwise we would interfere with the recreational use of the bay. That was true, too. That weekend, the dock was strewn from one end to the other with nets under intensive repair, people were charged, angry, and distant, and about a third of the fishermen were suffering from some kind of strange disease that burned with a fever over 102 degrees. We hadn't seen anything yet.

Sunday night, Katy and I ran over to Treasure Island on a bum report of fish. By the time we got there, reports had come in from all over the bay, and it sounded like no fish anywhere. It was all the excuse I needed to drop the hook. I had begun to feel the fever that was going around rising out of my skin by the hour. When I went to the bow to drop the anchor, I was so dizzy that I had to hold on to the rigging for balance. The light drops of drizzly rain felt like burning needles when they hit my skin. I was only in the bunk a couple of minutes when I caught myself smiling stupidly as I watched myself float around the forecastle like a big ball of cotton. A voice that came out of the radio said, "I'm going to drop a couple inside of you, Mat," and I started playing with it like a Ping-Pong ball echo that I could paddle around the inside of my head and make it repeat itself. "I'm going to drop a couple . . . I'm going to drop a couple . . ." Some part of the sound of his voice was becoming more and more prominent, a tension that was growing each time I listened.

Suddenly I jumped out of the bunk like I'd just been hit with 440 volts. "Katy, that guy's in fish, let's go." It is possible, I was learning from this fishery, to strip every gear in your mind, blast through some kind of warp, and come out on the other side of insanity running a boat and catching fish. The crazy speed, lightning mind, drive over pain, gut-based energy of birth, death, war, and herring season was teaching me to get there at the mere wish of my will. And I can't say it didn't turn me on. I loved it in fishing as much as I loved it in Vic.

Sausalito, I guessed. Sausalito was right. The action was full tilt boogie when we arrived. The sixty lamparas and seiners were there. We'd forgotten about them when we were working on the other side of the bay; now fifty-kilowatt floodlit boats were everywhere, circling, heaving, banging, and brailing. The thick, black clouds of fish had been marking on the Fathometer for a mile and a half before we reached the shallower water. Now the meter was black from top to bottom. The twelve fathom ledge that slowly dropped to twenty fathoms was the choice working area for gill netters, seiners, and lamparas. We looked in at all the blinking lights on the buoys, and we didn't have to count them to know that the whole gang was here. "Party time, Katy, are you ready?" Katy was broke, what could she say? She looked at me heavily, took a deep breath, and burst out laughing. And we were laughing right up to the moment I yelled from the bridge, "Let her go!" We were instantly rocketed back to a frenzy, trying to set our net in a fifteen-foot space between two nets and a tide running crosswise and seeing the running lights of a boat coming straight at us and setting from the other direction. All right, baby, we're going to fly tonight.

It was twenty-eight hours later before we could even draw a breath. We didn't bother to eat or take off our boots, the anchor went down, and we fell flat in the bunks. Not two whole lousy minutes had passed, and we heard the strangest sounds coming through the hull; the only thing I could imagine was a bunch of woodpeckers tapping on the planks. "Oh, God," said Katy in a drawn out groan of total exhaustion, "what the hell is it going to be this time?"

"I'm not going to look," I said. Bam! Glaring yellow light flashed into the cabin. Katy and I crashed into each other trying to get onto the deck.

The little woodpeckers were the corks of a gigantic three-hundred-fathom seine net wrapped completely around the boat. The sixty-foot seine boat was only ten feet away and coming toward us. The crew was frantically trying to retrieve their net but now, with the help of the tide, they had succeeded only to suck the two boats together; their stern was banging and lifting and crashing on ours. I could hear wood cracking not just in the stern but in the bow too. The webbing of his net had our anchor and chain all the way up to the bow, and the strain of their powerful winch was stuttering under the strain of pulling our bow stem loose with every pull. "Stop!" I screamed, "you're pulling the boat apart!"

"Shut up!" they screamed in panic. "You girls got no business out here in the first place." We screamed and cursed and yelled and dangerously hung each other over the side between the two boats with knives, and poles, and panicked, precision timing to keep from getting crushed. We rigged ropes from the corks at the bow, heaved them back to the seiner so they could pull from another angle, and three-quarter-inch line was snapping into deadly wild-flying whips under the strain, trying to think, think, think of solutions while the body reeled against the pain of hanging half under water, cutting hands on straining web and knives that slipped in the darkness. Two hours later and we were free. I looked around and every gill netter within my range of sight was caught in an equally horrifying encounter with a seiner or lampara. The radio was so full of terror, we turned it off. There was some kind of line of complete mental departure out here, and I don't think anyone knew which side they were on.

We lost another net to the ferryboat and another to a second seiner attack. Twenty-four hours later we got back to the dock to unload three tons of fish. Katy took care of loading another net on the boat while I took care of the weighing and fish tag. I got back to the boat and Katy was standing in the forecastle with her wet gear on, her hair soaked and covered with scales, her face drawn in an inhuman shape, and her seabag hoisted over her shoulder. "I quit," she said.

We looked at each other in long, silent recognition and complete stillness. Tears were running helplessly down our faces as if we didn't own them. Finally, I said, "I don't blame you, Katy, it's all right, but I have to keep working." I never did know when to quit.

By some stroke of luck, Vic and Jerry were on the dock. They offered to help me set the nets, but they needed to come right back so they could make the next tide. On the way out, they immediately went to the forecastle, switched on the lights, and broke out a deck of cards. I couldn't see a damn thing for the glare, but I was so glad they were there, I went up on the bridge, braced myself against a bitter cold winter wind, numbed my mind to all thought, and wound my way through the minefield of blinking lights.

Vic had suggested a look at Fort Baker. It was a good idea. The worst currents in the bay run through this rocky, treacherous area right beneath the awesome north tower of the Golden Gate. But there wasn't another boat in sight. Five or six sea lions barked out a welcome and a promise. We boldly set the nets tight into the rocks because that's the only spot that didn't plummet into the depths.

Running back to the dock, I cut behind the borderline at Richardson Bay to avoid the nets. Fred, a game warden, blasted me with the bullhorn from his boat. "Marie, don't set a net in there, you're over the line." I was furious.

"Goddamnit, Fred!" I screamed at the top of my lungs, "can't you see I haven't got a net on the boat?"

"Sorry," he said. "Good fishing to you."

"Fuck you!" I screamed even louder, and even as the words raged out of my mouth, I felt some horrible loss inside.

When I got back to the dock, I started looking all over for Crazy Frank, a hand of Vic's who works in his shop packing bait. Frank definitely wasn't all there or, as Vic put it, he was a little fifty-one-fifty, which is why Vic had him working the shop instead of the boat, but I didn't care; he could certainly help me pull a couple of nets.

At dawn, the early light was so beautiful as it wrapped around the Gate and splashed out on the ocean, I almost felt human as we pulled the first net back onto the boat. What a treat to work without a crowd, to once again have only the ocean, wind, and tides on my mind. Their force was more savage and ruthless than anything that humans could show, but they didn't make me hate.

The second net had a respectable amount of fish as we pulled the first few fathoms. When the net was halfway on the boat, I turned to Frank and said quickly, "Look, Frank, these fish are still gilling pretty good, I'm going to lay the net back out. I'm going to have to go fast because the current is setting us toward those rocks over there. All you have to do is stand back from the net until we get to the harness, but then you gotta be fast. Grab the anchor, clip the chain on the ring, and throw it over. Got it?'' He nodded and I kicked it in gear.

For some reason Frank reached over the net as it was going out, to try and grab the anchor. "Not now!" I yelled. "Get away from the net." He just started to step back when the webbing snagged something on his jacket and flipped him over the stern all in one second. He panicked immediately. Frank couldn't swim, I could see that right away as he flailed and choked and quickly went under, though he was still caught in the web. I slammed the engine into reverse, trying to get the net back onto the boat without getting it into the prop, without getting set farther toward the rocks. Frank was still fifteen feet away from me, choking and going under, choking and going under. If he ever got untangled from that net, he'd go to the bottom like a rock with those damn hip boots he had on. I tried not to panic as the moments stretched out unmercifully. The rest of the net came up and Frank was in it; he flopped out of the net, grabbed onto the rail, and gasped and choked, while I tried to keep the boat out of a worse scene yet.

I tied the boat up at a small nearby dock. I got off quickly, walked down the dock, put my head in my hands, pressed my body hard against a piling, and didn't move for a long time. It was torture, the feelings of guilt, the shaking, the horror of the whole season tearing through my mind. Safety first is what I told every crew member that got on my boat, and I always prided myself that I meant it. Now, I almost killed Frank because I was too exhausted to care anymore about the little things, like checking a crew member's jacket for snags, forbidding hip boots on the boat, taking a new crew member through at least one dry set, or picking the right person in the first place. Hell, I hadn't even thought of it. And here comes Frank, dancing around me like a Mexican jumping bean that just hit the sun. "Hey, I bet you never caught nothing like that before."

"Frank," I said, a little annoyed, "aren't you aware that you just almost died?"

"Ah, I always make it somehow."

The gill net quota was filled at noon that day. People were tying up their boats so fast and leaving for home, by two o'clock the dock looked like an abandoned beachhead.

The lampara boats were still fishing. I took advantage and sat in the bathtub for two whole days. I hadn't even gotten the energy to feed myself when Vic came walking in the door looking like he'd just stepped out of Guadalcanal. "Bad, huh?" I said.

Vic, who had one of the most vivid vocabularies of misery in the fleet, said nothing. He turned to look for something in the refrigerator and said, "Fred died of a heart attack last night while he was on patrol."

We lay awake long into the night, exhausted but unable to sleep. Fred was a friend, and you realize these things too late, on the eve of some ugly, greedy war that sucked the humanity out of everyone. And it's too damn late! Fred was one of a handful of game wardens who took the trouble over the years to form a lot of friendships with the fishermen. There was respect both ways. Fred knew what was going on with the fisheries, he always put his two cents in with the department, but beyond that he liked his job just like we liked ours.

For Vic, his feelings went a lot farther back to when he was a kid. Fred was their game warden in the East Bay. He sort of respected this handful of delinquent fishermen despite their techniques. In a way he was more of a father to them than their real fathers. He shared with them an interest in fishing and the workings of the bay that went beyond the money or the job. That's what made them good fishermen and that's what made Fred a good game warden. He tried, however much in vain, to get them to toe the line and to instill some sense of the law. He busted them all a lot more than once. But he also carried a picture in his wallet of Vic as a kid with a two-fathom smile on his face, surrounded by 250 illegal striped bass which Fred took when he caught Vic at six thirty in the morning delivering to Chinatown.

It was a long time before Vic no longer stopped, stunned, in the middle of whatever he was doing and said, "Why Fred? Why not the guy that sat at the desk and made this mess?" And I'll never forget my last words to him. "Fuck you, Fred." I'm stuck with it forever.

It was months before anyone recuperated from this battered herring season. Nobody worked on the boats much, and nobody laughed. The place was strewn with torn up old webbing, scarred boats, and enemies among friends. Herring disease was the name applied to the months-long malaise that had the proud fishermen propped around the dock like beat up old mops.

The fishermen who had worked and shared the ocean had been

pushed into each other's faces and shoved down each other's throats. And all they could see under the circumstances was a good close-up look of each other raging like animals after the almighty buck. The things that were said and done could not be easily forgotten. The wounds festered into hard-line arguments about what should be done, but when one group made a move in one direction, another group jumped down their throats and snagged their plans. The few people who went to the meetings often came back with reports that consisted entirely of shaking their heads. Relationships were all tangled up in a roaring tide of emotion that echoed the nightmares of the season.

The only thing that brought the fishermen together was cursing the Fish and Game. What was most disheartening to me was that Fish and Game just refused to learn. The experts they consult are at best the people with biology degrees; they wouldn't think of recognizing the knowledge of the fishermen who have daily spent their lives probing the depths, people who wouldn't eat a meal unless they're right about the fish, people who daily put their life on the line of their knowledge. "Maria," Freckles said to me after a hearing in Sacramento, "they think I'm stupid, but they'll never, ever be able to make me believe I'm stupid. I've forgotten more about this ocean than all their biologists put together ever knew."

What everyone said about the Fish and Game was true, but it couldn't disguise the real wounds. It was the fishermen who tore your net and left you to fume; it was fishermen who swore and cussed your inevitable mistakes. The so special fabric of the fishing community, woven with respect and cooperation, was shredding with ragged tears of suspicion. Even among acquaintances you wondered, was it you who stole my net, was it you I told to go to hell in the middle of a blind, stormy night, was it your propeller that ripped the corks from a net full of fish when I wasn't able to be there with armed guards? The name of the game was dog eat dog, but it was only ourselves who decided to play. The greed and need of the fishermen had opened a door that would be hard to close.

I swore on everything I held sacred that I wouldn't fish herring again.

12

Ocean Commotion

THE *EILEEN D.* was going to do it for me. This boat was going to catch so much salmon and albacore that the money I'd save in taxes alone would pay me to sit out the next herring season in front of the fireplace. And though important parts of this dream went unmaterialized, I was right about my boat. Aside from all the improvements in the layout and sturdiness of her hull, the *Eileen D.* fished.

Now it may seem a very far-fetched leap to say that a boat does anything more than float across the sea in this way or that. But what do you think when you hear stories about boats like the *Freddy J.* Three times on three different occasions she was seen running from the fleet in a suspicious direction. And on three different occasions when other fishermen called to see what was wrong, the captains of the *Freddy J.* did not answer because they were no longer aboard. The last time it happened, there had been two people aboard, and they were both missing. They were friends of mine, a young couple, experienced fishermen; the weather was good. Why? Coincidence, maybe. After all, it happens two or three times a year that someone gets thrown from his boat. But three times in a row for one boat?

Maybe that's not the way to explain it, because the real way I learned that these boats were more than just the wood and nails that held them together was day by day living in their bellies, feeling something inside of them that was for you or against you with a will that was beyond your control.

And the *Eileen D.* fished, from the first day, the first trip, and after the first month I was convinced. Tack for tack with other boats she'd always pick more fish than her share. It's been true ever since. Needless to say, though I've loved every boat I've had, the *Eileen D.* immediately occupied a special place in my heart. All I had to do was put her on fish and we'd have smiles on our faces by night.

"We" is another good thing on this boat—a crew, not just to share the work but to share the ocean, too. It's the only way to go, unless of course you get the wrong person, and on a boat at sea that includes just about everybody except the right person.

Captain and crew is probably the most intense relationship on earth. After days at sea, living and working in a space the size of a postage stamp, being tossed around by the moods of the fish and the sea, it can easily get right down to the full-scale nitty-gritty of who left the Oreo cookies at the dock. And no one can go for a walk.

Aside from a couple of very memorable, very short-term occasions, I've always been extremely lucky with the people I've worked with. They always took a lot of pride and interest in the boat beyond the 15 percent of the catch that was standard pay for the crew.

As far as being an actual salmon nut who wanted to catch every fish in the sea, Cindy stands out. She had a young, crazy, frantic energy that kept her in the back of the stern from morning to night no matter what the weather, as long as I kept the boat on top of the fish. The hard times on this boat came when the lines dragged for more than an hour without action, especially if Cindy had wanted to go the other way, and the guys at her spot were filling the radio with ten and twenty fish tacks, and the mood alone could part the seas. It didn't happen that way too often though. Cindy had a good instinct for the fish, I had six years' experience, *Eileen D.* was doing her magic below the surface, and our future looked very good, indeed.

The Farallon Islands were another ace in our hands. All those years following the Yukon gang through their perilous maze of pinnacles were about to pay off. This year over two hundred boats from Washington state had come to our area because of the restrictions put on their fishing by the *Boalt* decision. They were crowding the grounds badly, with the one exception that they didn't want anything to do with the Farallon Islands. They wanted to go home with their masts intact, and they could tell from one look at the chart that this place takes practice. To keep the impression alive, the locals spared no expletives on the radio when describing the latest illustrated island disaster. Not that we had to make up any of it; we just kept that kind of information in the foreground and neglected to mention that these savage, treacherous rocks were producing more fish than they had for years, and this is always a good spot.

For the next two years, these islands, located twenty miles out in one of the nastiest sections of ocean, became like a private niche on the Pacific for the thirty or forty boats that were willing to stretch their imaginations and endurance enough to call this place home. I had some of my most exquisite times fishing here on the stern of the *Eileen D.*, pulling more salmon than I ever expected out of the giant waves that moments later exploded on the craggy cliffs. The margin out here was so thin, the stakes so high, and the fishing so good that every sense in our bodies was opened to the fullest. Everything seemed doubly alive, the very soul of the rock seemed exposed.

No doubt we paid an endless variety of dues for the time spent, but at times even these could be turned to fun. One day as often happened, before the morning was over, the severity of the sea would force us to retreat to what can only mockingly be referred to as the shelter behind the southeast lee.

We pulled up to within fifty feet of a big sea cave in the familiar rock and dropped the hook. Home. An eighty-acre, grey black rock with thousands of seabirds sitting on its face and big herds of sea lions playing around the boat, oblivious to the waves that pitched the boat so violently that, even though we were anchored, you needed a hand grasp at all times. We finished up our chores and it was time to relax, but even a simple attempt of a meal ended up on the floor, the tape deck was broken, and reading was a blur. That left the San Francisco marine operator, twenty-four-hour, ship to shore entertainment. If you're just into the listening, it's the soaps of the high seas. Ships and fishermen talking to land: whose dog is at the vet's, whose kid got detention, who lies about their fish? Both sides of the conversation go out over every radio that's tuned to the channel, so it usually doesn't get too heavy, but on the other hand, many days at sea have passed since contact, and it never gets too dull, either.

"Hello, Mary," said Jake to his wife, whose voice I knew by now, "listen, we've had a lousy trip, the fishing's been real slow, so I'm going to try to push here for a couple more days." That conversation ended quickly, and right away Jake put in another call. Ring, ring.

"Hello?"

"Hi, sweetheart, meet me in an hour at the dock."

Oh, no, I thought, not Jake.

It was much more fun putting in your own calls anyway. Cindy wanted to call her eighty-year-old grandmother in Arkansas. "Hi, Grandma, I'm on a fishing boat anchored at the Farallon Islands, off California."

"Oh, dear, that's wonderful," said her grandmother with as much excitement as she could carry on her warm, southern drawl. "When I was a little girl, I had the best time of my life at those islands, dancing all night, big bands, strolling on the moonlit deck of the boat . . ."

"No, no, no, Grandma," said Cindy, trying to correct a horrible mistake, "you're thinking of southern California. You were at Catalina. That's five hundred miles away. It's different up here."

Grandma's image was not about to be changed. "It doesn't matter at all which island, honey, I just wish I could be there with you and see that beautiful blue water again. You all have a drink for me while you're there, you hear?"

We looked out the windows at the grey, windy fog that was settling over the rock and watched as wave after wave hurled itself at its jagged, cliffy shore, and we looked back at each other and burst out laughing. "Grandma," said Cindy at the same time that a wave rolled the boat on its side, threw her so suddenly against the door that she was forced to drop the microphone. "Sorry, Grandma, I dropped the microphone. You'd love it here; I'll send you a postcard."

"You all have yourselves a wonderful time out there, you hear?"

"OK, Grandma, good-bye, love you."

We sat down on the floor in the forecastle, braced our legs against one bunk and our backs against the other and broke open a bottle of brandy that was stashed for special occasions only. One drink for Grandma, one for the rock, and one for the fish in the hold. And though we could no longer read the bottle on the label, we had one more for the anchor so it wouldn't break loose in the night.

My dream for the *Eileen D.* was developing perfectly out here. It was back at the beach that our troubles began.

This year, the price we got for our fish, for a number of reasons that all came together at the wrong time, was seventy-five cents a pound lower than it had been for the last three years. The sting was more than any of us could afford.

Well, a lot of us had run our mouths off for a number of years about how we'd market our own fish if things got bad enough. If we didn't act now, we ought never to discuss it again.

Producing top quality food was as much a part of fishing's satisfaction as anything else. Actually, I'd always figured it would be fun taking the fish full circle from the ocean to the people. It turned out that it wasn't quite that clean an operation. For one thing, the salmon are so perishable that you can go from a five-thousand-dollar load to a garbage haul in a matter of hours if there's any shakiness or hang-ups in a deal. For another thing, we quickly found out, dealings in the fish business are synonymous with shakiness and hang-ups.

Typically, Cindy and I, on our first load, set out to cut the fattest hog we could find. We got one of our regular buyer's crew to give us the name of his New York City broker and we'd cut the local buyer right out of the picture. No small-time restaurant action for us!

We scored on the first phone call. The broker offered us $3.25 a pound for 3,000 pounds of salmon, over double the local price. In half a day we figured out about air freight containers, packing procedures, arranged a flight, and were ready to leave for the airport. One more phone call to give the broker flight information and arrange for a letter of credit. Everything was in order except that in five hours the price had dropped to $1.25 a pound, and we were stuck with the fish, with no ice and no chance of selling them until the next day. That's how they taught us the lesson of territory because, like they say, this way you don't make the same mistake twice, honey!

After that we confined ourselves to local Bay Area seafood restaurants and jobbers. This scene wasn't exactly a lemonade stand mentality, either. It was a song and dance every time. Muscle Lady, they called me in Chinatown as a little joke on the fact that I always carried my own fish boxes because we got tired of having them disappear on the way to the scale at the same time that everyone in the market would simultaneously forget the English language. Bum checks, deals broken on delivery, phony arguments over quality to try and get the price down, and on one finger I could count the buyers that didn't try to cheat us blind. I guess they saw two dumb girls walking in with a load of gold, and they couldn't help themselves. So one dumb girl learned how to distract the buyer with dumb questions while the other dumb girl shifted the boxes so the same fish got weighed twice.

In no time, every score had been evened. There was even a bonus thrown in. Whenever I was selling fish, I always took the opportunity to look around and check out the market's operation. Because it was interesting, and also because it was apparent to me as it was to many of the fishermen that somehow we had to get more control over the marketing end of the fishing even though it was just about impossible.

I was walking around this one buyer's freezer when what do I see but seven tons of shark stacked in the corner like cordwood. "Hey, Randy," I said to the buyer, knowing full well this swank, world-renowned restaurant didn't have a hint of shark on the menu, "is this for the cats in the back?"

"Oh, no," he said without blinking an eye, "that's for the bouillabaisse, the captain's plate, and the cioppino." And though he didn't mention it at the time, the shark was also euphemized as swordfish, scallops, and whitefish. Very interesting, I thought, and filed it away for a rainy day.

No sooner had Cindy and I developed an understanding with our clientele, then we didn't need them anymore. July came and the fish stopped. Just like that. Along the full coast of Oregon, Washington, and California, belly up was the word. It's actually a fascinating mystery if you can separate your mind from your stomach long enough to consider it. How can it be that salmon, separated by hundreds of miles, swimming in different conditions of current, weather, and feed, all go off the bite at the same time? And yet it happens frequently. The fascination, however, was long gone before we were even near finished with this particular episode. One week, two weeks, even three weeks, that's a normal lull;

but three *months*? Aside from the money lost, aside from the pressure, boredom, and tension, the constant humiliation of the ocean makes you start feeling like a chump—pumping five hundred dollars' worth of provisions on the boat just in case; baiting one hundred hooks before four in the morning just in case; running the empty gear, up and down, up and down, up and down, just in case what? There weren't any fish, and you get this image of yourself like a papaya farmer in Antartica watering the crop day after day after day after day.

The whole fleet got like that, torqued out and lobotomized. All you had to do was listen to the molasses dronings on the radio from three in the morning till ten at night, and you could tell. "I dunno, Jack, I dunno what I'm going to do here. What do you think?"

"I dunno, Joe, it looks bad."

"You said it, Jack, it sure don't look good."

"Maybe I'll take a look at the North Island."

"I dunno, Jack, Marty was up there yesterday, and he's not going back today."

"I dunno, Joe, it doesn't look good."

"Yeah, Jack, it looks bad, I dunno, why don't we give Tommy a call."

Only the old-timers seemed able to maintain their grip, but their musings didn't exactly help the mood. They wore their patience like Purple Hearts. "Yeah, Charlie, these young kids don't know you got to take the bad with the good; they think these fish are supposed to work like a clock. Remember the year when . . . ?" Just what we needed. Not only did we have to suffer the present, but we had to relive every bum year of the past as the old-timers with nothing better to do flaunted the undauntable ace of their age-experience.

If it weren't for the fact it was 1978, things would have gone the course they'd taken for ages, the progressive retardation acting like a cocoon you hide in until the fish come back and break you loose. But in the midst of all this the two-hundred-mile-limit bill, which seemed to be lying so harmlessly dormant three thousand miles away in the offices of Washington, now, suddenly emerged without warning as a fait accompli. The Pacific Fisheries Management Council, the arm of the Department of Commerce that had been created by the limit bill, made an announcement that since there weren't enough salmon left in the ocean, they were going to cut a month out of next year's season. The hostility had been growing between the fishermen and this group, but this latest move was Pearl Harbor. "How the hell do they know how many fish are in the ocean?" was the cry. Well, during a year of very bad drought in California, PFMC counted the fish at the end of the streams, and the numbers were very small.

"That proves it, Maria!" screamed Freckles. "That proves what I've been saying for years. The salmon is smarter than the biologists. Do you think that if the salmon gets to the bottom of the river and there's not much water, do you think the salmon's going to go all the way up the river to try and spawn? I don't know for sure, but I don't think so. The only place the salmon have to go up river every year is in the biology books."

What was more astounding to the fishermen was that PFMC made their decision to cut our season on the basis of the biologists' predictions that next year, because of the drought, was going to be one of the worst seasons the fishermen had ever seen. It was bad enough, they claimed, to be able to count the fish, but the idea of anyone trying to predict the fish of the sea was ludicrous.

Fishermen took the drastic measure of attending some of these meetings, and, in the process, the picture grew bleaker. Before the boards of lawyers, biologists, and resource management specialists, the fishermen tried over and over to explain that the salmon fishery, limited to the use of hook and line, was the most conservationally wise fishery on the coast. And they tried to explain the sea, that in all likelihood this lack of salmon was just part of an ocean cycle that no one could understand.

On the entire West Coast of the United States there are only two or three research vessels that operate full time. It's not like the land where naturalists have been poking in every nook and cranny for years. Jacques Cousteau can't cover the whole territory single-handed.

Fishermen have spent their lives daily probing the depths of the sea. They don't get paid a salary for putting in the time or writing books. They only get paid when they're right.

And after millions of hours of collective experience, there is one observation on which the fishermen agree to a man. Only a fool would say where the fish will be tomorrow. That's what they tried to tell the council, and that's what proved to the council that the fishermen were indeed ignorant. After all, the biologists had hard numbers that came out of computers, cold facts and solid predictions of the future. The uncertainty, which to the fishermen is the beauty of it all, is to the educated and civilized a dark and lowly thing.

One by one, or two by two, the fishermen came back from these meetings with a prediction as solid as concrete, "That's the last goddamned meeting I'll ever attend," and with very few exceptions, the fishermen kept their word.

Unfortunately, many important fishery policies were being formulated in the smoke-filled rooms, and no one who knew the sea was there. What had happened with the herring fishery was only an encapsulated version of what seemed about to take place in every ocean fishery on the West Coast.

Between the lack of salmon and the threat to next year's season, the mood on the fishing grounds was deadly. There was only one thing capable of instantaneously restoring our faith in the infinity of possibilities surging below the waves. It came across the radio one night in early September as we lay sound asleep on the anchor, a faraway conversation with the kind of news that over the years your ears have learned to sift from all other noise.

Albacore! A huge school of albacore had surfaced only forty miles off the beach. Before the conversation was done, I could hear the anchor chains on the boats around us clanking over their winches. No matter that it was 1:00 A.M., no matter that the fog was thick and black. I couldn't get sea room fast enough between me and the salmon grounds. Now that I had the *Eileen D.*, I figured I could stay on the grounds and make this fishery pay.

Cindy, who had never caught an albacore before, was chomping at the bit. I explained the simplicity of the gear on the way out and made a big deal of how easy it was to pull a fish by skipping it over the water.

Five hours out, the fog lifted to expose the sun just breaking over the horizon. At the same moment we crossed the line between the dark green cold water and hot blue water, the last jig got thrown in the water, and the first line pulled tight with a fish. You sure don't need coffee to wake you up on a morning like this.

Cindy was in the pit immediately, pulling on the fish and straining and pulling and trying to make it easy, but no sooner would she have a few fathoms of line coiled behind her when the fish would pull it all back in the water and she would have to start again from scratch. The next time she tried like anything to hold on to the line, but the fish jerked it out of her hand again and again. When she finally landed the fish, she turned around with a very puzzled look on her face, "That's what you call easy?" Every once in a while, I explained, you get a big fish that dives for the bottom; it's like a mack truck going in reverse, and you'd better focus every ounce of strength to overcome it. The next fish that hit, and the fish after that, dove to the bottom like ship anchors. When the fourth fish hit the line, Cindy turned to me and said, "Your turn." I jumped down from the bridge, put on my gloves, and easily glided the fish halfway in. Suddenly, before I could grip the line, it was burning a hole right through my glove. The next fish was the same. I could see the handwriting on the wall. We were in a school of large albacore. They're called cold water fish because they tend to break from the main school and congregate on the cold water edge.

In the next few days our arms would be stretched out of their sockets. In the evenings when the fish would go on the bite, we were literally making money hand over fist. But the strain of pulling these fish, like pulling one anchor after another, got so frustrating and painful, I'd wish the sun would set and end it. One night as a blood red sun set behind a purple horizon, the whole ocean turned a gelatinous purple grey, and as always the water seemed to hold the last light of the day, even after the sky was black. In a matter of minutes the sea released the day to darkness, but the albacore, like dragons that wouldn't die, kept snapping at the jigs. We pulled the fish from the black September sea, eerily caught in our own wished-for dream.

During the day, though, the pace was easy. The weather was good, and the sea was rich with whales and porpoises of all kinds that I hadn't seen before. We were off by ourselves when we spotted—are you ready?—a white whale, Moby Dick in the flesh. Actually, it was too small to be Moby Dick, but it was definitely much larger than a porpoise. It moved slowly and beautifully through the water. We followed it for quite a while to make sure our eyes got a good accurate look before we said anything. If you say something dumb on the air, you have to wear it for a long, long time. It wasn't until two days later that someone could identify it as a pilot whale. In a way, this whale took a lot of the juice out of the story of Moby Dick for me. There was nothing sinister at all in its beautiful, white, massive form moving through the blue water.

The whole trip, as a matter of fact, was like an artist's tour of the sea, so dramatically did one spectacular face of the sea transform to another. A squall of huge raindrops made the surface boil as dark clouds marched overhead. And in between the black clouds were giant shafts of light from the sun, and all this created the most awesome dance across the surface of the sea, the deep shadows and blinding silvery light in ever changing patterns. Then came the full arcs of double rainbows and sunsets of such deep, electrifying colors that made your mouth water as if you'd bit into a lemon. And every scene was given a heartbeat and pulse by the abundance of fish and the roll of the boat. The most jaded old-timers were caught in its spell.

The next day the ocean was as blue as the Caribbean, with multiple white shafts of sunlight beaming and dancing, reaching way down into the depths where they all converged. It was exactly as I imagine it would be to move across the surface of a planet-sized, liquid star sapphire. Around midday, when we found ourselves in the midst of a school of two to three hundred spinner dolphins leaping and twisting through the water, we could no longer be responsible for our actions. We shut the engine down, stretched out on the deck with a couple of cool drinks, and talked ourselves into a swim.

Hot and ready, I stepped onto the sternrail of the boat and looked around me. Except for Art and a couple of other boats which barely formed tiny specks in the distance, there was nothing but water all the way to the horizon. Suddenly this swimming pool seemed a little bit too big. Even comparing it to the size of Mount Everest or to the whole Himalayan range was a ridiculous mockery considering the actual vastness of this place. My feet felt like they were nailed to the rail, and Cindy kept saying "Well? Well?"

Each time I'd answer "Hmmmmm, hmmmmm." It was a great conversation.

So we hung a tire over the stern in order to stand on it and do the old "toe first in the water" trick. It was at least a half hour later before I managed to get all the way in and finally let go of the boat. I never did manage to mentally let go of how much water was below and around me.

I swam around with Cindy's face mask and looked at my legs and body dangling at the top of the light rays that went down forever. I saw the squid and all the other little creatures way down there swimming in the current. Then I looked over at my boat, the bright, sunlit red, beautifully curved hull and propeller, so confidently immersed in the surface of the shimmering sea. It was sculpturally perfect. Now it was Cindy's turn, and I kept saying "Well, well?" and she said, "Hmmmm, hmmmm."

By this time some of the other boats were calling us on the radio, not a few of them quite angry and disgusted that we would do something so stupid as jump off the boat in the middle of the ocean, particularly on the albacore grounds where so many sharks hang out. I never had the fleet come down so hard on me for anything before or since. They were right, really; you don't have to see the sharks on the surface for them to be there, and I know they were only speaking from real concern. What got to me a little was the recent history of some of those who spoke! In fact, Jerry, wasn't it less than a year ago when you were fishing over one hundred miles out, and you couldn't find your own boat? The night before it was calm, so he left his boat to drift, rowed over to a friend's boat, and they made like New Year's Eve way into the night. The next morning the sun was directly overhead before it finally blasted them awake, and Jerry's boat was nowhere to be seen. There wasn't one member of the fleet that didn't have to drop their fishing to go search the horizons for Jerry's boat. So, come on, Jerry, we all gotta tempt this place every once in a while or it's got us for sure.

Later that afternoon, the first sign of wind began roughing up the glassy surface; two o'clock that night, I woke up just as my head and elbow mashed into the floor from having been thrown out of my bunk. The twelve- to fourteen-foot seas were trampling the *Eileen D.* like an endless herd of wild elephants. Three in the morning, something had to be done. I tied one end of a line to a cleat on the rail and the other around my waist. "Cindy," I said as she stood ready for whatever was needed, and I could tell by the look on her face that I didn't have to say a word of what I was thinking. This sea was so thunderingly vicious, it seemed like any one of them could crush this miniature hull like a matchbox. I grabbed a hammer and a bag of four-inch ring nails and crawled to the back of the boat. Waves hurled themselves onto the deck, and the whole skyful of stars pitched wildly from the north to the south as if the universe itself had broken loose from its moorings. I certainly knew that this bag of nails wasn't about to tack it all back in place, and the hatch covers themselves were already secure with rope; it's just that one hundred miles to sea on a night like this, the illusion of control is the only comfort you've got.

With my foot hooked around the mast and my belly on the deck, I drove the nails through the hatch and into the coamings below. The ice hold done, I crawled my way to the stern hatch that was even more vulnerable to the roguish waves. As I pounded the last of the nails, a wave so big broke over the deck, I thought I'd been swept into the sea. My body was torqued in ten directions by the churning of the sea, the shock of the cold came into my back like a knife blade, and my eyes strained wide with fear against the blackness. And staring back at me was that overfamiliar, ugly, greedy, ravenous, motherless, bastard face of death. I hated it more every time I came within its grasp. My back slammed against the gunwale, the boat lurched back on its starboard side, and I scrambled into the cabin door faster than a cat coming in from the rain.

Cindy was lashing the wheel in place, and I went into the forecastle and braced myself against the rail of my bunk. This fear I used to think the fishermen somehow dissolved from their lives is a fear that only grows. Drenched, shaking, and breathing like an asthmatic, old horse, I listened to the sounds being made between the hull and the sea; hollow, watery, deep-throated gulping sounds; unearthly beautiful, secret, exploding, unfathomable sounds. What is it with the sea?

At five in the morning, someone yelled into the radio so loud you couldn't tell who it was. "Good morning all you crazy fishermen, fuck this place, I'm going in." For the next eighteen hours, half a dozen boats traveled at half speed, beam to the sea and bows on the distant city. Hour after hour after hour, my sturdy, streamlined hull was getting popped out of the water and dropped back so hard, I felt on every fall her massive planks could pop like a twig. It was literally getting pounded into my head, *no* boat was worthy of the sea, and somehow I loved the *Eileen D.* even more for her vulnerability.

When we hit the dock, they were as unprepared as we were when we hit the big fish. There were no bins, no reefer truck, and only a skeleton crew. It took forever to unload. But after the financial depression of a week ago, not even the hassle at the dock could dampen the beaming faces or put a dent in the hours of joking and laughing and recounting the trip's events as we waited our turns to unload. Later that day, Art dragged out the barbecue pit; the word passes and the party's on. The dock crew grabbed over fifty pounds of albacore from the freezer; beer, ice, booze, grass, French bread, watermelons, and soy sauce came out of the holds of the boats as the fishermen gathered like birds over bait.

Before the albacore on the grill had cooked, we had consumed over fifteen pounds of it raw. It's sashimi, a number one delicacy of the Japanese—raw albacore dipped in soy sauce and horse-radish, or just plain lemon juice. Followed by champagne, by big handfuls of barbecued albacore, half loaves of French bread, and big hunks of watermelon, and back to the sashimi to the rhythm of endless sea stories. Not even kings feast like fishermen!

I stared into the hot, glowing red embers with more peacefulness and security than I could ever feel staring into the sea, and I tried to get an honest answer from myself. Do I love it or hate it? This flirting with the margin, this grueling life cut off from the land, chasing the fish and fearing the sea? Now that I knew the answer, I realized the question was out of date.

13

Nectar in a Sieve

THE QUESTIONS BEFORE me now were entirely uninteresting and devoid of magic, but they had to be answered anyway, businesslike, concise, and without the interference of dreams. Is the small fisherman about to be muscled out? Is PCA going to pull the purse strings on small boat loans? Is the management council going to make it even quicker by pulling the rug on the salmon season? I sure would like to know because the thought of making six-thousand-dollar-a-year boat payments and three-thousand-dollar-a-year insurance payments on a boat that wasn't worth a dime was not appealing.

The one thing I could think of was to find a little niche, my own corner on an obscure market and develop it before it was too late. It was time for all good sharks to swim my way. I even found a couple of markets that would sell it by its name.

It's great food, firm, boneless, and tasty. Vic and I eat it often. But like so much other great food from the sea, Americans, the most unknowledgeable fish eaters in the world, are reluctant to try it. Then it gets labeled trash fish and thrown back in the sea along with hundreds of thousands of tons of other good food caught incidental to the big name species. Either that or it gets packed as crab, swordfish, scallops, you name it. Whatever your preference in seafood, I guarantee at some time you've paid a fortune for shark, hake, skatewings, etc. And the fishermen got three cents a pound and a line of grief from the buyer. "I ought to be charging you just to unload this junk," they scream while they work the hoist and the cash register rings in their mind.

213

All around it seemed like a worthwhile pursuit to try and develop my own market on shark. I bought a dozen shark hooks that looked like they could pull down a tree and a spool of three-hundred-pound test line because anything bigger than that deserved my humblest apologies, and I headed out on the bay.

Sharks in San Francisco Bay? Hate to tell all you weekenders, but it's loaded like most other marine estuaries. My major problem was that the game laws restricted commercial fishermen on the bay to two hooks and no mechanical gear. To my surprise, it turned out to be the most carefree fun I'd had in years.

All the joys of fishing without the worry of storms, away from the press of the fleet. I loved the hours exploring the quiet coves and inlets of the bay, trying to take in all the signs, my imagination reaching to live it like the shark. Exploring fantasy trips that all at once would explode into eerie, ancient battles when I suddenly found myself attached to the twelve-foot monsters below.

By December, I had to look at the reality. I figured the maximum potential of this business was about seventy-five dollars a day unless I sunk thousands of dollars into ocean-going gear. And seventy-five dollars wasn't going to cut it.

That left herring, and I realized more than ever I didn't want any part of its madness. "'It's a no-good fishery," I complained to Vic. "When we take thousands of tons of fish for the eggs just so the Japanese can keep a holiday tradition—it's just not right."

"Don't be ridiculous," Vic argued. "You see how many people want to eat the shark? Sure, the herring's a mess, but you can't change it, so take advantage of it. It's a quota anyway, and if you don't catch them, someone else will. Besides, you need the herring to survive."

This attitude of not caring was permeating the fleet like the stagnant water of a river dammed from the sea. A comment I heard at the dock seemed to sum up all the rest. "This year I don't give a fuck." It was hard to listen to because the things I liked the most about the fishermen was their ability to care about each other and the future of the fish. Whether it's greed or powerlessness or pressure or whatever that makes it turn around, I don't know, but one thing is clearer to me all the time. This business of people caring is the most fragile thing on earth, even more fragile than fish.

Unfortunately, Vic was right about one thing: I fish herring or I don't fish.

The first thing I got in the mail was a notice from the Fish and Game that my permit had been revoked for failure to properly fill out my log the previous year. Sixty other stupefied fishermen got the same notice. What this was all about was the situation; when we'd finished hauling the torn remains of a net from the jaws of chaos, we didn't then go into the cabin, wipe the blood and slime from our hands, and record the time, location, and tonnage of the set. If we wanted to appeal, we could appear at the next commission meeting to be held at the federal building in San Francisco. This all generated a lot of sarcastic remarks, but on the appointed day all sixty fishermen drove in from as far as Crescent City and flew in from as far as Seattle.

The fishermen sure looked ridiculous corralled by marble hallways. The Fish and Game commissioners all sat behind a polished wooden bench which was at least ten feet above the fishermen. They assumed such rigid poses of solemnity, I leaned over and asked Vic if he'd ever seen the movie, *The Trial of Billy Jack*. An official from the department lifted his gavel and pounded it against some kind of special platter so he wouldn't scratch the table. He leaned into the microphone and said, "The first thing I want to say to you all is that commercial fishing in the State of California is a privilege and not a right." I thought from the tension in the room that somebody was about to charge up there and ram that gavel down his throat. Instead, we all squirmed in our seats as this stern-faced man issued dictums for a full fifteen minutes. "Unless the fishermen start cooperating with the department, there is no way the department can cooperate with the fishermen. The fishermen must obey the letter of the law. You cannot ignore the importance of properly filling out the forms required." I was stunned by his tone. He really believed that we were ignorant natives and he was the colonialist charged with bringing us the ways of the white man. It was frightening. I wanted to get out of there with an intensity that was only matched by my desire to fish.

The commissioners had obviously decided ahead of time to reissue a permit to everyone in the room. But before they let this be known, they made each and every fisherman, one by one, come before the bench. "Speak into the microphone; tell us the reasons you have for not filling in the log, and state why you think this commission should reconsider your permit."

One by one the fishermen shuffled up to the front and sucked on the microphone. "I was tired, sirs, it was a tough year out there. I didn't realize how important this log was since it was the first year we were asked to do this, and if I get my permit back, I'll record everything." One by one the commissioners argued every case, taking turns opposing and defending its merits. Why no one tore into this facade and called it for what it was I'll never know. I was ashamed of myself and ashamed of the fishermen. I had never before seen a fisherman not speak his mind. Something died in me that day, watching every last one of us relinquish the dignity of our lives just so we could participate in its demise.

A whole new series of laws made the season even more difficult and frustrating than the year before. It was a source of shocked amazement to everyone that each year this fishery became more of a mess and at the same time never accomplished a thing in terms of protecting the fish. Even so, at the end of the season, as the boats were unburdened of ripped-up nets and busted gear, thoughts of straightening out the herring laws were the last thing on everyone's mind. In this new age of bureaucratic control one urgent question was replaced by another before there was a moment's time to respond.

Now we all walked around scratching our heads, trying to decide whether or not to mount the salmon gear on the boats. Pacific Fisheries Management Council was still arguing about whether or not there were enough salmon in the ocean to proceed with a normal season. Unbelievably, they waited until the very last minute to tell us that two weeks were taken from the month of April and the month of June was closed completely. That constitutes almost a 30 percent cut, 30 percent of our gross income, which means good-by profit because expenses never get cut.

An incredible thing happened. That May more salmon were caught than had been caught in the same month for the past twenty years. I was ending trips early because the boat was full of fish before the groceries were gone. And for Freckles there was the added joy of at least once a day broadcasting his personal pride in the performance of his beloved ocean. "I can't wait," he said, ecstatic, "I can't wait to hear how the biologists are going to explain this one."

Did the council then say, "Sorry, we made a mistake, we predicted no fish, and now there's more fish than anyone would have guessed. We give you back the month of June"? Hell, no. It takes time to make a decision like that. But after the closure, when we went back on the ocean and the fish still bubbled like a fountain from the sea, the council began contemplating decisions at an alarming rate. Now, they said, we had "caught too many fish" and threatened another emergency closure. There was also talk of a quota on the salmon, which would pit fisherman against fisherman on the much more dangerous arena of the open sea. It would mean pushing in weather we never would have considered bucking without the pressure of a quota. There was also a plan drawn up to block the ocean into territories that would open and close at different times of the year, as if the water of the ocean stays put like the soil on a mountain, as if the fish travel by itinerary. But the council was nodding their heads in approval even as we worked outside San Francisco and caught fish that originated in Alaska.

As the echoes of the herring mismanagement seemed amplified by the sheer scope and reach of the council's domain, it became more and more clear that the goal of protecting the fish was at odds with the goals of the political process. The council was the one government agency that had been given real power over the fish and their habitat. But not even a voice was raised to insist that the hydroelectric pumps have proper strainers so the baby fish won't get mashed by the millions, nor was there any objection to diverting major portions of the Sacramento River and sending it down to Los Angeles, the river that at one time supported the largest runs of king salmon in the U.S.; and the intensive lumbering practices that gorge the rivers with silt, which clogs the gills of the fish, never even made it to the council's agendas. Of course not. The power and lumber companies have mammoth lobbies and high men in high places, and the fishermen meet three or four times in the winter over coffee and doughnuts. The predator naturally goes for the weakest prey. So the council goes for the fishermen with a hook and line in the water and makes it look to the world like they're doing their job. The goal of the council is met, it all looks good in the press, and the council is funded for another year.

Still, I would have thought with all the fish we were catching, the fishermen would have been lost in their full euphoric glory. Instead, in the midst of making some of the biggest hauls of their lives, the radio was full of disharmony over the overcrowding, despair over the future of the fisheries, and some sad conversations among the old-timers, wondering if they could ever make their way on the beach. There was even a new catch phrase that filled the pauses of their talks. Instead of the "better days are coming," which I had heard from the first day I ventured on the sea, now, over and over, the fishermen passed the word: "The thrill is gone," they said over the radio, even as their deckhands piled the fish on the stern. "The thrill is gone," they said at the docks, even as they unloaded their record catches. "The thrill is gone!" And in a way this lament restored my faith in the fishermen; I always knew they were out here coursing the seas in search of something much more than a load of fish to fill the bins.

Epilogue

I sold my boat six months after the end of that salmon season. My timing was perfect—economically. That salmon season and the following herring season were a bonanza for me. It was unlikely I could ever leave the business in better shape financially. Not three weeks after I sold my boat, Production Credit drastically cut back on its loans for trollers, and the prices dropped out of the fishing boats. Simultaneously, the Pacific Management Council began steadfast implementation of its policies of quotas, borders, and schedules with such disregard for the natural order of the sea, that it showed the events of the herring to be but the first meek tear in the shredding of the fabric of the entire American fishery.

Over and over, when I wander down to the docks to catch a barbecue and hear the latest news, my friends keep telling me the same thing. "Maria, you played it smart; you got out at just the right time." And I look at the unruliness of the sea wind still caught in their hair and the gaze of distant horizons reflected in their eyes, and taste the wild, sweet flavor of fresh-caught fish, and feel the tugging of the boat on the dock lines like a wild horse trying to throw off the reins, and I wonder if I did indeed do the right thing. Only Freckles seemed to read my mind. "Didn't I tell you, Maria, you leave the ocean and it's like living the rest of your life in a closet?"